Matthew Arnold's *Culture and Anarchy*, first published in 1869, is one of the most celebrated works of social criticism ever written. It has become an inescapable reference-point for all subsequent discussion of the relations between politics and culture, and it has exercised a profound influence both on conceptions of the distinctive nature of British society, and on ideas about education and the teaching of literature more generally. This edition establishes the authoritative text of this much-revised work, and places it alongside Arnold's three most important essays on political subjects – 'Democracy', 'Equality', and 'The Function of Criticism at the Present Time'. The editor's substantial introduction situates these works in the context both of Arnold's life and other writings, and of nineteenth-century intellectual and political history. In order to make Arnold's work accessible to students, this edition also contains a chronology of Arnold's life, a bibliographical guide and full notes on the names, books, and historical events mentioned in the texts.

CAMBRIDGE TEXTS IN THE
HISTORY OF POLITICAL THOUGHT

———

MATTHEW ARNOLD

*Culture and Anarchy*

*and other writings*

# CAMBRIDGE TEXTS IN THE
# HISTORY OF POLITICAL THOUGHT

*Series Editors:*
RAYMOND GEUSS, *Columbia University*
QUENTIN SKINNER, *Christ's College, Cambridge*

This series is intended to make available to students the most important texts required for an understanding of the history of political thought. The scholarship of the present generation has greatly expanded our sense of the range of authors indispensable for such an understanding, and the series will reflect those developments. It will also include a number of less well-known works, in particular those needed to establish the intellectual contexts that in turn help to make sense of the major texts. The principal aim, however, will be to produce new versions of the major texts themselves, based on the most up-to-date scholarship. The preference will always be for complete texts, and a special feature of the series will be to complement individual texts, within the compass of a single volume, with subsidiary contextual material. Each volume will contain an introduction on the historical identity and contemporary significance of the text concerned, as well as such student aids as notes for further reading and chronologies of the principal events in a thinker's life.

*For a complete list of titles published in the series, see end of book*

# MATTHEW ARNOLD

# *Culture and Anarchy*

## *and other writings*

EDITED BY

STEFAN COLLINI

*University Lecturer in English and
Fellow of Clare Hall, Cambridge*

CAMBRIDGE
UNIVERSITY PRESS

Published by the Press Syndicate of the University of Cambridge
The Pitt Building, Trumpington Street, Cambridge CB2 1RP
40 West 20th Street, New York, NY 10011–4211, USA
10 Stamford Road, Oakleigh, Victoria 3166, Australia

© Cambridge University Press 1993

First published 1993
Reprinted 1995

Printed in Great Britain by Athenæum Press Ltd, Gateshead, Tyne & Wear

*A catalogue record for this book is available from the British Library*

*Library of Congress cataloguing in publication data*

Arnold, Matthew, 1822–1888
Culture and anarchy and other writings / Matthew Arnold: edited by Stefan Collini
p.    cm. — (Cambridge texts in the history of political thought)
Includes bibliographical references and index
Contents: Democracy (1861) — The function of criticism at the
present time (1864) — Culture and anarchy (1867–9) — 'Preface' to
Culture and anarchy (1869) — Equality (1878)

ISBN 0 521 37440 5 (hc). — ISBN 0 521 37796 X (pb)

1. Great Britain—Social conditions—19th century. 2. Culture.
3. Democracy. 4. Criticism. 5. Equality. I. Collini, Stefan,
1947–   . II. Title. III. Series.

HN389.A72   1993
306–dc20   92–7595   CIP

ISBN 0 521 37440 5 hardback
ISBN 0 521 37796 X (paperback)

# Contents

# Introduction

Matthew Arnold is not primarily read or remembered for his contribution to the history of what has come to be known as 'political thought', and at first sight it may seem surprising to find him in such company. 'Literary critic' is the label most readily applied to him today; certainly, he did more than any other single figure to endow the role of the critic with the cultural centrality it has come to enjoy in the English-speaking world. At the same time, his poetry, including such frequently anthologized pieces as 'Dover Beach' and 'The Scholar-Gypsy', has earned him a secure place in the canon of English literature. He also wrote extensively and influentially on religion and education, among other topics, and at his death in 1888 he was recognized as the leading man-of-letters in Victorian Britain. Nonetheless, his best-known work, *Culture and Anarchy*, first published in 1869, has left a lasting impress upon subsequent debate about the relation between politics and culture, not least by provoking vigorous disagreement, and this book and the selection of his other writings included here reveal him to have been a social critic and political commentator of rare power and persuasiveness.

*Culture and Anarchy*, which may be one of the most frequently cited non-fiction prose works in the English language, is hard to classify in terms of modern academic disciplines. However, its subtitle (misleadingly omitted in some selections from his writings) points us in the right direction: 'An Essay in Political and Social Criticism'. It is an 'essay', intended to be readable and stimulating: it is neither a treatise nor a text-book. And it is a work of 'political and social criticism', closely engaging with the beliefs and assumptions manifested in the public life of its time: it is neither a policy proposal nor a work of systematic theory. The book requires, if it is to exercise its subtle power, a certain willing complicity on the part of the reader. Both Arnold's distinctive style and the high degree of allusion and local reference in his writing can, on first acquaintance, obstruct this process. The notes to this edition are designed to remove the second of these obstacles, and the following discussion of Arnold's character-istic literary strategies and leading ideas is intended to help the reader who is coming for the first time to this elusive, but ultimately deeply rewarding writer.

## The purpose and style of Arnold's social criticism

Arnold wrote as a critic of his own society, constantly attempting to correct the exaggeration and one-sidedness which in his view disfi-gured much of its political and intellectual debate. With some justice, he identified the besetting sins of the public life of Victorian England as parochialism, complacency, and (in a term of German origin which he did much to put into general circulation) 'philistinism'. His response was to try to open up English consciousness to European ideas and perspectives, and to provoke his readers into an uneasy awareness of the limitations of their established mental habits. He did not, therefore, occupy a position that can easily be characterized as 'radical' or 'conservative', in either intellectual or political terms. Although he was, like most of his educated contemporaries, appre-hensive about the dangers involved in the as yet untried experiment of democracy, he was firmly committed to reducing existing inequalities and he could be a stinging critic of the failings of the English govern-ing classes.

There is an important general question here about the degree of distance from one's society required by such a task. A certain reflec-tive detachment is obviously indispensable, but effective cultural critics need to be sufficiently intimate with the assumptions and tradi-tions of their society to criticize with the requisite discrimination, and they have to share enough of its values to be able to bring them to bear in inducing that kind of self-criticism which is the condition of per-suasion. Complete outsiders, by contrast, can only denounce; they may disturb those within the walls who hear their curses, but they are unlikely to lead them to reform their ways. Arnold was in no sense an outsider: he belonged, by upbringing and style of life, to the most comfortable stratum of the Victorian professional class, mixing easily with the more sympathetic members of the political and social elite. In intellectual style, he was, in Carlyle's adaptation of a biblical phrase that Arnold was fond of quoting, 'terribly at ease in Zion' (e.g. p. 130). Moreover, he took for granted much that men of his rank and time took for granted. Inevitably, this has left him vulnerable to the reproaches of an age more alert to some of the injustices of class, gender, and race. But it also gave him an insider's ear for significance and nuance, and it meant that he very rarely indulged in that deceptive form of self-flattery which consists in dramatizing oneself as locked in heroically lonely combat with forces that are both alien and overwhelming.

In engaging in such criticism, Arnold's tone of voice was at once his chief weapon and his most distinctive quality. It was not a matter of forcing his readers to abandon one position in favour of another, but of putting them in the way of the experience which, when reflected upon, would bring home to them the defects of the frame of mind that had found expression in the erroneous 'position' in the first place. This is one of the reasons why the sense of the engaging conversational presence of the author is exceptionally vivid when reading Arnold's prose. Arnold, as one might expect of such a self-conscious writer, could be knowingly aware of this effect (indeed, a sense of this awareness is sometimes allowed to edge into the prose itself, thereby drawing the reader further into complicity). As his essays began to attract attention, he took the measure of his powers with a frank confidence:

> It is very animating to think that one at last has a chance of *getting at* the English public. Such a public as it is, and such a work as one wants to do with it! Partly nature, partly time and study, have also by this time taught me thoroughly the precious truth that everything turns upon one's exercising the power of *persuasion*, of *charm*; that without this all fury, energy, reasoning power, acquirement, are thrown away and only render their owner more miserable. Even in one's ridicule one must preserve a sweetness and good-humour.
>
> (Letter, 29 Oct. 1863)

One cannot read very far into Arnold's prose, however, without recognizing that much the most important, if also potentially the most troublesome, feature of his style is his irony, and this is closely related to his characteristic strategy of taking the higher ground than his opponents. Irony is a particularly vital resource for a writer who wishes to embody as well as recommend an alternative to stridency, exaggeration and over-simplification. Skilfully used, irony can conjure up the suggestion of much wisdom and judgement held in reserve, accumulated stocks of experience that are not drawn on directly but which enable the too-simple or too-loud to be seen for what they are. Such a tone came naturally to Arnold, though he was also fully aware of its effectiveness. 'For my part', he reflected in a letter of 1867, 'I see more and more what an effective weapon, in a confused, loud-talking, clap-trappy country like this, where every writer and speaker to the public tends to say rather more than he means, is *irony* . . . The main effect I have had on the mass of noisy claptrap and inert prejudice which chokes us has been, I can see, by the use of this weapon.' Arnold's light touch has misled some readers into thinking him merely flippant. But what he called his 'vivacities' were not only a necessary form of artistic self-assertion on his part: they were in themselves also an essential element in the realization of a purpose which was, at bottom, profoundly serious. Moreover, he was surely right to take satisfaction from the thought that 'however much I may be attacked, my manner of writing is certainly one that takes hold of people and proves effective.'

## 'Democracy'

In 1859 Arnold was sent by the Newcastle Commission on Elementary Education on a five-month tour of the schools of France, Holland, and the French cantons of Switzerland, and two years later he published a revised version of his official report under the title *The Popular Education of France*. For this volume he composed a long introduction, reflecting upon the whole question of the proper role of the state in a modern society, and when he later republished this introduction as a separate essay, he entitled it 'Democracy'. This title, and still more the tenor of his reflections themselves, indicated an important affinity with the French political theorist Alexis de Tocqueville, whose *De la démocratie en Amérique* (which had appeared some twenty years earlier and had immediately been published in an influential English translation) explored the kinds of social as well as political relations entailed by the inevitable movement of modern societies towards greater 'equality of conditions'.

That five-month visit to France was as much the occasion as the catalyst for the thirty-seven-year-old Arnold, hitherto known as a poet and essayist, to emerge in a new role as a social critic. His admiration of French intellectuality, of the 'idea-moved masses' of their democracy, and of the embodiment of these values in a rational, active state was already of long standing in 1859. Moreover, his experience in the dismally provincial society of the Dissenters (as members of the Protestant Nonconformist churches and sects were called), whose schools in central England he had been inspecting for the last eight years, formed the strongest counterpoint to this selectively perceived ideal.

The essay was his first extended statement of what was to become a familiar Arnoldian theme, namely that an hereditary aristocracy, whatever its political achievements in the past, was ill-equipped to understand a modern world that was essentially governed by ideas and inevitably moving towards greater social equality. Characteristically, Arnold focused not upon democracy as a set of political institutions, still less upon the economic arrangements these might presuppose, but upon the question of cultural values and intellectual and aesthetic standards. 'The difficulty for democracy', he declared, 'is, how to find and keep high ideals' (p. 14). It was a variant on a problem that preoccupied many nineteenth-century social thinkers: how were increasingly democratic societies to sustain those cultural and political activities which had in the past depended upon the existence of a wealthy and leisured aristocracy? Arnold thought that there were two reasons why the problem assumed a particularly acute form in England. The first was the way in which the sturdy independence which was claimed to be such a feature of the English national character had combined with a peculiar political history to produce a very deep antipathy to allowing the state to play a more active part. And secondly, from a rather similar combination of causes, the English middle class, which was thus left to determine the future tone of national life, exhibited a painfully narrow and impoverished conception of what that life might be.

Faced with this diagnosis, Arnold turned in the first instance to education. At that date, there was, in sad contrast to countries like France or Prussia, no national system of education in England.

Arnold deplored this neglect of what he took to be one of the most fundamental tasks of the state in a civilized community, and he frequently insisted that the superiority of educational arrangements in France lay not just in their practical effectiveness, but also in the example they provided of looking to the state to uphold and promote the highest ideals of civilization. Indeed, at times Arnold seems less concerned with the actual merits of a public system of education in its own right, and more with the way it instantiated a more expansive conception of the state as the embodiment of the national life:

> The question is whether ... the nation may not thus acquire in the State an ideal of high reason and right feeling, representing its best self, commanding general respect, and forming a rallying-point for the intelligence and for the worthiest instincts of the community, which will herein find a true bond of union. (p. 15)

On this question of the role of the state, Arnold was self-consciously challenging the established pieties of the day. He argued that there was little danger in England of the state exceeding its powers; the safeguards, especially the fierce public antagonism to such action, were too strong for that. Arnold was not indifferent to the dangers an over-mighty state could pose to the liberties of the individual; but he perceived that this case did not want for advocates in mid-nineteenth-century England, and he concentrated on pressing the claims of the opposite position. This led to a notable difference of view with the most obviously comparable social critic among his contemporaries, John Stuart Mill. The question of education crystallized the difference. Mill, fearful of the coercive power of an unchallenged democracy, argued that schools should not actually be run by the state lest that give it the power to impose its own views and press uniformity upon the next generation (though he accepted the need for the public setting and monitoring of minimal educational standards); he saw in the variety of private provision of education the best defence of individuality. Arnold, by contrast, feared that the danger of leaving education in private hands was that it would only be conducted by the narrowest or most eccentric or provincial of criteria. As he put it in 1861:

> By giving to schools ... a public character, the state can bring the instruction in them under a criticism which the stock of know-

ledge and judgment in our middle classes is not itself at present
able to supply. By giving to them a national character, it can
confer on them a greatness and a noble spirit, which the tone of
these classes is not of itself at present able to impart. (p. 19)

In Arnold's mind, the contrast to 'national' or 'public' – terms which
he always endowed with strong positive connotations – was 'provincial' or 'sectarian'; even in this relatively early essay, the idea that what
is 'central' is *in itself* superior to what is marginal or merely local is
already evident.

## 'The Function of Criticism at the Present Time'

'The Function of Criticism at the Present Time' was written in the
autumn of 1864 to serve as the introductory essay in his *Essays in
Criticism* which appeared early in the following year. Partly because
the majority of pieces in that volume are on literary subjects, and
partly because Arnold has been retrospectively recruited as one of the
founding fathers of the academic study of English literature, it is often
assumed that this essay defines the function of what the twentieth
century has come to understand by the term 'literary criticism'. The
discussion in its opening pages of the English literature of the
Romantic period may at first seem to reinforce this assumption, but
closer inspection reveals that Arnold was discussing a much broader
notion, an ideal which embraced social and political as well as literary
criticism.

The organizing contrast which lies at the heart of the essay is
between the intellectual as well as political energy released by the
French Revolution – which he, with an enthusiasm rare among the
Victorian educated classes, saw as 'the greatest, the most animating
event in history' (p. 32) – and the insularity, complacency, and mud-
dle-headed practicality which he found to be characteristic of public
life in mid-nineteenth-century England. The essay pleads for all
established practices and beliefs to be subjected to critical, sceptical
scrutiny and to judgement by the highest standards. The term he
famously used to represent the essential spirit of this activity was
'disinterestedness', and he glossed this much-misunderstood word in
the passage which begins: 'And how is criticism to show disinterestedness? By keeping aloof from what is called "the practical view

of things" ...' (p. 37). What Arnold was attacking here was any attempt to subordinate criticism to some other purpose. By urging the critic to practise a kind of 'disinterestedness', he was not encouraging a posture of withdrawal from the world – 'disinterested', it ought to be unnecessary to say, does not mean 'uninterested'. The aim of criticism, as he had already insisted more than once, is 'to see the object as in itself it really is', and his reference later in that same passage to the situation in England gives the clue to what he was trying to avoid. Books and ideas were judged, he was complaining, by whether they were consistent with the true tenets of the Protestant religion, or supported a Whig or Tory view of the English constitution, or had an immediate bearing upon the great policy issues of the moment. It was precisely this habit of appealing to 'ulterior, political, practical considerations about ideas' (p. 37) that in his view narrowed and stultified the intellectual life of Victorian England.

With late-twentieth-century condescension, we may feel that Victorian society provided Arnold with altogether too easy a target, all earnest humbug and ugly antimacassars. But that was not how it seemed at the time. Arnold was attacking a society that was at the peak of its self-confidence: it was not used to having some of its most cherished beliefs treated with scornful mockery, and still less to having the virtues of other nations held up for emulation. John Bull had shown his superiority over the foreigner at Waterloo, just as he was doing again in every workshop and factory in the land; he felt he could pride himself, and often did, on being heir to a unique tradition of political liberty, sensible religion, and respectable manners. Arnold himself was certainly not without deep patriotic feelings, but this emotional allegiance only made him detest English complacency and parochialism the more, and his diverse essays in social criticism were united by the purpose, much frustrated but resourcefully prosecuted, of teasing, educating, and shaming his countrymen into a greater awareness of these shortcomings.

Among those who did not take kindly to being schooled in this way was James Fitzjames Stephen, a leading representative of Benthamite Utilitarianism and a pugnacious controversialist. He had no patience with what he took to be Arnold's fastidious nose-holding about the unintellectual English in 'The Function of Criticism', and responded with the delicacy of a wounded rhinoceros in an article entitled 'Mr Arnold and his Countrymen'. This and other attacks led Arnold to write a further series of articles; not until the majority of these had already been published did he decide to bring them together as a book, and the title *Culture and Anarchy*, which now seems so inevitably right, appears to have been settled on only a month or two before its publication in January 1869. Thus Fitzjames Stephen had, indirectly but not inappropriately, helped to provoke the work which has since become recognized as the classic indictment of English philistinism.

## *Culture and Anarchy*

The piecemeal composition of the book over a period of more than a year left its mark in various ways, as generations of puzzled readers have had cause to testify. One chapter will make reference to published criticisms of the periodical form of the preceding chapter (see, for example, the opening paragraphs of Chapter Two, pp. 81–2), and the long Preface, which was written last, is clearly addressing a rather different political and religious situation from that supposed by the first few chapters proper. At the same time, the periodical origins of the work are also a source of strengths, such as its conversational, at times almost intimate, discursive tone. Arnold's prose more generally has been criticized as a monologue masquerading as a dialogue, but there is a genuinely responsive rhythm to much of his writing in this book: which of the other great English prose writers, after all, could get away with beginning not just a sentence or a paragraph but a *chapter* with the argumentative conjunction 'But' (p. 153)?

The book is linked to *Essays in Criticism* both by the thread of controversy and by the purpose signalled in its subtitle. No section of English society entirely escaped his 'political and social criticism', and among the happy coinages for which the work is remembered was his characterization of the three main classes as Barbarians, Philistines, and Populace. (Interestingly, the first and last of these terms are in effect classical allusions, while the middle one is, of course, biblical: these two sources always remained the chief reference-points of Arnold's thought and sensibility.) But although the aristocracy and the working class by no means escaped censure (the former perhaps being let off a little more lightly than the latter), the central target of the book, as of Arnold's work in general, was 'the bad civilization of the English middle class'. Revealingly, he dated the malaise of

English life not from the Industrial Revolution of the late eighteenth century, but from the linked religious and commercial developments of the early seventeenth. Like several subsequent English critics, T. S. Eliot and F. R. Leavis among them, he tended to idealize what he took to be the vigorous and expressive life of Elizabethan England, the great creative epoch of English history and literature alike, when English culture was not yet divorced from the mainstream of the European tradition. But then, as he had memorably put it in *Essays in Criticism*, 'the great English middle class, the kernel of the nation, the class whose intelligent sympathy had upheld a Shakespeare, entered the prison of Puritanism and had the key turned on its spirit there for two hundred years.'

The 'prison of Puritanism' is a striking phrase, but like many of Arnold's more resonant categories it is not always clear how far 'Puritanism' here is intended to stand for some ideal–typical set of qualities and how far it is supposed to refer to a particular historical embodiment of those qualities (the question will arise again with his famous pairing of 'Hellenism' and 'Hebraism'). Certainly, in this case he was less concerned with the details of seventeenth-century denominational strife than with the way the severer strains of Protestantism – those sects which had refused to acquiesce in the Anglican Settlement and hence were known as Nonconformists or, more commonly, Dissenters – had coloured, in drab and sombre hues, the texture of English life more generally. Ultimately, the importance Arnold assigned to Puritanism in English history was itself a reflection of his preoccupation with the part played by its descendants in Victorian Britain.

It is almost impossible to overestimate the importance of Arnold's response to Dissent in shaping his social criticism. We need to remember how deeply, fiercely, and consistently religious issues divided Victorian society. Arnold, of course, had ample first-hand experience of this sectarian temper from his school-inspecting duties. As he wrote in a letter in 1869, the year of *Culture and Anarchy*'s publication: 'The feeling of the harm their [the Dissenters'] isolation from the main current of thought and culture does in the nation, a feeling that has been developed in me by going about among them for years, is the source of all that I have written on religious, political and social subjects.' But his discussion of this topic soon reveals itself to be just one more example of the role he assigned to criticism discussed above, and hence to be part of his constant search for correctives to all forms of one-sidedness and obsessiveness. That the Church of England was the ideal corrective in this case, or even an acceptable one, may seem more doubtful. Arnold's own religious beliefs were complex and far from orthodox, but his conviction of the *cultural* value of sharing in the traditions and rites of an established church was a central feature of his social criticism. Writing as someone temperamentally antipathetic to both biblical literalism and theological abstractions, Arnold arguably failed to show sufficient sympathy with the views of those for whom these matters were more important than life or death; Dissenters could hardly be responsive to the beautiful cadences of *The Book of Common Prayer* when they believed that its use might entail eternal damnation.

Of course, the wilful, sectarian temper Arnold was criticizing expressed itself in political as well as religious terms. It issued in the doctrine that Arnold pilloried (in ch. II) as 'Doing as One Likes'. This represented that central strain in Victorian political attitudes (powerfully expressed in, but not confined to, the Liberal Party, the natural home of the Dissenters in this period) which insisted on the right of the individual to go about his business – the 'individual' was usually assumed to be male – without let or hindrance from his fellow-citizens or from the state. Clearly, this could issue in a strict policy of *laissez-faire* in social and economic matters, and this is the aspect of Victorian Liberalism that has most engaged the attention of later historians. But Arnold was, as ever, concerned less with particular policies than with the deeper attitudes they expressed. In this exaggerated individualism he detected both a low aspiration, in being content with one's existing wants, and a kind of hubris in assuming that the isolated individual can adequately determine his pattern of life for himself. The ethos of popular Liberalism – on the one hand jealous of its rights and touchy about being patronized, on the other proud of its material achievements and dismissive of cultivation and refinement – had no room for 'high ideals' or notions of a 'best self', still less for seeing these embodied in a conception of 'the state' as the highest expression of the national community. *Culture and Anarchy* was a bravura attempt to domesticate these alien notions and to make such elevated language part of the common currency of English thought.

Arnold had the shrewd controversialist's eye for ways of gaining attention for his ideas, and a talent for condensing an argument into a catch-phrase. His teasing labels for the three great classes of English society caught on almost immediately, but these were if anything overshadowed by a yet more lasting coinage (which he adapted from Heine): the binary categories of 'Hebraism' and 'Hellenism'. These terms characterize the two great traditions of thought and feeling that had influenced the Western world, but also stand for the two tendencies which are constantly struggling for dominance within each individual. His various definitions of these two terms prove, as so often in Arnold, to be diverse and not always obviously compatible, but the outlines are clear enough. 'The governing idea of Hellenism', as he puts it most pithily, 'is *spontaneity of consciousness*; that of Hebraism, *strictness of conscience*' (p. 128). Hebraism, that is, fixes above all on the idea of duty, of moral rules, of the subjugation of the self: its chief concern is to act rightly, and the emphasis here falls not only on the 'rightly', but also on the 'acting', for Hebraism is an ethic which stresses the exercise of will. Hellenism, by contrast, concerns itself more with knowledge and beauty, with the play of ideas and the charm of form. Hebraism attacks wrongdoing, moral laxness, and weakness of will; Hellenism attacks ignorance, ugliness, and rigidity of mind. Arnold constantly asserts that society needs a balance between these two forces, since both are essential to the full development of the human spirit, but that it must genuinely be a balance. It will already be obvious that, in his view, Victorian England was far too dominated by the ethic of Hebraism, and his work may be seen as a series of attempts to bring some of the resources of the tradition of Hellenism to bear upon the cramped consciousness of his contemporaries – indeed, the Greeks (albeit very selectively characterized) are the unacknowledged heroes of *Culture and Anarchy*.

The term, to come to it finally, which stands for the animating idea of the book, the term with which Arnold's name is now indissolubly linked, is, of course, 'culture'. In one of his many phrases which have subsequently become part of our common language, Arnold said that by culture he meant 'the best that has been thought and said'. In implicitly assigning priority to the literary and philosophical over the visual and musical, the phrase faithfully represents Arnold's own cultural tastes, yet in other ways it expresses rather poorly the richness of the idea behind his use of the term, since he treats culture not just as something that we can acquire or possess, but as an active force in its own right. One indication of this is the frequency with which he uses the word with an active verb: culture '*endeavours* to see and learn, and to *make* what it sees and learns prevail', culture '*conceives* of perfection ... as a harmonious expansion of all the powers which make the beauty and worth of human nature', 'culture has a rough *task to achieve* in this country', and so on.

This simple stylistic fact alone should suggest that he is not talking about some passive body of art and learning whose natural home is the museum and the library, nor simply a set of high-status social activities encased in an aura of snobbery and pretentiousness. He is talking, rather, about an ideal of human life, a standard of excellence and fulness for the development of our capacities, aesthetic, intellectual, and moral. The ideal which culture holds up before us is that of 'perfection' or the 'harmonious expansion of *all* the powers which make the beauty and worth of human nature' (p. 62). Of course, the assumption that *all* our capacities could even in principle be compatible with each other is itself doubtful, unless, with a hint of circularity, there is an implicit restriction to our 'positive' capacities. In his other works, Arnold, like several other prominent Victorian moralists, oscillated a little unsteadily between, on the one hand, affirming the possibility of a harmonious development of *all* our impulses, and, on the other, endorsing the view that the self was a battleground where the forces of the higher self of conscience and rationality were perpetually in conflict with those of the lower self of appetite and animality. In some of his later writings, which were the work of a more sombre Arnold, sobered by bereavement and prolonged meditation on religion, he most often inclines to the latter view, but in *Culture and Anarchy* it is the former emphasis which predominates.

He recognized, of course, that even in this active sense culture is not innate: a true understanding of it is acquired only by effort and by exposure to the results of the efforts of previous generations. But it is certainly something that is, in his view, within reach of everybody, given the right opportunities, not something confined to a small class. Culture, he argued in an important passage, has to be 'carr[ied] from one end of society to the other', and the task is to divest 'the best knowledge' of all that is 'harsh, uncouth, difficult, abstract, professional, exclusive; to humanise it, to make it efficient outside the clique of the cultivated and the learned, yet still remaining the *best* knowledge and thought of the time, and a true source, therefore, of sweetness and light' (p. 79). As the negatives indicate, he is arguing that 'the best knowledge' should not be imprisoned in a form of expression that is specialized, technical, idiosyncratic, or private, but should rather be accessible, shareable, public – part, as we have since come to say, of a common culture. This idea of the capacity of culture to unify and heal the divisions in society has been one of Arnold's most potent legacies.

*Culture and Anarchy* is not a work of 'political philosophy', and Arnold does not attempt to justify the idea of a higher or common reason, transcending individual preferences, in some purportedly more fundamental principles. He takes its existence and value for granted, and uses it to show up the shortcomings of existing liberal attitudes and to cast doubt (it cannot operate more conclusively than that) on that deep liberal conviction that all opinions are equally 'valid'. Similarly, the book should not be approached as a political programme proposing specific policies. The final chapter on 'Our Liberal Practitioners' deals with issues which were at the forefront of contemporary politics, such as the Disestablishment of the Irish Church and the Real Estate Intestacy Bill. Arnold's discussion of these topics is, however, noticeably devoid of practical suggestions. Rather, these issues simply furnish examples of how culture, as Arnold understood it, that reflective possession of an ideal of human wholeness, disposes us to view the political enthusiasms of the day, of any day, from a broader and less dogmatic perspective.

## 'Equality'

The question of where the author of *Culture and Anarchy* should be placed on the political spectrum as conventionally understood puzzled some of its first readers, and has continued to vex commentators ever since. The fact that his most vehement critics at the time would all have described themselves as Liberals and that the work was praised by the Tory leader, Disraeli, does not by itself establish the book's conservative identity, though it indicates why the question insists on being asked. Arnold's subsequent political essays are an important source of evidence here, especially those written in the last decade of his life when he was a well-known public figure whose utterances were eagerly solicited by the editors of the leading reviews. 'Equality', which first appeared as a periodical article in 1878, was one of his most trenchant and outspoken statements, and should dispel any suggestion that Arnold's elevated notion of the state entailed an uncritical endorsement of the conventional wisdom of the governing class of his day.

'Equality' expresses a view that was at the time deliberately heterodox and remarkably radical (the more so for the fact that it was first given as an address to the gathering of scientists, literati, and members of high society who made up the audience at the Royal Institution). The essay is a sustained denunciation of the extreme inequality of the distribution of property in Britain, and of the impress which that had left on social relations. 'Our inequality materialises our upper class, vulgarises our middle class, brutalises our lower' (p. 236). He particularly deplored the way in which the laws of bequest and inheritance permitted and even encouraged this excessive concentration of property in a few hands, and, as so often, he made his point by means of a running contrast with France where, since the Revolution, the law had reinforced tradition to *prevent* such concentration, and where social life was consequently much freer and less deferential. In this essay, Arnold was willing to be entirely pragmatic about what system of property-holding it may be in society's interests to endorse, vigorously repudiating any idea of 'natural rights': 'all rights are created by law and are based on expediency, and are alterable as the public advantage may require' (p. 220). Even in this passionate indictment of the poisonous consequences of the extremes of wealth encountered in Victorian England, Arnold took certain forms of inequality for granted, and his case was addressed, as he undefensively declared, to 'the thoughts of those who think' (p. 239). But his commitment to a more egalitarian form of social life is evident throughout, notably in his observation that, in contrast to England, 'France is the country where the people, as distinguished from a wealthy refined class, most lives what we call a humane life, the life of civilised man' (p. 225). Here, as elsewhere, Arnold did not shrink from telling his English audience truths he knew they did not wish to hear.

## The identity of Arnold's political thought

Arnold described himself as a Liberal, but usually with some qualification such as 'a Liberal tempered by experience' or, in a phrase he particularly favoured, 'a Liberal of the Future'. However, some of the presiding spirits who did most to influence his social thought make, when taken together, what might seem to be an odd pedigree for a Liberal: Burke, Newman, Carlyle, to name the most obvious. Actually, he had never been entirely comfortable with the blacker side of Carlyle's reactionary politics, and explicitly repudiated his increasingly unconfined authoritarianism. Similarly, for all his reverence for John Henry Newman, both personally and as the embodiment of the spirit of his beloved Oxford, Arnold was undeniably and unshakeably a liberal in the intellectual and religious senses which Newman had spent his life denouncing. On such matters, Arnold ranged himself on the side of Goethe and Heine and all those whom he described (borrowing another phrase of Heine's) as 'soldiers in the Liberation War of humanity' for their attempts to carry through the best features of the programme of the Enlightenment.

His relation to Burke is more teasing. He fully shared the deep admiration that was so common in nineteenth-century England, calling him 'our greatest political thinker', quoting him often, and, suggestively, taking from him the epigraph to both *The Popular Education of France* and *Essays in Criticism*. But as these and the other contexts in which he cites Burke make clear, Arnold valued him as a writer and as one who 'treats politics with . . . thought and imagination', and not, as he has increasingly been treated in the twentieth century, as the chief source for conservative political theory. He noticeably preferred Burke writing about Ireland or America, where he displayed a magnanimity and balance Arnold could identify with, to Burke writing about France, where both Arnold's general Francophilia and his specific enthusiasm for 1789 were sorely taxed ('there is much in his view of France and her destinies which is narrow and erroneous' he observed in 1864). No writer who estimated the French Revolution as highly as Arnold did could be regarded as an unproblematic disciple of Burke, still less could he be anything but an extremely awkward recruit to the ranks of conservatism.

Among the phrases from Burke that Arnold adapted to his own purposes was his characterization of the state as 'the nation in its collective and corporate character' (indeed, Arnold so liked the phrase, which was rather a paraphrase of Burke than a direct quotation, that he used it at least sixteen times in his essays, beginning at pp. 22–3). The liberal emphasis upon leaving individuals alone to pursue their own self-interest prevented the English, Arnold insisted, from properly understanding the very notion of a political community: 'We have not the notion, so familiar on the Continent and to anti-quity, of *the State*, – the nation in its collective and corporate charac-ter, entrusted with stringent powers for the general advantage, and controlling individual wills in the name of an interest wider than that of individuals' (p. 83). Arnold was aware, of course, that such a conception of the state had not been entirely unknown even among English political philosophers, but he was surely right to insist that it did not inform wider social attitudes and practices. Yet again he used a contrast with France to underline the point: 'Whereas in France, since the Revolution, a man feels that the power which represses him is *the State*, is *himself*, here a man feels that the power which represses him is the Tories, the upper class, the aristocracy, and so on' (Letter, 27 July 1866). It is typical of Arnold's elusiveness that the thought underlying this remark may as easily suggest affinities with Rousseau as with Burke.

It has been well said of Arnold that he had a strong, almost Roman, sense of the state, but little feel for the people: in this sense, he was a republican but not a democrat (the influence of his father, the historian of the Roman Republic, was strong here). Similarly, his affinities with the Idealist tradition of political thought lead back from Rousseau and Hegel to Aristotle and, above all, Plato. Though he found systematic philosophy uncongenial, Arnold was temperamen-tally something of a Platonist, with all the Platonist's vulnerability to being dazzled by the beauty of ideals to the neglect of their abuse in practice. This surely helps to explain why Arnold has attracted charges of authoritarianism. But this deep intellectual affinity also suggests what might be described as the 'anti-political' character of his thought. This is well caught by a passage in *Culture and Anarchy* where he is talking about what is involved in coming to recognize ourselves as members of a state in his elevated sense. We come, he wrote (here very much the residuary legatee of Coleridge and English Broad Church historiography and hence, indirectly, of German Ideal-ism), 'to make the State more and more the expression, as we say, of our best self, which is not manifold, and vulgar, and unstable, and contentious, and ever-varying, but one, and noble, and secure, and peaceful, and the same for all mankind' (p. 181). The juxtaposition of the five negatives in the first part of this sentence expresses Arnold's aversion to conflict, shapelessness, disorder, or, in a word, to anarchy, while his temperamental affinity for the opposite of these characteristics is evident in the five positive terms, which are all suggestive of rest and order, and, once more, of his deep feeling for centrality and unity.

No one with such a strong aversion to conflict as Arnold came to manifest could be an altogether satisfactory writer on politics, and, as we have seen, he deliberately distanced himself from the ambitions of the philosopher or theorist. As should by now be evident, we do not turn to him for that kind of intellectual architectonic, based on rigorous analysis of the nature of the state or the logic of political obligation, which had for so long been the staple of the Western tradition of political theory. *Culture and Anarchy* and the other essays included in this volume are, rather, works of social criticism, deploying a range of rhetorical resources to cajole, mock, provoke, and persuade. But this is a genre which, at the close of the twentieth century, appears to be taking over much of the territory formerly occupied by systematic social and political theory. For intellectual and practical reasons, confidence in the very possibility of proceeding from putatively universal first principles to generally applicable normative conclusions has declined sharply in recent decades, and it may be that contributions to 'political thought' in the future will be increasingly local in scope and informal in manner. Arnold's acuity in discerning the emotional and psychological roots of political attitudes, together with his capacity for bringing a vision of human wholeness to bear upon the practical and everyday, enabled him to characterize the contentious public life of his time with a sharpness and stylishness which continue to provide a model for this form of social criticism.

# Chronology

1822    Born (24 December) at Laleham in the Thames valley, second child and eldest son of Thomas Arnold, Headmaster of Rugby School (1828–41) and Regius Professor of Modern History at Oxford (1841–2), and of Mary Arnold, *née* Penrose

1841–4    Undergraduate at Balliol College, Oxford; graduates with 2nd-class degree

1845    Elected Fellow of Oriel College, Oxford

1847    Becomes personal secretary to Lord Lansdowne, a leading Whig politician

1849    Publishes (anonymously) first volume of poetry, *The Strayed Reveller, and Other Poems*

1850    Meets and (1851) marries Frances Lucy Wightman, daughter of a prominent judge

1851–86    Inspector, eventually Chief Inspector, of Schools; his duties involve frequent travelling, the inspection chiefly of Nonconformist schools, and several tours of European schools

1852–4    Publishes three more volumes of poetry (*Empedocles on Etna and other Poems; Poems. A New Edition; Poems. Second Series*)

1857    Elected to the (largely honorary) post of Professor of Poetry at Oxford (re-elected 1862), in which he is required to deliver three public lectures a year

1859    Visits and reports on Continental schools for the Newcastle Commission on Elementary Education

| | |
|---|---|
| 1861 | *The Popular Education of France* (the 'Introduction' later republished as 'Democracy') |
| 1862 | Publishes his first periodical article ('The Twice-Revised Code', *Fraser's Magazine*); thereafter publishes a very large number of articles in the main cultural and political journals of the time, nearly all his books first appearing in this form |
| 1864 | 'The Function of Criticism at the Present Time' published in *The National Review* (republished as the opening essay in his *Essays in Criticism* in 1865) |
| 1867 | 'Culture and Its Enemies' published in *The Cornhill Magazine*, the first of the series of articles that were to make up *Culture and Anarchy* |
| 1869 | *Culture and Anarchy: An Essay in Political and Social Criticism* |
| 1873 | *Literature and Dogma*, his major work on religion |
| 1878 | 'Equality' published in *The Fortnightly Review* (and republished in his *Mixed Essays* in 1879) |
| 1883 | Awarded Civil List pension 'in public recognition of service to the poetry and literature of England' |
| 1883–4 | Makes lecture tour of the USA |
| 1886 | Retires from school inspecting |
| 1888 | Dies (15 April) at Liverpool while awaiting the arrival of his married daughter from America |

# Bibliographical note

The standard edition of Arnold's prose is *The Complete Prose Works of Matthew Arnold*, edited by R.H. Super, 11 vols. (Ann Arbor, 1960–77). This superb edition not only establishes the authoritative texts of his works and records textual variants, but it also provides a great deal of useful historical, critical, and bibliographical information, and I have relied upon it heavily. For the poetry, the standard edition is *The Poems of Matthew Arnold*, edited by Kenneth Allott, 2nd edition revised by Miriam Allott (London, 1979). Selections fron Arnold's writings are available in various modern editions: two of the most accessible are *Matthew Arnold: Selected Prose*, edited by P.J. Keating in the 'Penguin English Library' (Harmondsworth, 1970); and *Matthew Arnold: Selected Works*, edited by Miriam Allott and R.H. Super in the 'Oxford Authors' series (Oxford, 1986), though neither of these selections prints the complete text of *Culture and Anarchy*. A new edition of Arnold's correspondence is in preparation, but meanwhile one has to fall back on the (somewhat unreliable) *Letters of Matthew Arnold 1848–1888*, collected and arranged by George W.E. Russell, 2 vols. (London, 1895); this should be supplemented by *Unpublished Letters of Matthew Arnold*, edited by Arnold Whitridge (New Haven, Conn., 1923), and *The Letters of Matthew Arnold to Arthur Hugh Clough*, edited by Howard Foster Lowry (Oxford, 1932). Much the fullest biography, which draws extensively on these and the as yet unpublished letters, is Park Honan, *Matthew Arnold: a Life* (London, 1981).

There is a large secondary literature on Arnold, and what follows is an introductory selection intended to be of help primarily to the student of Arnold's political and social thought. For fuller and more authoritative guides, one should consult David J. DeLaura (ed.), *Victorian Prose: A Guide to Research* (New York, 1973), and the annual bibliographies provided in three periodicals: *Victorian Studies, Victorian Poetry*, and *The Arnoldian*. Some indication of the range of contemporary response to Arnold may be gathered from the relevant volumes in the 'Critical Heritage' series: *Matthew Arnold: the Poetry*, edited by Carl Dawson (London, 1973), and *Matthew Arnold: Prose Writings*, edited by Carl Dawson and John Pfordresher (London, 1979).

Among studies which deal with Arnold's work as a whole, a special interest attaches, despite its datedness, to Lionel Trilling's *Matthew Arnold* (New York, 1939; repr. Oxford, 1982). Two particularly good collections of essays, which deal with both the poetry and the prose, are David J. DeLaura (ed.), *Matthew Arnold: a Collection of Critical Essays* (Englewood Cliffs, N.J., 1973) and Kenneth Allott (ed.), *Matthew Arnold*, 'Writers and their Background', (London, 1975). Three further collections, of rather more variable quality, are Robert Giddings (ed.), *Matthew Arnold: Between Two Worlds* (London, 1986); Miriam Allott (ed.), *Matthew Arnold 1988: A Centennial Review (Essays and Studies*, vol. 41) (London 1988); and Clinton Machann and Forrest D. Burt (eds.), *Matthew Arnold in his Time and Ours* (Charlottesville, Va., 1988). The most recent general study is Stefan Collini, *Arnold* (Oxford, 1988).

Among more detailed works, two are particularly outstanding: Sidney Coulling, *Matthew Arnold and his Critics: A Study of Arnold's Controversies* (Athens, Ohio, 1974), and David J. DeLaura, *Hebrew and Hellene in Victorian England: Newman, Arnold, Pater* (Austin, Texas, 1969). The chapter on Arnold in John Holloway, *The Victorian Sage: Studies in Argument* (London, 1953) is extremely perceptive. Arnold's literary and cultural criticism has been the subject of several classic essays which are reprinted in the collections of essays edited by DeLaura and Allott, cited above; two books which are interesting and very learned, but which perhaps ride their particular interpretations a little hard, are William A. Madden, *Matthew Arnold: A Study of the Aesthetic Temperament in Victorian England* (Bloomington, 1967) and Joseph Carroll, *The Cultural Theory of Matthew Arnold* (Berkeley, 1982). Arnold's religious and moral thought has been discussed very thoroughly in William Robbins, *The Ethical Idealism of Matthew*

*Arnold: A Study of the Nature and Sources of his Moral Ideas* (Toronto, 1959), in the chapters on Arnold in Vincent Buckley, *Poetry and Morality* (London, 1959), in Ruth apRoberts, *Arnold and God* (Berkeley, 1983), and in James C. Livingston, *Matthew Arnold and Christianity* (Columbia, South Carolina, 1986).

His social and political writings have been less well served: F. G. Walcott, *The Origins of 'Culture and Anarchy': Matthew Arnold and Popular Education in England* (Toronto, 1970) is useful on Arnold's educational writings in the 1860s, but Patrick J. McCarthy, *Matthew Arnold and the Three Classes* (New York, 1964) must be used with caution. R. H. Super's brief *The Time-Spirit of Matthew Arnold* (Ann Arbor, 1970) contains a helpful discussion of Arnold as 'a Liberal of the future'. Edward Alexander, *Matthew Arnold and John Stuart Mill* (New York, 1965) is a full comparison, though now somewhat dated. For brief general assessments of his social thought, which give due attention to 'Democracy', 'Equality', and other essays, see Peter Keating, 'Arnold's Social and Political Thought', in Allott (ed.), *Matthew Arnold*, and Collini, *Arnold*, ch. 5, 'The Social Critic'.

For the intellectual context of Arnold's social criticism see, among recent studies, Christopher Harvie, *The Lights of Liberalism: Academic Liberals and the Challenge of Democracy 1860–1886* (London, 1976); Christopher Kent, *Brains and Numbers: Elitism, Comtism, and Democracy in Mid-Victorian England* (Toronto, 1978); Richard Jenkyns, *The Victorians and Ancient Greece* (London, 1980); T. W. Heyck, *The Transformation of Intellectual Life in Victorian England* (Beckenham, 1982); Richard Bellamy (ed.), *Victorian Liberalism: Nineteenth-Century Political Thought and Practice* (London, 1989); Stefan Collini, *Public Moralists: Political Thought and Intellectual Life in Britain 1850–1930* (Oxford, 1991).

# Note on the texts and acknowledgements

Following the dominant modern editorial practice, the texts reprinted here are those of the last editions to appear in Arnold's lifetime over which he is known (or may reasonably be presumed) to have exercised any supervision. Arnold often revised his writings quite substantially for later editions, generally reducing the merely topical allusions and the sometimes sharp comments on named contemporaries. The textual variants are given in full in Super's edition of the complete prose.

'Democracy', as noted above (p. xii), has a complex history. After his official 'Report on the Systems of Popular Education in France, Holland, and the French Cantons of Switzerland' had been published as part of the Newcastle Commission's Report in 1861, Arnold decided to publish it separately at his own expense. The present essay, simply entitled 'Introduction', first appeared in this version of the report; Arnold revised it, adding its present title, when he included it in his *Mixed Essays* of 1879. The present text is that of the 1883 edition of his *Mixed Essays, Irish Essays, and Others*.

'The Functions of Criticism at the Present Time' was first given as a lecture at Oxford in October 1864, and published in the *National Review* for November of that year. With 'Functions' reduced to the singular, it appeared (as Arnold had intended in composing it) as the opening essay in his *Essays in Criticism* (1st edn, 1865; 2nd edn, 1869; 3rd enlarged edn, 1875). The present text is that of the 1884 edition of *Essays in Criticism*.

*Culture and Anarchy* also had a somewhat complicated publishing history. 'Culture and its Enemies' was the last of his Oxford lectures, delivered in June 1867 and published in the *Cornhill Magazine* in July. This provoked a considerable number of critical reponses, to which Arnold replied with a series of articles entitled 'Anarchy and Authority' published in the *Cornhill* between January and August 1868. These articles were then combined to form *Culture and Anarchy*, first published (without chapter titles) in 1869; this was the first appearance of the 'Preface', which contained further replies to critics. For the second edition of 1875, Arnold made numerous changes, including the addition of the chapter titles; a third edition appeared in 1882. The present text is that of this edition as printed, together with *Friendship's Garland*, in 1883. Since the 'Preface' in effect assumes some prior familiarity with the periodical publication of the chapters it is ostensibly intended to introduce, I have followed Super's example in placing it after the main text. It should perhaps be noted that the hitherto most widely available edition of *Culture and Anarchy*, edited by J. Dover Wilson (Cambridge, 1932 and frequently reprinted), is textually something of a mishmash. Essentially, it is the text of the first book edition of 1869, but it includes some (though by no means all) of the revisions introduced by Arnold in the second edition, including the chapter titles, and even a few small corrections he made for the third edition. In his 'Editor's Preface' Dover Wilson acknowledged that this 'textual combination' might seem to raise some 'problems involving editorial authority', but these do not appear to have deterred him ('another passage which I have enjoyed restoring ...' gives the flavour of his editorial practice).

'Equality' was given as a lecture at the Royal Institution in February 1878, and published in the *Fortnightly Review* in March. Arnold included it in his *Mixed Essays* of 1879; the present text (which is essentially identical with that of 1879) is that of the 1883 edition of his *Mixed Essays, Irish Essays, and Others*.

The texts reprinted here also incorporate the correction of one or two printer's errors as noted in Super's edition.

Arnold's (very few) footnotes are indicated by arabic numerals. Editorial footnotes are signalled by letters. These notes have been kept to the minimum, but Arnold's topical and allusive writing inevitably requires a certain amount of annotation for the modern reader. References to well-known writers (such as Plato or Burke) have not been annotated, and Arnold's many biblical quotations have not been identified. Translations of quotations in foreign languages have only been given where Arnold does not himself translate or give the sense of the passage in the text.

I am grateful to R.H. Super for generously encouraging me to make use of his edition of Arnold's prose, and to Oxford University Press for permission to draw upon my *Arnold*. I also owe thanks to Raymond Geuss and Quentin Skinner for their stringent editorial comments. Above all, I am grateful to 'the usual suspects' – John Burrow, Geoffrey Hawthorn, Ruth Morse, John Thompson, and Donald Winch – for good judgment, good will, and good cheer.

# Democracy

*I know that, since the Revolution, along with many dangerous, many
useful powers of Government have been weakened.*

BURKE (1770)

In giving an account of education in certain countries of the Continent, I have often spoken of the State and its action in such a way as
to offend, I fear, some of my readers, and to surprise others. With
many Englishmen, perhaps with the majority, it is a maxim that the
State, the executive power, ought to be entrusted with no more means
of action than those which it is impossible to withhold from it; that the
State neither would nor could make a safe use of any more extended
liberty; would not, because it has in itself a natural instinct of despotism, which, if not jealously checked, would become outrageous; could
not, because it is, in truth, not at all more enlightened, or fit to assume
a lead, than the mass of this enlightened community.

No sensible man will lightly go counter to an opinion firmly held by
a great body of his countrymen. He will take for granted, that for any
opinion which has struck deep root among a people so powerful, so
successful, and so well worthy of respect as the people of this country,
there certainly either are, or have been, good and sound reasons. He
will venture to impugn such an opinion with real hesitation, and only
when he thinks he perceives that the reasons which once supported it
exist no longer, or at any rate seem about to disappear very soon. For
undoubtedly there arrive periods, when, the circumstances and conditions of government having changed, the guiding maxims of govern-

ment ought to change also. *J'ai dit souvent*, says Mirabeau,[1] admonishing the Court of France in 1790, *qu'on devait changer de manière de gouverner, lorsque le gouvernement n'est plus le même.* And these decisive changes in the political situation of a people happen gradually as well as violently. "In the silent lapse of events," says Burke,[2] writing in England twenty years before the French Revolution, "as material alterations have been insensibly brought about in the policy and character of governments and nations, as those which have been marked by the tumult of public revolutions."

I propose to submit to those who have been accustomed to regard all State-action with jealousy, some reasons for thinking that the circumstances which once made that jealousy prudent and natural have undergone an essential change. I desire to lead them to consider with me, whether, in the present altered conjuncture, that State-action, which was once dangerous, may not become, not only without danger in itself, but the means of helping us against dangers from another quarter. To combine and present the considerations upon which these two propositions are based, is a task of some difficulty and delicacy. My aim is to invite impartial reflection upon the subject, not to make a hostile attack against old opinions, still less to set on foot and fully equip a new theory. In offering, therefore, the thoughts which have suggested themselves to me, I shall studiously avoid all particular applications of them likely to give offence, and shall use no more illustration and development than may be indispensable to enable the reader to seize and appreciate them.

The dissolution of the old political parties which have governed this country since the Revolution of 1688 has long been remarked. It was repeatedly declared to be happening long before it actually took place, while the vital energy of these parties still subsisted in full vigour, and was threatened only by some temporary obstruction. It has been eagerly deprecated long after it had actually begun to take place, when it was in full progress, and inevitable. These parties, differing in so much else, were yet alike in this, that they were both, in a certain broad sense, *aristocratical* parties. They were combinations of persons considerable, either by great family and estate, or by Court favour, or lastly, by eminent abilities and popularity; this last body, however,

---

[1] *Correspondence entre le Comte de Mirabeau et le Comte de la Marck*, publiée par M. de Bacourt, Paris, 1851, vol. ii. p. 143.

[2] Burke's *Works* (edit. of 1852), vol. iii. p. 115.

attaining participation in public affairs only through a conjunction with one or other of the former. These connections, though they contained men of very various degrees of birth and property, were still wholly leavened with the feelings and habits of the upper class of the nation. They had the bond of a common culture; and, however their political opinions and acts might differ, what they said and did had the stamp and style imparted by this culture, and by a common and elevated social condition.

Aristocratical bodies have no taste for a very imposing executive, or for a very active and penetrating domestic administration. They have a sense of equality among themselves, and of constituting in themselves what is greatest and most dignified in the realm, which makes their pride revolt against the overshadowing greatness and dignity of a commanding executive. They have a temper of independence, and a habit of uncontrolled action, which makes them impatient of encountering, in the management of the interior concerns of the country, the machinery and regulations of a superior and peremptory power. The different parties amongst them, as they successively get possession of the government, respect this jealous disposition in their opponents, because they share it themselves. It is a disposition proper to them as great personages, not as ministers; and as they are great personages for their whole life, while they may probably be ministers but for a very short time, the instinct of their social condition avails more with them than the instinct of their official function. To administer as little as possible, to make its weight felt in foreign affairs rather than in domestic, to see in ministerial station rather the means of power and dignity than a means of searching and useful administrative activity, is the natural tendency of an aristocratic executive. It is a tendency which is creditable to the good sense of aristocracies, honourable to their moderation, and at the same time fortunate for their country, of whose internal development they are not fitted to have the full direction.

One strong and beneficial influence, however, the administration of a vigorous and high-minded aristocracy is calculated to exert upon a robust and sound people. I have had occasion, in speaking of Homer, to say very often, and with much emphasis, that he is *in the grand style*. It is the chief virtue of a healthy and uncorrupted aristocracy, that it is, in general, in this grand style. That elevation of character, that noble way of thinking and behaving, which is an eminent gift of nature to

3

some individuals, is also often generated in whole classes of men (at least when these come of a strong and good race) by the possession of power, by the importance and responsibility of high station, by habitual dealing with great things, by being placed above the necessity of constantly struggling for little things. And it is the source of great virtues. It may go along with a not very quick or open intelligence; but it cannot well go along with a conduct vulgar and ignoble. A governing class imbued with it may not be capable of intelligently leading the masses of a people to the highest pitch of welfare for them; but it sets them an invaluable example of qualities without which no really high welfare can exist. This has been done for their nation by the best aristocracies. The Roman aristocracy did it; the English aristocracy has done it. They each fostered in the mass of the peoples they governed, — peoples of sturdy moral constitution and apt to learn such lessons, — a greatness of spirit, the natural growth of the condition of magnates and rulers, but not the natural growth of the condition of the common people. They made, the one of the Roman, the other of the English people, in spite of all the shortcomings of each, great peoples, peoples *in the grand style*. And this they did, while wielding the people according to their own notions, and in the direction which seemed good to them; not as servants and instruments of the people, but as its commanders and heads; solicitous for the good of their country, indeed, but taking for granted that of that good they themselves were the supreme judges, and were to fix the conditions.

The time has arrived, however, when it is becoming impossible for the aristocracy of England to conduct and wield the English nation any longer. It still, indeed, administers public affairs; and it is a great error to suppose, as many persons in England suppose, that it administers but does not govern. He who administers, governs,[3] because he infixes his own mark and stamps his own character on all public affairs as they pass through his hands; and, therefore, so long as the English aristocracy administers the commonwealth, it still governs it. But signs not to be mistaken show that its headship and leadership of the nation, by virtue of the substantial acquiescence of the body of the nation in its predominance and right to lead, is nearly over. That acquiescence was the tenure by which it held its power; and it is fast giving way. The superiority of the upper class over all

---

[3] *Administrer, c'est gouverner*, says Mirabeau; *gouverner, c'est régner; tout se réduit là.*

4

others is no longer so great; the willingness of the others to recognise that superiority is no longer so ready.

This change has been brought about by natural and inevitable causes, and neither the great nor the multitude are to be blamed for it. The growing demands and audaciousness of the latter, the encroaching spirit of democracy, are, indeed, matters of loud complaint with some persons. But these persons are complaining of human nature itself, when they thus complain of a manifestation of its native and ineradicable impulse. Life itself consists, say the philosophers, in the effort *to affirm one's own essence*; meaning by this, to develop one's own existence fully and freely, to have ample light and air, to be neither cramped nor overshadowed. Democracy is trying *to affirm its own essence*; to live, to enjoy, to possess the world, as aristocracy has tried, and successfully tried, before it. Ever since Europe emerged from barbarism, ever since the condition of the common people began a little to improve, ever since their minds began to stir, this effort of democracy has been gaining strength; and the more their condition improves, the more strength this effort gains. So potent is the charm of life and expansion upon the living; the moment men are aware of them, they begin to desire them, and the more they have of them, the more they crave.

This movement of democracy, like other operations of nature, merits properly neither blame nor praise. Its partisans are apt to give it credit which it does not deserve, while its enemies are apt to upbraid it unjustly. Its friends celebrate it as the author of all freedom. But political freedom may very well be established by aristocratic founders; and, certainly, the political freedom of England owes more to the grasping English barons than to democracy. Social freedom,—equality,— that is rather the field of the conquests of democracy. And here what I must call the injustice of its enemies comes in. For its seeking after equality, democracy is often, in this country above all, vehemently and scornfully blamed; its temper contrasted with that worthier temper which can magnanimously endure social distinctions; its operations all referred, as of course, to the stirrings of a base and malignant envy. No doubt there is a gross and vulgar spirit of envy, prompting the hearts of many of those who cry for equality. No doubt there are ignoble natures which prefer equality to liberty. But what we have to ask is, when the life of democracy is admitted as something natural and inevitable, whether this or that product of democracy is a necessary growth from its parent stock, or merely an excrescence upon it. If it be the latter, certainly it may be due to the meanest and most culpable passions. But if it be the former, then this product, however base and blameworthy the passions which it may sometimes be made to serve, can in itself be no more reprehensible than the vital impulse of democracy is in itself reprehensible; and this impulse is, as has been shown, identical with the ceaseless vital effort of human nature itself.

Now, can it be denied, that a certain approach to equality, at any rate a certain reduction of signal inequalities, is a natural, instinctive demand of that impulse which drives society as a whole,—no longer individuals and limited classes only, but the mass of a community,—to develop itself with the utmost possible fulness and freedom? Can it be denied, that to live in a society of equals tends in general to make a man's spirits expand, and his faculties work easily and actively; while, to live in a society of superiors, although it may occasionally be a very good discipline, yet in general tends to tame the spirits and to make the play of the faculties less secure and active? Can it be denied, that to be heavily overshadowed, to be profoundly insignificant, has, on the whole, a depressing and benumbing effect on the character? I know that some individuals react against the strongest impediments, and owe success and greatness to the efforts which they are thus forced to make. But the question is not about individuals. The question is about the common bulk of mankind, persons without extraordinary gifts or exceptional energy, and who will ever require, in order to make the best of themselves, encouragement and directly favouring circumstances. Can any one deny, that for these the spectacle, when they would rise, of a condition of splendour, grandeur, and culture, which they cannot possibly reach, has the effect of making them flag in spirit, and of disposing them to sink despondingly back into their own condition? Can any one deny, that the knowledge how poor and insignificant the best condition of improvement and culture attainable by them must be esteemed by a class incomparably richer-endowed, tends to cheapen this modest possible amelioration in the account of those classes also for whom it would be relatively a real progress, and to disenchant their imaginations with it? It seems to me impossible to deny this. And therefore a philosophic observer,[4] with no love for

---

[4] M. de Tocqueville. See his *Démocratie en Amérique* (edit. of 1835), vol. i. p. 11. "Le peuple est plus grossier dans les pays aristocratiques que partout ailleurs. Dans ces lieux,

democracy, but rather with a terror of it, has been constrained to remark, that "the common people is more uncivilised in aristocratic countries than in any others;" because there "the lowly and the poor feel themselves, as it were, overwhelmed with the weight of their own inferiority." He has been constrained to remark[5] that "there is such a thing as a manly and legitimate passion for equality, prompting men to desire to be, *all* of them, in the enjoyment of power and consideration." And, in France, that very equality, which is by us so impetuously decried, while it has by no means improved (it is said) the upper classes of French society, has undoubtedly given to the lower classes, to the body of the common people, a self-respect, an enlargement of spirit, a consciousness of counting for something in their country's action, which has raised them in the scale of humanity. The common people, in France, seems to me the soundest part of the French nation. They seem to me more free from the two opposite degradations of multitudes, brutality and servility, to have a more developed human life, more of what distinguishes elsewhere the cultured classes from the vulgar, than the common people in any other country with which I am acquainted.

I do not say that grandeur and prosperity may not be attained by a nation divided into the most widely distinct classes, and presenting the most signal inequalities of rank and fortune. I do not say that great national virtues may not be developed in it. I do not even say that a popular order, accepting this demarcation of classes as an eternal providential arrangement, not questioning the natural right of a superior order to lead it, content within its own sphere, admiring the grandeur and highmindedness of its ruling class, and catching on its own spirit some reflex of what it thus admires, may not be a happier body, as to the eye of the imagination it is certainly a more beautiful body, than a popular order, pushing, excited, and presumptuous; a popular order, jealous of recognising fixed superiorities, petulantly claiming to be as good as its betters, and tastelessly attiring itself with the fashions and designations which have become unalterably associated with a wealthy and refined class, and which, tricking out those who have neither wealth nor refinement, are ridiculous. But a popular

où se rencontrent des hommes si forts et si riches, les faibles et les pauvres se sentent comme accablés de leur bassesse; ne découvrant aucun point par lequel ils puissent regagner l'égalité, ils désespèrent entièrement d'eux-mêmes, et se laissent tomber au-dessous de la dignité humaine."

[5] *Démocratie en Amérique*, vol. i. p. 60.

order of that old-fashioned stamp exists now only for the imagination. It is not the force with which modern society has to reckon. Such a body may be a sturdy, honest, and sound-hearted lower class; but it is not a democratic people. It is not that power, which at the present day in all nations is to be found existing; in some, has obtained the mastery; in others, is yet in a state of expectation and preparation.

The power of France in Europe is at this day mainly owing to the completeness with which she has organised democratic institutions. The action of the French State is excessive; but it is too little understood in England that the French people has adopted this action for its own purposes, has in great measure attained those purposes by it, and owes to its having done so the chief part of its influence in Europe. The growing power in Europe is democracy; and France has organised democracy with a certain indisputable grandeur and success. The ideas of 1789 were working everywhere in the eighteenth century; but it was because in France the State adopted them that the French Revolution became an historic epoch for the world, and France the lode-star of Continental democracy. Her airs of superiority and her overweening pretensions come from her sense of the power which she derives from this cause. Every one knows how Frenchmen proclaim France to be at the head of civilisation, the French army to be the soldier of God, Paris to be the brain of Europe, and so on. All this is, no doubt, in a vein of sufficient fatuity and bad taste; but it means, at bottom, that France believes she has so organised herself as to facilitate for all members of her society full and free expansion; that she believes herself to have remodelled her institutions with an eye to reason rather than custom, and to right rather than fact; it means, that she believes the other peoples of Europe to be preparing themselves, more or less rapidly, for a like achievement, and that she is conscious of her power and influence upon them as an initiatress and example. In this belief there is a part of truth and a part of delusion. I think it is more profitable for a Frenchman to consider the part of delusion contained in it; for an Englishman, the part of truth.

It is because aristocracies almost inevitably fail to appreciate justly, or even to take into their mind, the instinct pushing the masses towards expansion and fuller life, that they lose their hold over them. It is the old story of the incapacity of aristocracies for ideas,—the secret of their want of success in modern epochs. The people treats them with flagrant injustice, when it denies all obligation to them. They can, and often do, impart a high spirit, a fine ideal of grandeur, to the people; thus they lay the foundations of a great nation. But they leave the people still the multitude, the crowd; they have small belief in the power of the ideas which are its life. Themselves a power reposing on all which is most solid, material, and visible, they are slow to attach any great importance to influences impalpable, spiritual, and viewless. Although, therefore, a disinterested looker-on might often be disposed, seeing what has actually been achieved by aristocracies, to wish to retain or replace them in their preponderance, rather than commit a nation to the hazards of a new and untried future; yet the masses instinctively feel that they can never consent to this without renouncing the inmost impulse of their being; and that they should make such a renunciation cannot seriously be expected of them. Except on conditions which make its expansion, in the sense understood by itself, fully possible, democracy will never frankly ally itself with aristocracy; and on these conditions perhaps no aristocracy will ever frankly ally itself with it. Even the English aristocracy, so politic, so capable of compromises, has shown no signs of being able so to transform itself as to render such an alliance possible. The reception given by the Peers to the bill for establishing life-peerages was, in this respect, of ill omen.[a] The separation between aristocracy and democracy will probably, therefore, go on still widening.

And it must in fairness be added, that as in one most important part of general human culture, — openness to ideas and ardour for them, — aristocracy is less advanced than democracy, to replace or keep the latter under the tutelage of the former would in some respects be actually unfavourable to the progress of the world. At epochs when new ideas are powerfully fermenting in a society, and profoundly changing its spirit, aristocracies, as they are in general not long suffered to guide it without question, so are they by nature not well fitted to guide it intelligently.

In England, democracy has been slow in developing itself, having met with much to withstand it, not only in the worth of the aristocracy, but also in the fine qualities of the common people. The aristocracy has been more in sympathy with the common people than perhaps any

---

[a] In 1856 the House of Lords refused to allow Sir James Parke to be created a life peer, arguing that the Crown had lost by disuse the power of creating life peerages. In effect this amounted to a defence of the hereditary principle.

other aristocracy. It has rarely given them great umbrage; it has neither been frivolous, so as to provoke their contempt, nor impertinent, so as to provoke their irritation. Above all, it has in general meant to act with justice, according to its own notions of justice. Therefore the feeling of admiring deference to such a class was more deep-rooted in the people of this country, more cordial, and more persistent, than in any people of the Continent. But, besides this, the vigour and high spirit of the English common people bred in them a self-reliance which disposed each man to act individually and independently; and so long as this disposition prevails through a nation divided into classes, the predominance of an aristocracy, of the class containing the greatest and strongest individuals of the nation, is secure. Democracy is a force in which the concert of a great number of men makes up for the weakness of each man taken by himself; democracy accepts a certain relative rise in their condition, obtainable by this concert for a great number, as something desirable in itself, because though this is undoubtedly far below grandeur, it is yet a good deal above insignificance. A very strong, self-reliant people neither easily learns to act in concert, nor easily brings itself to regard any middling good, any good short of the best, as an object ardently to be coveted and striven for. It keeps its eye on the grand prizes, and these are to be won only by distancing competitors, by getting before one's comrades, by succeeding all by one's self; and so long as a people works thus individually, it does not work democratically. The English people has all the qualities which dispose a people to work individually; may it never lose them! A people without the salt of these qualities, relying wholly on mutual co-operation, and proposing to itself second-rate ideals, would arrive at the pettiness and stationariness of China. But the English people is no longer so entirely ruled by them as not to show visible beginnings of democratic action; it becomes more and more sensible to the irresistible seduction of democratic ideas, promising to each individual of the multitude increased self-respect and expansion with the increased importance and authority of the multitude to which he belongs, with the diminished preponderance of the aristocratic class above him.

While the habit and disposition of deference are thus dying out among the lower classes of the English nation, it seems to me indisputable that the advantages which command deference, that eminent superiority in high feeling, dignity, and culture, tend to diminish among the highest class. I shall not be suspected of any inclination to underrate the aristocracy of this country. I regard it as the worthiest, as it certainly has been the most successful, aristocracy of which history makes record. If it has not been able to develop excellences which do not belong to the nature of an aristocracy, yet it has been able to avoid defects to which the nature of an aristocracy is peculiarly prone. But I cannot read the history of the flowering time of the English aristocracy, the eighteenth century, and then look at this aristocracy in our own century, without feeling that there has been a change. I am not now thinking of private and domestic virtues, of morality, of decorum. Perhaps with respect to these there has in this class, as in society at large, been a change for the better. I am thinking of those public and conspicuous virtues by which the multitude is captivated and led,—lofty spirit, commanding character, exquisite culture. It is true that the advance of all classes in culture and refinement may make the culture of one class, which, isolated, appeared remarkable, appear so no longer; but exquisite culture and great dignity are always something rare and striking, and it is the distinction of the English aristocracy, in the eighteenth century, that not only was their culture something rare by comparison with the rawness of the masses, it was something rare and admirable in itself. It is rather that this rare culture of the highest class has actually somewhat declined,[6] than that it has come to look less by juxtaposition with the augmented culture of other classes.

Probably democracy has something to answer for in this falling off of her rival. To feel itself raised on high, venerated, followed, no doubt stimulates a fine nature to keep itself worthy to be followed, venerated, raised on high; hence that lofty maxim, *noblesse oblige*. To feel its culture something precious and singular, makes such a nature zealous to retain and extend it. The elation and energy thus fostered by the sense of its advantages, certainly enhances the worth, strengthens the behaviour, and quickens all the active powers of the class enjoying it. *Possunt quia posse videntur.*[b] The removal of the stimulus a

---

[6] This will appear doubtful to no one well acquainted with the literature and memoirs of the last century. To give but two illustrations out of a thousand. Let the reader refer to the anecdote told by Robert Wood in his *Essay on the Genius of Homer* (London, 1775), p. vii. and to Lord Chesterfield's *Letters* (edit. of 1845), vol. i. pp. 115, 143; vol. ii. p. 54; and then say, whether the culture there indicated as the culture of a *class* has maintained itself at that level.

[b] 'They succeed because they are seen to succeed'; Virgil, *Aeneid* v, 231.

little relaxes their energy. It is not so much that they sink to be somewhat less than themselves, as that they cease to be somewhat more than themselves. But, however this may be, whencesoever the change may proceed, I cannot doubt that in the aristocratic virtue, in the intrinsic commanding force of the English upper class, there is a diminution. Relics of a great generation are still, perhaps, to be seen amongst them, surviving exemplars of noble manners and consummate culture; but they disappear one after the other, and no one of their kind takes their place. At the very moment when democracy becomes less and less disposed to follow and to admire, aristocracy becomes less and less qualified to command and to captivate.

On the one hand, then, the masses of the people in this country are preparing to take a much more active part than formerly in controlling its destinies; on the other hand, the aristocracy (using this word in the widest sense, to include not only the nobility and landed gentry, but also those reinforcements from the classes bordering upon itself, which this class constantly attracts and assimilates), while it is threatened with losing its hold on the rudder of government, its power to give to public affairs its own bias and direction, is losing also that influence on the spirit and character of the people which it long exercised.

I know that this will be warmly denied by some persons. Those who have grown up amidst a certain state of things, those whose habits, and interests, and affections, are closely concerned with its continuance, are slow to believe that it is not a part of the order of nature, or that it can ever come to an end. But I think that what I have here laid down will not appear doubtful either to the most competent and friendly foreign observers of this country, or to those Englishmen who, clear of all influences of class or party, have applied themselves steadily to see the tendencies of their nation as they really are. Assuming it to be true, a great number of considerations are suggested by it; but it is my purpose here to insist upon one only.

That one consideration is: On what action may we rely to replace, for some time at any rate, that action of the aristocracy upon the people of this country, which we have seen exercise an influence in many respects elevating and beneficial, but which is rapidly, and from inevitable causes, ceasing? In other words, and to use a short and significant modern expression which every one understands, what influence may help us to prevent the English people from becoming, with the growth of democracy, *Americanised?* I confess I am disposed to answer: On the action of the State.

I know what a chorus of objectors will be ready. One will say: Rather repair and restore the influence of aristocracy. Another will say: It is not a bad thing, but a good thing, that the English People should be Americanised. But the most formidable and the most widely entertained objection, by far, will be that which founds itself upon the present actual state of things in another country; which says: Look at France! there you have a signal example of the alliance of democracy with a powerful State-action, and see how it works.

This last and principal objection I will notice at once. I have had occasion to touch upon the first already, and upon the second I shall touch presently. It seems to me, then, that one may save one's self from much idle terror at names and shadows if one will be at the pains to remember what different conditions the different character of two nations must necessarily impose on the operation of any principle. That which operates noxiously in one, may operate wholesomely in the other; because the unsound part of the one's character may be yet further inflamed and enlarged by it, the unsound part of the other's may find in it a corrective and an abatement. This is the great use which two unlike characters may find in observing each other. Neither is likely to have the other's faults, so each may safely adopt as much as suits him of the other's qualities. If I were a Frenchman I should never be weary of admiring the independent, individual, local habits of action in England, of directing attention to the evils occasioned in France by the excessive action of the State; for I should be very sure that, say what I might, the part of the State would never be too small in France, nor that of the individual too large. Being an Englishman, I see nothing but good in freely recognising the coherence, rationality, and efficaciousness which characterise the strong State-action of France, of acknowledging the want of method, reason, and result which attend the feeble State-action of England; because I am very sure that, strengthen in England the action of the State as one may, it will always find itself sufficiently controlled. But when either the *Constitutionnel* sneers at the do-little talkativeness of parliamentary government, or when the *Morning Star* inveighs against the despotism of a centralised administration, it seems to me that they lose their labour, because they are hardening themselves against dangers to which they are neither of them liable.ᶜ Both the one and the other, in plain truth,

> "Compound for sins they are inclined to,
> By damning those they have no mind to."

They should rather exchange doctrines one with the other, and each might thus, perhaps, be profited.

So that the exaggeration of the action of the State, in France, furnishes no reason for absolutely refusing to enlarge the action of the State in England; because the genius and temper of the people of this country are such as to render impossible that exaggeration which the genius and temper of the French rendered easy. There is no danger at all that the native independence and individualism of the English character will ever belie itself, and become either weakly prone to lean on others, or blindly confiding in them.

English democracy runs no risk of being overmastered by the State; it is almost certain that it will throw off the tutelage of aristocracy. Its real danger is, that it will have far too much its own way, and be left far too much to itself. "What harm will there be in that?" say some; "are we not a self-governing people?" I answer: "We have never yet been a *self-governing democracy*, or anything like it." The difficulty for democracy is, how to find and keep high ideals. The individuals who compose it are, the bulk of them, persons who need to follow an ideal, not to set one; and one ideal of greatness, high feeling, and fine culture, which an aristocracy once supplied to them, they lose by the very fact of ceasing to be a lower order and becoming a democracy. Nations are not truly great solely because the individuals composing them are numerous, free, and active; but they are great when these numbers, this freedom, and this activity are employed in the service of an ideal higher than that of an ordinary man, taken by himself. Our society is probably destined to become much more democratic; who or what will give a high tone to the nation then? That is the grave question.

The greatest men of America, her Washingtons, Hamiltons,

---

ᶜ The *Constitutionnel*, founded in 1815, was Bonapartist in sympathies and supported the *coup d'état* by which Napoleon III became Emperor in 1851. The *Morning Star*, a Radical newspaper founded in 1856, supported the laissez-faire views of the 'Manchester School' associated with Cobden and Bright (see below p. 168).

Madisons, well understanding that aristocratical institutions are not in all times and places possible; well perceiving that in their Republic there was no place for these; comprehending, therefore, that from these that security for national dignity and greatness, an ideal commanding popular reverence, was not to be obtained, but knowing that this ideal was indispensable, would have been rejoiced to found a substitute for it in the dignity and authority of the State. They deplored the weakness and insignificance of the executive power as a calamity. When the inevitable course of events has made our self-government something really like that of America, when it has removed or weakened that security for national dignity, which we possessed in *aristocracy*, will the substitute of the *State* be equally wanting to us? If it is, then the dangers of America will really be ours; the dangers which come from the multitude being in power, with no adequate ideal to elevate or guide the multitude.

It would really be wasting time to contend at length, that to give more prominence to the idea of the State is now possible in this country, without endangering liberty. In other countries the habits and dispositions of the people may be such that the State, if once it acts, may be easily suffered to usurp exorbitantly; here they certainly are not. Here the people will always sufficiently keep in mind that any public authority is a trust delegated by themselves, for certain purposes, and with certain limits; and if that authority pretends to an absolute, independent character, they will soon enough (and very rightly) remind it of its error. Here there can be no question of a paternal government, of an irresponsible executive power, professing to act for the people's good, but without the people's consent, and, if necessary, against the people's wishes; here no one dreams of removing a single constitutional control, of abolishing a single safeguard for securing a correspondence between the acts of government and the will of the nation. The question is, whether, retaining all its power of control over a government which should abuse its trust, the nation may not now find advantage in voluntarily allowing to it purposes somewhat ampler, and limits somewhat wider within which to execute them, than formerly; whether the nation may not thus acquire in the State an ideal of high reason and right feeling, representing its best self, commanding general respect, and forming a rallying-point for the intelligence and for the worthiest instincts of the community, which will herein find a true bond of union.

I am convinced that if the worst mischiefs of democracy ever happen in England, it will be, not because a new condition of things has come upon us unforeseen, but because, though we all foresaw it, our efforts to deal with it were in the wrong direction. At the present time, almost every one believes in the growth of democracy, almost every one talks of it, almost every one laments it; but the last thing people can be brought to do is to make timely preparation for it. Many of those who, if they would, could do most to forward this work of preparation, are made slack and hesitating by the belief that, after all, in England, things may probably never go very far; that it will be possible to keep much more of the past than speculators say. Others, with a more robust faith, think that all democracy wants is vigorous putting-down; and that, with a good will and strong hand, it is perfectly possible to retain or restore the whole system of the Middle Ages. Others, free from the prejudices of class and position which warp the judgment of these, and who would, I believe, be the first and greatest gainers by strengthening the hands of the State, are averse from doing so by reason of suspicions and fears, once perfectly well-grounded, but, in this age and in the present circumstances, well-grounded no longer.

I speak of the middle classes. I have already shown how it is the natural disposition of an aristocratical class to view with jealousy the development of a considerable State-power. But this disposition has in England found extraordinary favour and support in regions not aristocratical, — from the middle classes; and, above all, from the kernel of these classes, the Protestant Dissenters. And for a very good reason. In times when passions ran high, even an aristocratical executive was easily stimulated into using, for the gratification of its friends and the abasement of its enemies, those administrative engines which, the moment it chose to stretch its hand forth, stood ready for its grasp. Matters of domestic concern, matters of religious profession and religious exercise, offered a peculiar field for an intervention gainful and agreeable to friends, injurious and irritating to enemies. Such an intervention was attempted and practised. Government lent its machinery and authority to the aristocratical and ecclesiastical party, which it regarded as its best support. The party which suffered comprised the flower and strength of that middle class of society, always very flourishing and robust in this country. That powerful class, from this specimen of the administrative activity of government, conceived a strong antipathy against all intervention of the State in certain spheres. An active, stringent administration in those spheres, meant at that time a High Church and Prelatic administration in them, an administration galling to the Puritan party and to the middle class; and this aggrieved class had naturally no proneness to draw nice philosophical distinctions between State-action in these spheres, as a thing for abstract consideration, and State-action in them as they practically felt it and supposed themselves likely long to feel it, guided by their adversaries. In the minds of the English middle class, there-fore, State-action in social and domestic concerns became inextric-ably associated with the idea of a Conventicle Act, a Five-Mile Act, an Act of Uniformity.[d] Their abhorrence of such a State-action as this they extended to State-action in general; and, having never known a beneficent and just State-power, they enlarged their hatred of a cruel and partial State-power, the only one they had ever known, into a maxim that no State-power was to be trusted, that the least action, in certain provinces, was rigorously to be denied to the State, whenever this denial was possible.

Thus that jealousy of an important, sedulous, energetic executive, natural to grandees unwilling to suffer their personal authority to be circumscribed, their individual grandeur to be eclipsed, by the auth-ority and grandeur of the State, became reinforced in this country by a like sentiment among the middle classes, who had no such authority or grandeur to lose, but who, by a hasty reasoning, had theoretically condemned for ever an agency which they had practically found at times oppressive. *Leave us to ourselves!* magnates and middle classes alike cried to the State. Not only from those who were full and abounded went up this prayer, but also from those whose condition admitted of great amelioration. Not only did the whole repudiate the physician, but also those who were sick.

For it is evident, that the action of a diligent, an impartial, and a national government, while it can do little to better the condition, already fortunate enough, of the highest and richest class of its people, can really do much, by institution and regulation, to better that of the middle and lower classes. The State can bestow certain broad collective benefits, which are indeed not much if compared with the advantages already possessed by individual grandeur, but

---

[d] These Acts were passed by the first Restoration Parliament (1661–5) to restrict the activities of the Nonconformists.

which are rich and valuable if compared with the make-shifts of mediocrity and poverty. A good thing meant for the many cannot well be so exquisite as the good things of the few; but it can easily, if it comes from a donor of great resources and wide power, be incomparably better than what the many could, unaided, provide for themselves.

In all the remarks which I have been making, I have hitherto abstained from any attempt to suggest a positive application of them. I have limited myself to simply pointing out in how changed a world of ideas we are living; I have not sought to go further, and to discuss in what particular manner the world of facts is to adapt itself to this changed world of ideas. This has been my rule so far; but from this rule I shall here venture to depart, in order to dwell for a moment on a matter of practical institution, designed to meet new social exigencies: on the intervention of the State in public education.

The public secondary schools of France, decreed by the Revolution and established under the Consulate, are said by many good judges to be inferior to the old colleges. By means of the old colleges and of private tutors, the French aristocracy could procure for its children (so it is said, and very likely with truth) a better training than that which is now given in the lyceums. Yes; but the boon conferred by the State, when it founded the lyceums, was not for the aristocracy; it was for the vast middle class of Frenchmen. This class, certainly, had not already the means of a better training for its children, before the State interfered. This class, certainly, would not have succeeded in procuring by its own efforts a better training for its children, if the State had not interfered. Through the intervention of the State this class enjoys better schools for its children, not than the great and rich enjoy (that is not the question), but than the same class enjoys in any country where the State has not interfered to found them. The lyceums may not be so good as Eton or Harrow; but they are a great deal better than a *Classical and Commercial Academy*.[e]

The aristocratic classes in England may, perhaps, be well content to rest satisfied with their Eton and Harrow. The State is not likely to do better for them. Nay, the superior confidence, spirit, and style, engendered by a training in the great public schools, constitute for these classes a real privilege, a real engine of command, which they

---

[e] Arnold uses this term to refer, somewhat disparagingly, to the various schools set up for the sons of the commercial middle class.

might, if they were selfish, be sorry to lose by the establishment of schools great enough to beget a like spirit in the classes below them. But the middle classes in England have every reason not to rest content with their private schools; the State can do a great deal better for them. By giving to schools for these classes a public character, it can bring the instruction in them under a criticism which the stock of knowledge and judgment in our middle classes is not of itself at present able to supply. By giving to them a national character, it can confer on them a greatness and a noble spirit, which the tone of these classes is not of itself at present adequate to impart. Such schools would soon prove notable competitors with the existing public schools; they would do these a great service by stimulating them, and making them look into their own weak points more closely. Economical, because with charges uniform and under severe revision, they would do a great service to that large body of persons who, at present, seeing that on the whole the best secondary instruction to be found is that of the existing public schools, obtain it for their children from a sense of duty, although they can ill afford it, and although its cost is certainly exorbitant. Thus the middle classes might, by the aid of the State, better their instruction, while still keeping its cost moderate. This in itself would be a gain; but this gain would be slight in comparison with that of acquiring the sense of belonging to great and honourable seats of learning, and of breathing in their youth the air of the best culture of their nation. This sense would be an educational influence for them of the highest value. It would really augment their self-respect and moral force; it would truly fuse them with the class above, and tend to bring about for them the equality which they are entitled to desire.

So it is not State-action in itself which the middle and lower classes of a nation ought to deprecate; it is State-action exercised by a hostile class, and for their oppression. From a State-action reasonably, equitably, and nationally exercised, they may derive great benefit; greater, by the very nature and necessity of things, than can be derived from this source by the class above them. For the middle or lower classes to obstruct such a State-action, to repel its benefits, is to play the game of their enemies, and to prolong for themselves a condition of real inferiority.

This, I know, is rather dangerous ground to tread upon. The great middle classes of this country are conscious of no weakness, no inferiority; they do not want any one to provide anything for them. Such as they are, they believe that the freedom and prosperity of England are their work, and that the future belongs to them. No one esteems them more than I do; but those who esteem them most, and who most believe in their capabilities, can render them no better service than by pointing out in what they underrate their deficiencies, and how their deficiencies, if unremedied, may impair their future. They want culture and dignity; they want ideas. Aristocracy has culture and dignity; democracy has readiness for new ideas, and ardour for what ideas it possesses. Of these, our middle class has the last only: ardour for the ideas it already possesses. It believes ardently in liberty, it believes ardently in industry; and, by its zealous belief in these two ideas, it has accomplished great things. What it has accomplished by its belief in industry is patent to all the world. The liberties of England are less its exclusive work than it supposes; for these, aristocracy has achieved nearly as much. Still, of one inestimable part of liberty, liberty of thought, the middle class has been (without precisely intending it) the principal champion. The intellectual action of the Church of England upon the nation has been insignificant; its social action has been great. The social action of Protestant Dissent, that genuine product of the English middle class, has not been civilising; its positive intellectual action has been insignificant; its negative intellectual action, — in so far as by strenuously maintaining for itself, against persecution, liberty of conscience and the right of free opinion, it at the same time maintained and established this right as a universal principle—has been invaluable. But the actual results of this negative intellectual service rendered by Protestant Dissent, — by the middle class, — to the whole community, great as they undoubtedly are, must not be taken for something which they are not. It is a very great thing to be able to think as you like; but, after all, an important question remains: *what* you think. It is a fine thing to secure a free stage and no favour; but, after all, the part which you play on that stage will have to be criticised. Now, all the liberty and industry in the world will not ensure these two things: a high reason and a fine culture. They may favour them, but they will not of themselves produce them; they may exist without them. But it is by the appearance of these two things, in some shape or other, in the life of a nation, that it becomes something more than an independent, an energetic, a successful nation, — that it becomes a *great* nation.

In modern epochs the part of a high reason, of ideas, acquires constantly increasing importance in the conduct of the world's affairs. A fine culture is the complement of a high reason, and it is in the conjunction of both with character, with energy, that the ideal for men and nations is to be placed. It is common to hear remarks on the frequent divorce between culture and character, and to infer from this that culture is a mere varnish, and that character only deserves any serious attention. No error can be more fatal. Culture without character is, no doubt, something frivolous, vain, and weak; but character without culture is, on the other hand, something raw, blind, and dangerous. The most interesting, the most truly glorious peoples, are those in which the alliance of the two has been effected most successfully, and its result spread most widely. This is why the spectacle of ancient Athens has such profound interest for a rational man; that it is the spectacle of the culture of a *people*. It is not an aristocracy, leavening with its own high spirit the multitude which it wields, but leaving it the unformed multitude still; it is not a democracy, acute and energetic, but tasteless, narrow-minded, and ignoble; it is the middle and lower classes in the highest development of their humanity that these classes have yet reached. It was the *many* who relished those arts, who were not satisfied with less than those monuments. In the conversations recorded by Plato, or even by the matter-of-fact Xenophon, which for the free yet refined discussion of ideas have set the tone for the whole cultivated world, shopkeepers and tradesmen of Athens mingle as speakers. For any one but a pedant, this is why a handful of Athenians of two thousand years ago are more interesting than the millions of most nations our contemporaries. Surely, if they knew this, those friends of progress, who have confidently pronounced the remains of the ancient world to be so much lumber, and a classical education an aristocratic impertinence, might be inclined to reconsider their sentence.

The course taken in the next fifty years by the middle classes of this nation will probably give a decisive turn to its history. If they will not seek the alliance of the State for their own elevation, if they go on exaggerating their spirit of individualism, if they persist in their jealousy of all governmental action, if they cannot learn that the antipathies and the shibboleths of a past age are now an anachronism for them—that will not prevent them, probably, from getting the rule of their country for a season, but they will certainly *Americanise* it.

They will rule it by their energy, but they will deteriorate it by their low ideals and want of culture. In the decline of the aristocratical element, which in some sort supplied an ideal to ennoble the spirit of the nation and to keep it together, there will be no other element present to perform this service. It is of itself a serious calamity for a nation that its tone of feeling and grandeur of spirit should be lowered or dulled. But the calamity appears far more serious still when we consider that the middle classes, remaining as they are now, with their narrow, harsh, unintelligent, and unattractive spirit and culture, will almost certainly fail to mould or assimilate the masses below them, whose sympathies are at the present moment actually wider and more liberal than theirs. They arrive, these masses, eager to enter into possession of the world, to gain a more vivid sense of their own life and activity. In this their irrepressible development, their natural educators and initiators are those immediately above them, the middle classes. If these classes cannot win their sympathy or give them their direction, society is in danger of falling into anarchy.

Therefore, with all the force I can, I wish to urge upon the middle classes of this country, both that they might be very greatly profited by the action of the State, and also that they are continuing their opposition to such action out of an unfounded fear. But at the same time I say that the middle classes have the right, in admitting the action of government, to make the condition that this government shall be one of their own adoption, one that they can trust. To ensure this is now in their own power. If they do not as yet ensure this, they ought to do so, they have the means of doing so. Two centuries ago they had not; now they have. Having this security, let them now show themselves jealous to keep the action of the State equitable and rational, rather than to exclude the action of the State altogether. If the State acts amiss, let them check it, but let them no longer take it for granted that the State cannot possibly act usefully.

*The State—but what is the State?* cry many. Speculations on the idea of a State abound, but these do not satisfy them; of that which is to have practical effect and power they require a plain account. The full force of the term, *the State*, as the full force of any other important term, no one will master without going a little deeply, without resolutely entering the world of ideas; but it is possible to give in very plain language an account of it sufficient for all practical purposes. The State is properly just what Burke called it—*the nation in its collective and corporate character.*[f] The State is the representative acting-power of the nation; the action of the State is the representative action of the nation. Nominally emanating from the Crown, as the ideal unity in which the nation concentrates itself, this action, by the constitution of our country, really emanates from the ministers of the Crown. It is common to hear the depreciators of State-action run through a string of ministers' names, and then say: "Here is really your *State*; would you accept the action of these men as your own representative action? In what respect is their judgment on national affairs likely to be any better than that of the rest of the world?" In the first place I answer: Even supposing them to be originally no better or wiser than the rest of the world, they have two great advantages from their position: access to almost boundless means of information, and the enlargement of mind which the habit of dealing with great affairs tends to produce. Their position itself, therefore, if they are men of only average honesty and capacity, tends to give them a fitness for acting on behalf of the nation superior to that of other men of equal honesty and capacity who are not in the same position. This fitness may be yet further increased by treating them as persons on whom, indeed, a very grave responsibility has fallen, and from whom very much will be expected;—nothing less than the representing, each of them in his own department, under the control of Parliament, and aided by the suggestions of public opinion, the collective energy and intelligence of his nation. By treating them as men on whom all this devolves to do, to their honour if they do it well, to their shame if they do it ill, one probably augments their faculty of well-doing; as it is excellently said: "To treat men as if they were better than they are, is the surest way to *make* them better than they are." But to treat them as if they had been shuffled into their places by a lucky accident, were most likely soon to be shuffled out of them again, and meanwhile ought to magnify themselves and their office as little as possible; to treat them as if they and their functions could without much inconvenience be quite dispensed with, and they ought perpetually to be admiring their own inconceivable good fortune in being permitted to discharge them;—this is the way to paralyse all high effort in the

[f] According to R.H. Super (*Complete Prose Works* II, p. 377), Burke never used exactly this phrase, which Arnold cites so often, but closely similar wording about the state occurs in both his *Reflections on the Revolution in France* and his *An Appeal from the New to the Old Whigs*; see also Introduction above, p. xxiv.

executive government, to extinguish all lofty sense of responsibility; to make its members either merely solicitous for the gross advantages, the emolument and self-importance, which they derive from their offices, or else timid, apologetic, and self-mistrustful in filling them; in either case, formal and inefficient.

But in the second place I answer: If the executive government is really in the hands of men no wiser than the bulk of mankind, of men whose action an intelligent man would be unwilling to accept as representative of his own action, whose fault is that? It is the fault of the nation itself, which, not being in the hands of a despot or an oligarchy, being free to control the choice of those who are to sum up and concentrate its action, controls it in such a manner that it allows to be chosen agents so little in its confidence, or so mediocre, or so incompetent, that it thinks the best thing to be done with them is to reduce their action as near as possible to a nullity. Hesitating, blundering, unintelligent, inefficacious, the action of the State may be; but, such as it is, it is the collective action of the nation itself, and the nation is responsible for it. It is our own action which we suffer to be thus unsatisfactory. Nothing can free us from this responsibility. The conduct of our affairs is in our own power. To carry on into its executive proceedings the indecision, conflict, and discordance of its parliamentary debates, may be a natural defect of a free nation, but it is certainly a defect; it is a dangerous error to call it, as some do, a perfection. The want of concert, reason, and organisation in the State, is the want of concert, reason, and organisation in the collective nation.

Inasmuch, therefore, as collective action is more efficacious than isolated individual efforts, a nation having great and complicated matters to deal with must greatly gain by employing the action of the State. Only, the State-power which it employs should be a power which really represents its best self, and whose action its intelligence and justice can heartily avow and adopt; not a power which reflects its inferior self, and of whose action, as of its own second-rate action, it has perpetually to be ashamed. To offer a worthy initiative, and to set a standard of rational and equitable action,—this is what the nation should expect of the State; and the more the State fulfils this expectation, the more will it be accepted in practice for what in idea it must always be. People will not then ask the State, what title it has to commend or reward genius and merit, since commendation and reward imply an attitude of superiority, for it will then be felt that the State truly acts for the English nation; and the genius of the English nation is greater than the genius of any individual, greater even than Shakspeare's genius, for it includes the genius of Newton also.

I will not deny that to give a more prominent part to the State would be a considerable change in this country; that maxims once very sound, and habits once very salutary, may be appealed to against it. The sole question is, whether those maxims and habits are sound and salutary at this moment. A yet graver and more difficult change, — to reduce the all-effacing prominence of the State, to give a more prominent part to the individual, — is imperiously presenting itself to other countries. Both are the suggestions of one irresistible force, which is gradually making its way everywhere, removing old conditions and imposing new, altering long-fixed habits, undermining venerable institutions, even modifying national character: *the modern spirit*.

Undoubtedly we are drawing on towards great changes; and for every nation the thing most needful is to discern clearly its own condition, in order to know in what particular way it may best meet them. Openness and flexibility of mind are at such a time the first of virtues. *Be ye perfect*, said the Founder of Christianity; *I count not myself to have apprehended*, said its greatest Apostle. Perfection will never be reached; but to recognise a period of transformation when it comes, and to adapt themselves honestly and rationally to its laws, is perhaps the nearest approach to perfection of which men and nations are capable. No habits or attachments should prevent their trying to do this; nor indeed, in the long run, can they. Human thought, which made all institutions, inevitably saps them, resting only in that which is absolute and eternal.

# The Function of Criticism at the
# Present Time

Many objections have been made to a proposition which, in some remarks of mine on translating Homer, I ventured to put forth; a proposition about criticism, and its importance at the present day. I said: "Of the literature of France and Germany, as of the intellect of Europe in general, the main effort, for now many years, has been a critical effort; the endeavour, in all branches of knowledge, theology, philosophy, history, art, science, to see the object as in itself it really is." I added, that owing to the operation in English literature of certain causes, "almost the last thing for which one would come to English literature is just that very thing which now Europe most desires,—criticism;" and that the power and value of English literature was thereby impaired.[a] More than one rejoinder declared that the importance I here assigned to criticism was excessive, and asserted the inherent superiority of the creative effort of the human spirit over its critical effort. And the other day, having been led by Mr. Shairp's excellent notice of Wordsworth[1] to turn again to his biogra-

[1] I cannot help thinking that a practice, common in England during the last century, and still followed in France, of printing a notice of this kind,—a notice by a competent critic,—to serve as an introduction to an eminent author's works, might be revived among us with advantage. To introduce all succeeding editions of Wordsworth, Mr. Shairp's notice might, it seems to me, excellently serve; it is written from the point of view of an admirer, nay, of a disciple, and that is right; but then the disciple must be also, as in this case he is, a critic, a man of letters, not, as too often happens, some relation or friend with no qualification for his task except affection for his author.[b]

[a] *On Translating Homer* (1861), Lect.2.
[b] [John Campbell Shairp], 'Wordsworth: the Man and the Poet', *North British Review* (1864).

phy, I found, in the words of this great man, whom I, for one, must always listen to with the profoundest respect, a sentence passed on the critic's business, which seems to justify every possible disparagement of it. Wordsworth says in one of his letters: —

"The writers in these publications" (the Reviews), "while they prosecute their inglorious employment, can not be supposed to be in a state of mind very favourable for being affected by the finer influences of a thing so pure as genuine poetry."

And a trustworthy reporter of his conversation quotes a more elaborate judgment to the same effect: —

"Wordsworth holds the critical power very low, infinitely lower than the inventive; and he said to-day that if the quantity of time consumed in writing critiques on the works of others were given to original composition, of whatever kind it might be, it would be much better employed; it would make a man find out sooner his own level, and it would do infinitely less mischief. A false or malicious criticism may do much injury to the minds of others; a stupid invention, either in prose or verse, is quite harmless."

It is almost too much to expect of poor human nature, that a man capable of producing some effect in one line of literature, should, for the greater good of society, voluntarily doom himself to impotence and obscurity in another. Still less is this to be expected from men addicted to the composition of the "false or malicious criticism" of which Wordsworth speaks. However, everybody would admit that a false or malicious criticism had better never have been written. Everybody, too, would be willing to admit, as a general proposition, that the critical faculty is lower than the inventive. But is it true that criticism is really, in itself, a baneful and injurious employment; is it true that all time given to writing critiques on the works of others would be much better employed if it were given to original composi-tion, of whatever kind this may be? Is it true that Johnson had better have gone on producing more *Irenes* instead of writing his *Lives of the Poets*; nay, is it certain that Wordsworth himself was better employed in making his Ecclesiastical Sonnets than when he made his celebrated Preface, so full of criticism, and criticism of the works of others? Wordsworth was himself a great critic, and it is to be sincerely regretted that he has not left us more criticism; Goethe was one of the greatest of critics, and we may sincerely congratulate ourselves that he has left us so much criticism. Without wasting time over the exaggera-tion which Wordsworth's judgment on criticism clearly contains, or over an attempt to trace the causes,—not difficult, I think, to be traced,—which may have led Wordsworth to this exaggeration, a critic may with advantage seize an occasion for trying his own conscience, and for asking himself of what real service at any given moment the practice of criticism either is or may be made to his own mind and spirit, and to the minds and spirits of others.

The critical power is of lower rank than the creative. True; but in assenting to this proposition, one or two things are to be kept in mind. It is undeniable that the exercise of a creative power, that a free creative activity, is the highest function of man; it is proved to be so by man's finding in it his true happiness. But it is undeniable, also, that men may have the sense of exercising this free creative activity in other ways than in producing great works of literature or art; if it were not so, all but a very few men would be shut out from the true happiness of all men. They may have it in well-doing, they may have it in learning, they may have it even in criticising. This is one thing to be kept in mind. Another is, that the exercise of the creative power in the production of great works of literature or art, however high this exercise of it may rank, is not at all epochs and under all conditions possible; and that therefore labour may be vainly spent in attempting it, which might with more fruit be used in preparing for it, in rendering it possible. This creative power works with elements, with materials; what if it has not those materials, those elements, ready for its use? In that case it must surely wait till they are ready. Now, in literature,—I will limit myself to literature, for it is about literature that the question arises,—the elements with which the creative power works are ideas; the best ideas, on every matter which literature touches, current at the time. At any rate we may lay it down as certain that in modern literature no manifestation of the creative power not working with these can be very important or fruitful. And I say *current* at the time, not merely accessible at the time; for creative literary genius does not principally show itself in discovering new ideas, that is rather the business of the philosopher. The grand work of literary genius is a work of synthesis and exposition, not of analysis and discovery; its gift lies in the faculty of being happily inspired by a certain intellectual and spiritual atmosphere, by a certain order of ideas, when it finds itself in them; of dealing divinely with these ideas, presenting them in the most effective and attractive combinations, – making beautiful works with them, in short. But it must have the atmosphere, it must find itself amidst the order of ideas, in order to work freely; and these it is not so easy to command. This is why great creative epochs in literature are so rare, this is why there is so much that is unsatisfactory in the productions of many men of real genius; because for the creation of a master-work of literature two powers must concur, the power of the man and the power of the moment, and the man is not enough without the moment; the creative power has, for its happy exercise, appointed elements, and those elements are not in its own control.

Nay, they are more within the control of the critical power. It is the business of the critical power, as I said in the words already quoted, "in all branches of knowledge, theology, philosophy, history, art, science, to see the object as in itself it really is." Thus it tends, at last, to make an intellectual situation of which the creative power can profitably avail itself. It tends to establish an order of ideas, if not absolutely true, yet true by comparison with that which it displaces; to make the best ideas prevail. Presently these new ideas reach society, the touch of truth is the touch of life, and there is a stir and growth everywhere; out of this stir and growth come the creative epochs of literature.

Or, to narrow our range, and quit these considerations of the general march of genius and of society,—considerations which are apt to become too abstract and impalpable,—every one can see that a poet, for instance, ought to know life and the world before dealing with them in poetry; and life and the world being in modern times very complex things, the creation of a modern poet, to be worth much, implies a great critical effort behind it; else it must be a comparatively poor, barren, and short-lived affair. This is why Byron's poetry had so little endurance in it, and Goethe's so much; both Byron and Goethe had a great productive power, but Goethe's was nourished by a great critical effort providing the true materials for it, and Byron's was not; Goethe knew life and the world, the poet's necessary subjects, much more comprehensively and thoroughly than Byron. He knew a great deal more of them, and he knew them much more as they really are.

It has long seemed to me that the burst of creative activity in our literature, through the first quarter of this century, had about it in fact something premature; and that from this cause its productions are doomed, most of them, in spite of the sanguine hopes which accompanied and do still accompany them, to prove hardly more lasting than the productions of far less splendid epochs. And this prematureness comes from its having proceeded without having its proper data, without sufficient materials to work with. In other words, the English poetry of the first quarter of this century, with plenty of energy, plenty of creative force, did not know enough. This makes Byron so empty of matter, Shelley so incoherent, Wordsworth even, profound as he is, yet so wanting in completeness and variety. Wordsworth cared little for books, and disparaged Goethe. I admire Wordsworth, as he is, so much that I cannot wish him different; and it is vain, no doubt, to imagine such a man different from what he is, to suppose that he *could* have been different. But surely the one thing wanting to make Wordsworth an even greater poet than he is,—his thought richer, and his influence of wider application,—was that he should have read more books, among them, no doubt, those of that Goethe whom he disparaged without reading him.

But to speak of books and reading may easily lead to a misunderstanding here. It was not really books and reading that lacked to our poetry at this epoch; Shelley had plenty of reading, Coleridge had immense reading. Pindar and Sophocles—as we all say so glibly, and often with so little discernment of the real import of what we are saying—had not many books; Shakspeare was no deep reader. True; but in the Greece of Pindar and Sophocles, in the England of Shakspeare, the poet lived in a current of ideas in the highest degree animating and nourishing to the creative power; society was, in the fullest measure, permeated by fresh thought, intelligent and alive. And this state of things is the true basis for the creative power's exercise, in this it finds its data, its materials, truly ready for its hand; all the books and reading in the world are only valuable as they are helps to this. Even when this does not actually exist, books and reading may enable a man to construct a kind of semblance of it in his own mind, a world of knowledge and intelligence in which he may live and work. This is by no means an equivalent to the artist for the nationally diffused life and thought of the epochs of Sophocles or Shakspeare; but, besides that it may be a means of preparation for such epochs, it does really constitute, if many share in it, a quickening and sustaining atmosphere of great value. Such an atmosphere the many-sided learning and the long and widely-combined critical effort of Germany formed for Goethe, when he lived and worked. There was no national glow of life and thought there as in the Athens of

Pericles or the England of Elizabeth. That was the poet's weakness. But there was a sort of equivalent for it in the complete culture and unfettered thinking of a large body of Germans. That was his strength. In the England of the first quarter of this century there was neither a national glow of life and thought, such as we had in the age of Elizabeth, nor yet a culture and a force of learning and criticism such as were to be found in Germany. Therefore the creative power of poetry wanted, for success in the highest sense, materials and a basis; a thorough interpretation of the world was necessarily denied to it.

At first sight it seems strange that out of the immense stir of the French Revolution and its age should not have come a crop of works of genius equal to that which came out of the stir of the great productive time of Greece, or out of that of the Renascence, with its powerful episode the Reformation. But the truth is that the stir of the French Revolution took a character which essentially distinguished it from such movements as these. These were, in the main, disinterestedly intellectual and spiritual movements; movements in which the human spirit looked for its satisfaction in itself and in the increased play of its own activity. The French Revolution took a political, practical character. The movement which went on in France under the old *régime*, from 1700 to 1789, was far more really akin than that of the Revolution itself to the movement of the Renascence; the France of Voltaire and Rousseau told far more powerfully upon the mind of Europe than the France of the Revolution. Goethe reproached this last expressly with having "thrown quiet culture back." Nay, and the true key to how much in our Byron, even in our Wordsworth, is this! — that they had their source in a great movement of feeling, not in a great movement of mind. The French Revolution, however, — that object of so much blind love and so much blind hatred, — found undoubtedly its motive-power in the intelligence of men, and not in their practical sense; this is what distinguishes it from the English Revolution of Charles the First's time. This is what makes it a more spiritual event than our Revolution, an event of much more powerful and world-wide interest, though practically less successful; it appeals to an order of ideas which are universal, certain, permanent. 1789 asked of a thing, Is it rational? 1642 asked of a thing, Is it legal? or, when it went furthest, Is it according to conscience? This is the English fashion, a fashion to be treated, within its own sphere, with the highest respect; for its success, within its own sphere, has been prodigious. But what is law in one place is not law in another; what is law here to-day is not law even here tomorrow; and as for conscience, what is binding on one man's conscience is not binding on another's. The old woman who threw her stool at the head of the surpliced minister in St. Giles's Church at Edinburgh obeyed an impulse to which millions of the human race may be permitted to remain strangers.[c] But the prescriptions of reason are absolute, unchanging, of universal validity; *to count by tens is the easiest way of counting*—that is a proposition of which every one, from here to the Antipodes, feels the force; at least I should say so if we did not live in a country where it is not impossible that any morning we may find a letter in the *Times* declaring that a decimal coinage is an absurdity.[d] That a whole nation should have been penetrated with an enthusiasm for pure reason, and with an ardent zeal for making its prescriptions triumph, is a very remarkable thing, when we consider how little of mind, or anything so worthy and quickening as mind, comes into the motives which alone, in general, impel great masses of men. In spite of the extravagant direction given to this enthusiasm, in spite of the crimes and follies in which it lost itself, the French Revolution derives from the force, truth, and universality of the ideas which it took for its law, and from the passion with which it could inspire a multitude for these ideas, a unique and still living power; it is—it will probably long remain—the greatest, the most animating event in history. And as no sincere passion for the things of the mind, even though it turn out in many respects an unfortunate passion, is ever quite thrown away and quite barren of good, France has reaped from hers one fruit—the natural and legitimate fruit, though not precisely the grand fruit she expected: she is the country in Europe where *the people* is most alive.

But the mania for giving an immediate political and practical application to all these fine ideas of the reason was fatal. Here an Englishman is in his element: on this theme we can all go on for hours. And all we are in the habit of saying on it has undoubtedly a great deal of truth. Ideas cannot be too much prized in and for themselves, cannot

[c] On Sunday, 23 July 1637, Jenny Geddes threw a stool at the Bishop of Edinburgh as a (Presbyterian) protest against his Laudian tendencies.

[d] The decimal system had been adopted by most European countries in the years since the French Revolution; a bill proposing the decimalization of weights and measures was introduced in Parliament in 1863 but withdrawn before becoming law. Britain did not adopt decimal coinage until 1971.

be too much lived with; but to transport them abruptly into the world of politics and practice, violently to revolutionise this world to their bidding,—that is quite another thing. There is the world of ideas and there is the world of practice; the French are often for suppressing the one and the English the other; but neither is to be suppressed. A member of the House of Commons said to me the other day: "That a thing is an anomaly, I consider to be no objection to it whatever." I venture to think he was wrong; that a thing is an anomaly *is* an objection to it, but absolutely and in the sphere of ideas: it is not necessarily, under such and such circumstances, or at such and such a moment, an objection to it in the sphere of politics and practice. Joubert has said beautifully: "C'est la force et le droit qui règlent toutes choses dans le monde; la force en attendant le droit." (Force and right are the governors of this world; force till right is ready.)[e] *Force till right is ready*; and till right is ready, force, the existing order of things, is justified, is the legitimate ruler. But right is something moral, and implies inward recognition, free assent of the will; we are not ready for right,—*right*, so far as we are concerned, *is not ready*,— until we have attained this sense of seeing it and willing it. The way in which for us it may change and transform force, the existing order of things, and become, in its turn, the legitimate ruler of the world, should depend on the way in which, when our time comes, we see it and will it. Therefore for other people enamoured of their own newly discerned right, to attempt to impose it upon us as ours, and violently to substitute their right for our force, is an act of tyranny, and to be resisted. It sets at nought the second great half of our maxim, *force till right is ready*. This was the grand error of the French Revolution; and its movement of ideas, by quitting the intellectual sphere and rushing furiously into the political sphere, ran, indeed, a prodigious and memorable course, but produced no such intellectual fruit as the movement of ideas of the Renascence, and created, in opposition to itself, what I may call an *epoch of concentration*. The great force of that epoch of concentration was England; and the great voice of that epoch of concentration was Burke. It is the fashion to treat Burke's writings on the French Revolution as superannuated and conquered by the event; as the eloquent but unphilosophical tirades of bigotry and prejudice. I will not deny that they are often disfigured by the violence

---

[e] Joseph Joubert (1754–1824), *Penseés* (1838); the French critic was the subject of another of Arnold's essays in *Essays in Criticism*.

33

and passion of the moment, and that in some directions Burke's view was bounded, and his observation therefore at fault. But on the whole, and for those who can make the needful corrections, what distinguishes these writings is their profound, permanent, fruitful, philosophical truth. They contain the true philosophy of an epoch of concentration, dissipate the heavy atmosphere which its own nature is apt to engender round it, and make its resistance rational instead of mechanical.

But Burke is so great because, almost alone in England, he brings thought to bear upon politics, he saturates politics with thought. It is his accident that his ideas were at the service of an epoch of concentration, not of an epoch of expansion; it is his characteristic that he so lived by ideas, and had such a source of them welling up within him, that he could float even an epoch of concentration and English Tory politics with them. It does not hurt him that Dr. Price[f] and the Liberals were enraged with him; it does not even hurt him that George the Third and the Tories were enchanted with him. His greatness is that he lived in a world which neither English Liberalism nor English Toryism is apt to enter; – the world of ideas, not the world of catchwords and party habits. So far is it from being really true of him that he "to party gave up what was meant for mankind," that at the very end of his fierce struggle with the French Revolution, after all his invectives against its false pretensions, hollowness, and madness, with his sincere conviction of its mischievousness, he can close a memorandum on the best means of combating it, some of the last pages he ever wrote, — the *Thoughts on French Affairs*, in December 1791, — with these striking words: —

"The evil is stated, in my opinion, as it exists. The remedy must be where power, wisdom, and information, I hope, are more united with good intentions than they can be with me. I have done with this subject, I believe, for ever. It has given me many anxious moments for the last two years. *If a great change is to be made in human affairs, the minds of men will be fitted to it; the general opinions and feelings will draw that way. Every fear, every hope will forward it; and then they who persist in opposing this mighty current in human affairs, will appear rather to resist the decrees of Providence itself, than the mere designs of men. They will not be resolute and firm, but perverse and obstinate.*"

[f] Richard Price (1723–91) was a Unitarian minister whose sermon praising the French Revolution provoked Burke to write his *Reflections on the Revolution in France* (1790).

34

That return of Burke upon himself has always seemed to me one of the finest things in English literature, or indeed in any literature. That is what I call living by ideas: when one side of a question has long had your earnest support, when all your feelings are engaged, when you hear all round you no language but one, when your party talks this language like a steam-engine and can imagine no other, —still to be able to think, still to be irresistibly carried, if so it be, by the current of thought to the opposite side of the question, and, like Balaam, to be unable to speak anything *but what the Lord has put in your mouth.* I know nothing more striking, and I must add that I know nothing more un-English.

For the Englishman in general is like my friend the Member of Parliament, and believes, point-blank, that for a thing to be an anomaly is absolutely no objection to it whatever. He is like the Lord Auckland of Burke's day, who, in a memorandum on the French Revolution, talks of "certain miscreants, assuming the name of philosophers, who have presumed themselves capable of establishing a new system of society."[g] The Englishman has been called a political animal, and he values what is political and practical so much that ideas easily become objects of dislike in his eyes, and thinkers "miscreants," because ideas and thinkers have rashly meddled with politics and practice. This would be all very well if the dislike and neglect confined themselves to ideas transported out of their own sphere, and meddling rashly with practice; but they are inevitably extended to ideas as such, and to the whole life of intelligence; practice is everything, a free play of the mind is nothing. The notion of the free play of the mind upon all subjects being a pleasure in itself, being an object of desire, being an essential provider of elements without which a nation's spirit, whatever compensations it may have for them, must, in the long run, die of inanition, hardly enters into an Englishman's thoughts. It is noticeable that the word *curiosity*, which in other languages is used in a good sense, to mean, as a high and fine quality of man's nature, just this disinterested love of a free play of the mind on all subjects, for its own sake, —it is noticeable, I say, that this word has in our language no sense of the kind, no sense but a rather bad and disparaging one. But criticism, real criticism, is essentially the exercise of this very quality. It obeys an instinct prompting it to try

[g] William Eden, Lord Auckland (1744–1814) in a memorandum, dated 25 January 1793, to the States General at The Hague where he was British Ambassador.

to know the best that is known and thought in the world, irrespectively of practice, politics, and everything of the kind; and to value knowledge and thought as they approach this best, without the intrusion of any other considerations whatever. This is an instinct for which there is, I think, little original sympathy in the practical English nature, and what there was of it has undergone a long benumbing period of blight and suppression in the epoch of concentration which followed the French Revolution.

But epochs of concentration cannot well endure for ever; epochs of expansion, in the due course of things, follow them. Such an epoch of expansion seems to be opening in this country. In the first place all danger of a hostile forcible pressure of foreign ideas upon our practice has long disappeared; like the traveller in the fable, therefore, we begin to wear our cloak a little more loosely. Then, with a long peace, the ideas of Europe steal gradually and amicably in, and mingle, though in infinitesimally small quantities at a time, with our own notions. Then, too, in spite of all that is said about the absorbing and brutalising influence of our passionate material progress, it seems to me indisputable that this progress is likely, though not certain, to lead in the end to an apparition of intellectual life; and that man, after he has made himself perfectly comfortable and has now to determine what to do with himself next, may begin to remember that he has a mind, and that the mind may be made the source of great pleasure. I grant it is mainly the privilege of faith, at present, to discern this end to our railways, our business, and our fortune-making; but we shall see if, here as elsewhere, faith is not in the end the true prophet. Our ease, our travelling, and our unbounded liberty to hold just as hard and securely as we please to the practice to which our notions have given birth, all tend to beget an inclination to deal a little more freely with these notions themselves, to canvass them a little, to penetrate a little into their real nature. Flutterings of curiosity, in the foreign sense of the word, appear amongst us, and it is in these that criticism must look to find its account. Criticism first; a time of true creative activity, perhaps,—which, as I have said, must inevitably be preceded amongst us by a time of criticism,—hereafter, when criticism has done its work.

It is of the last importance that English criticism should clearly discern what rule for its course, in order to avail itself of the field now opening to it, and to produce fruit for the future, it ought to take. The rule may be summed up in one word,—*disinterestedness*. And how is criticism to show disinterestedness? By keeping aloof from what is called "the practical view of things;" by resolutely following the law of its own nature, which is to be a free play of the mind on all subjects which it touches. By steadily refusing to lend itself to any of those ulterior, political, practical considerations about ideas, which plenty of people will be sure to attach to them, which perhaps ought often to be attached to them, which in this country at any rate are certain to be attached to them, quite sufficiently, but which criticism has really nothing to do with. Its business is, as I have said, simply to know the best that is known and thought in the world, and by in its turn making this known, to create a current of true and fresh ideas. Its business is to do this with inflexible honesty, with due ability; but its business is to do no more, and to leave alone all questions of practical consequences and applications, questions which will never fail to have due prominence given to them. Else criticism, besides being really false to its own nature, merely continues in the old rut which it has hitherto followed in this country, and will certainly miss the chance now given to it. For what is at present the bane of criticism in this country? It is that practical considerations cling to it and stifle it. It subserves interests not its own. Our organs of criticism are organs of men and parties having practical ends to serve, and with them those practical ends are the first thing and the play of mind the second; so much play of mind as is compatible with the prosecution of those practical ends is all that is wanted. An organ like the *Revue des Deux Mondes*, having for its main function to understand and utter the best that is known and thought in the world, existing, it may be said, as just an organ for a free play of the mind, we have not. But we have the *Edinburgh Review*, existing as an organ of the old Whigs, and for as much play of the mind as may suit its being that; we have the *Quarterly Review*, existing as an organ of the Tories, and for as much play of mind as may suit its being that; we have the *British Quarterly Review*, existing as an organ of the political Dissenters, and for as much play of mind as may suit its being that; we have the *Times*, existing as an organ of the common, satisfied, well-to-do Englishman, and for as much play of mind as may suit its being that. And so on through all the various fractions, political and religious, of our society; every fraction has, as such, its organ of criticism, but the notion of combining all fractions in the common pleasure of a free disinterested play of mind meets with no favour. Directly this play of mind wants to have more scope, and to forget the pressure of practical considerations a little, it is checked, it is made to feel the chain. We saw this the other day in the extinction, so much to be regretted, of the *Home and Foreign Review*.[h] Perhaps in no organ of criticism in this country was there so much knowledge, so much play of mind; but these could not save it. The *Dublin Review* subordinates play of mind to the practical business of English and Irish Catholicism, and lives. It must needs be that men should act in sects and parties, that each of these sects and parties should have its organ, and should make this organ subserve the interests of its action; but it would be well, too, that there should be a criticism, not the minister of these interests, not their enemy, but absolutely and entirely independent of them. No other criticism will ever attain any real authority or make any real way towards its end, — the creating a current of true and fresh ideas.

It is because criticism has so little kept in the pure intellectual sphere, has so little detached itself from practice, has been so directly polemical and controversial, that it has so ill accomplished, in this country, its best spiritual work; which is to keep man from a self-satisfaction which is retarding and vulgarising, to lead him towards perfection, by making his mind dwell upon what is excellent in itself, and the absolute beauty and fitness of things. A polemical practical criticism makes men blind even to the ideal imperfection of their practice, makes them willingly assert its ideal perfection, in order the better to secure it against attack; and clearly this is narrowing and baneful for them. If they were reassured on the practical side, speculative considerations of ideal perfection they might be brought to entertain, and their spiritual horizon would thus gradually widen. Sir Charles Adderley says to the Warwickshire farmers: —

"Talk of the improvement of breed! Why, the race we ourselves represent, the men and women, the old Anglo-Saxon race, are the best breed in the whole world. . . . The absence of a too enervating climate, too unclouded skies, and a too luxurious nature, has produced so vigorous a race of people, and has rendered us so superior to all the world."[i]

---

[h] A liberal Catholic quarterly, edited by Lord Acton, which was discontinued after two years (1862–4) following pressure from the Catholic hierarchy.
[i] Sir Charles Adderley, Conservative MP for North Staffordshire, addressing the Warwickshire Agricultural Association on 16 September 1863.

Mr. Roebuck says to the Sheffield cutlers:—

"I look around me and ask what is the state of England? Is not property safe? Is not every man able to say what he likes? Can you not walk from one end of England to the other in perfect security? I ask you whether, the world over or in past history, there is anything like it? Nothing. I pray that our unrivalled happiness may last."[j]

Now obviously there is a peril for poor human nature in words and thoughts of such exuberant self-satisfaction, until we find ourselves safe in the streets of the Celestial City.

> "Das wenige verschwindet leicht dem Blicke
> Der vorwärts sieht, wie viel noch übrig bleibt—"

says Goethe; "the little that is done seems nothing when we look forward and see how much we have yet to do." Clearly this is a better line of reflection for weak humanity, so long as it remains on this earthly field of labour and trial.

But neither Sir Charles Adderley nor Mr. Roebuck is by nature inaccessible to considerations of this sort. They only lose sight of them owing to the controversial life we all lead, and the practical form which all speculation takes with us. They have in view opponents whose aim is not ideal, but practical; and in their zeal to uphold their own practice against these innovators, they go so far as even to attribute to this practice an ideal perfection. Somebody has been wanting to introduce a six-pound franchise, or to abolish church-rates, or to collect agricultural statistics by force, or to diminish local self-government. How natural, in reply to such proposals, very likely improper or ill-timed, to go a little beyond the mark, and to say stoutly, "Such a race of people as we stand, so superior to all the world! The old Anglo-Saxon race, the best breed in the whole world! I pray that our unrivalled happiness may last! I ask you whether, the world over or in past history, there is anything like it?" And so long as criticism answers this dithyramb by insisting that the old Anglo-Saxon race would be still more superior to all others if it had no church-rates, or that our unrivalled happiness would last yet longer with a six-pound franchise, so long will the strain, "The best breed in the whole world!" swell louder and louder, everything ideal and refining will be lost out of sight, and both the assailed and their critics will remain in a

---

[j] John Arthur Roebuck (1801–79), Radical MP for Sheffield, addressing his constituents on 18 August 1864.

sphere, to say the truth, perfectly unvital, a sphere in which spiritual progression is impossible. But let criticism leave church-rates and the franchise alone, and in the most candid spirit, without a single lurking thought of practical innovation, confront with our dithyramb this paragraph on which I stumbled in a newspaper immediately after reading Mr. Roebuck: —

"A shocking child murder has just been committed at Nottingham. A girl named Wragg left the workhouse there on Saturday morning with her young illegitimate child. The child was soon afterwards found dead on Mapperly Hills, having been strangled. Wragg is in custody."[k]

Nothing but that; but, in juxtaposition with the absolute eulogies of Sir Charles Adderley and Mr. Roebuck, how eloquent, how suggestive are those few lines! "Our old Anglo-Saxon breed, the best in the whole world!"—how much that is harsh and ill-favoured there is in this best! *Wragg!* If we are to talk of ideal perfection, of "the best in the whole world," has any one reflected what a touch of grossness in our race, what an original shortcoming in the more delicate spiritual perceptions, is shown by the natural growth amongst us of such hideous names,—Higginbottom, Stiggins, Bugg! In Ionia and Attica they were luckier in this respect than "the best race in the world;" by the Ilissus there was no Wragg, poor thing! And "our unrivalled happiness,"—what an element of grimness, bareness, and hideousness mixes with it and blurs it; the workhouse, the dismal Mapperly Hills,—how dismal those who have seen them will remember;—the gloom, the smoke, the cold, the strangled illegitimate child! "I ask you whether, the world over or in past history, there is anything like it?" Perhaps not, one is inclined to answer; but at any rate, in that case, the world is [not] very much to be pitied. And the final touch,—short, bleak, and inhuman: *Wragg is in custody.* The sex lost in the confusion of our unrivalled happiness; or (shall I say?) the superfluous Christian name lopped off by the straight-forward vigour of our old Anglo-Saxon breed! There is profit for the spirit in such contrasts as this; criticism serves the cause of perfection by establishing them. By eluding sterile conflict, by refusing to remain in the sphere where alone narrow and relative conceptions have any worth and validity,

[k] The crime was committed on 10 September 1864. Elizabeth Wragg was eventually found guilty of manslaughter and sentenced to twenty years penal servitude; the trial was reported in *The Times*, 15 March 1865.

criticism may diminish its momentary importance, but only in this way has it a chance of gaining admittance for those wider and more perfect conceptions to which all its duty is really owed. Mr. Roebuck will have a poor opinion of an adversary who replies to his defiant songs of triumph only by murmuring under his breath, *Wragg is in custody*; but in no other way will these songs of triumph be induced gradually to moderate themselves, to get rid of what in them is excessive and offensive, and to fall into a softer and truer key.

It will be said that it is a very subtle and indirect action which I am thus prescribing for criticism, and that, by embracing in this manner the Indian virtue of detachment and abandoning the sphere of practical life, it condemns itself to a slow and obscure work. Slow and obscure it may be, but it is the only proper work of criticism. The mass of mankind will never have any ardent zeal for seeing things as they are; very inadequate ideas will always satisfy them. On these inadequate ideas reposes, and must repose, the general practice of the world. That is as much as saying that whoever sets himself to see things as they are will find himself one of a very small circle; but it is only by this small circle resolutely doing its own work that adequate ideas will ever get current at all. The rush and roar of practical life will always have a dizzying and attracting effect upon the most collected spectator, and tend to draw him into its vortex; most of all will this be the case where that life is so powerful as it is in England. But it is only by remaining collected, and refusing to lend himself to the point of view of the practical man, that the critic can do the practical man any service; and it is only by the greatest sincerity in pursuing his own course, and by at last convincing even the practical man of his sincerity, that he can escape misunderstandings which perpetually threaten him.

For the practical man is not apt for fine distinctions, and yet in these distinctions truth and the highest culture greatly find their account. But it is not easy to lead a practical man,—unless you reassure him as to your practical intentions, you have no chance of leading him,—to see that a thing which he has always been used to look at from one side only, which he greatly values, and which, looked at from that side, quite deserves, perhaps, all the prizing and admiring which he bestows upon it,—that this thing, looked at from another side, may appear much less beneficent and beautiful, and yet retain all its claims to our practical allegiance. Where shall we find language

innocent enough, how shall we make the spotless purity of our intentions evident enough, to enable us to say to the political Englishman
that the British Constitution itself, which, seen from the practical
side, looks such a magnificent organ of progress and virtue, seen from
the speculative side,—with its compromises, its love of facts, its horror of theory, its studied avoidance of clear thoughts,—that, seen
from this side, our august Constitution sometimes looks,—forgive
me, shade of Lord Somers!—a colossal machine for the manufacture
of Philistines? How is Cobbett to say this and not be misunderstood,
blackened as he is with the smoke of a lifelong conflict in the field of
political practice?[m] how is Mr. Carlyle to say it and not be misunderstood, after his furious raid into this field with his *Latter-day
Pamphlets?*[n] how is Mr. Ruskin, after his pugnacious political
economy?[o] I say, the critic must keep out of the region of immediate
practice in the political, social, humanitarian sphere, if he wants to
make a beginning for that more free speculative treatment of things,
which may perhaps one day make its benefits felt even in this sphere,
but in a natural and thence irresistible manner.

Do what he will, however, the critic will still remain exposed to
frequent misunderstandings, and nowhere so much as in this country.
For here people are particularly indisposed even to comprehend that
without this free disinterested treatment of things, truth and the
highest culture are out of the question. So immersed are they in
practical life, so accustomed to take all their notions from this life and
its processes, that they are apt to think that truth and culture themselves can be reached by the processes of this life, and that it is an
impertinent singularity to think of reaching them in any other. "We
are all *terræ filii*," cries their eloquent advocate; "all Philistines
together. Away with the notion of proceeding by any other course
than the course dear to the Philistines; let us have a social movement,
let us organise and combine a party to pursue truth and new thought,

[l] Lord Somers (1651–1716), Whig politician and lawyer, who presided over the drafting
of the Declaration of Rights in 1688.

[m] William Cobbett (1762–1835), radical journalist, fierce critic of Tory governments, and
author of *Rural Rides* (1830).

[n] Thomas Carlyle (1795–1881) was the most influential social critic of the 1830s and
1840s, but the exaggerated vehemence of his *Latter-Day Pamphlets* (1850) repelled many
of his former admirers.

[o] John Ruskin (1819–1900) was already a celebrated cultural critic when he first
attempted to formulate his unorthodox and rather amateur criticisms of political
economy in *Unto This Last* (1862).

let us call it *the liberal party*, and let us all stick to each other, and back each other up. Let us have no nonsense about independent criticism, and intellectual delicacy, and the few and the many. Don't let us trouble ourselves about foreign thought; we shall invent the whole thing for ourselves as we go along. If one of us speaks well, applaud him; if one of us speaks ill, applaud him too; we are all in the same movement, we are all liberals, we are all in pursuit of truth." In this way the pursuit of truth becomes really a social, practical, pleasurable affair, almost requiring a chairman, a secretary, and advertisements; with the excitement of an occasional scandal, with a little resistance to give the happy sense of difficulty overcome; but, in general, plenty of bustle and very little thought. To act is so easy, as Goethe says; to think is so hard! It is true that the critic has many temptations to go with the stream, to make one of the party of movement, one of these *terræ filii*; it seems ungracious to refuse to be a *terræ filius*, when so many excellent people are; but the critic's duty is to refuse, or, if resistance is vain, at least to cry with Obermann: *Périssons en résistant.*[p]

How serious a matter it is to try and resist, I had ample opportunity of experiencing when I ventured some time ago to criticise the celebrated first volume of Bishop Colenso.[2] The echoes of the storm which was then raised I still, from time to time, hear grumbling round me. That storm arose out of a misunderstanding almost inevitable. It is a result of no little culture to attain to a clear perception that science and religion are two wholly different things. The multitude will for ever confuse them; but happily that is of no great real importance, for while the multitude imagines itself to live by its false science, it does

---

[2] So sincere is my dislike to all personal attack and controversy, that I abstain from reprinting, at this distance of time from the occasion which called them forth, the essays in which I criticised Dr. Colenso's book;[q] I feel bound, however, after all that has passed, to make here a final declaration of my sincere impenitence for having published them. Nay, I cannot forbear repeating yet once more, for his benefit and that of his readers, this sentence from my original remarks upon him: *There is truth of science and truth of religion; truth of science does not become truth of religion till it is made religious.* And I will add: Let us have all the science there is from the men of science; from the men of religion let us have religion.

[p] 'Let us die resisting'; *Obermann*, a romantic novel by the French author Senancour (1770–1846), was greatly admired by Arnold, who wrote two poems dealing with it.

[q] John William Colenso (1814–83), Bishop of Natal, was the author of *The Pentateuch and the Book of Joshua Critically Examined*, which Arnold had savaged in 'The Bishop and the Philosopher', *Macmillian's Magazine* (1863). In the following number of the same periodical Arnold had praised the *Lectures on the History of the Jewish Church* by his friend Arthur Penrhyn Stanley (1815–81).

really live by its true religion. Dr. Colenso, however, in his first volume did all he could to strengthen the confusion,[3] and to make it dangerous. He did this with the best intentions, I freely admit, and with the most candid ignorance that this was the natural effect of what he was doing; but, says Joubert, "Ignorance, which in matters of morals extenuates the crime, is itself, in intellectual matters, a crime of the first order." I criticised Bishop Colenso's speculative confusion. Immediately there was a cry raised: "What is this? here is a liberal attacking a liberal. Do not you belong to the movement? are not you a friend of truth? Is not Bishop Colenso in pursuit of truth? then speak with proper respect of his book. Dr. Stanley is another friend of truth, and you speak with proper respect of his book; why make these invidious differences? both books are excellent, admirable, liberal; Bishop Colenso's perhaps the most so, because it is the boldest, and will have the best practical consequences for the liberal cause. Do you want to encourage to the attack of a brother liberal his, and your, and our implacable enemies, the *Church and State Review* or the *Record*, — the High Church rhinoceros and the Evangelical hyæna? Be silent, therefore; or rather speak, speak as loud as ever you can! and go into ecstasies over the eighty and odd pigeons."[r]

But criticism cannot follow this coarse and indiscriminate method. It is unfortunately possible for a man in pursuit of truth to write a book which reposes upon a false conception. Even the practical consequences of a book are to genuine criticism no recommendation of it, if the book is, in the highest sense, blundering. I see that a lady who herself, too, is in pursuit of truth, and who writes with great ability, but a little too much, perhaps, under the influence of the practical spirit of the English liberal movement, classes Bishop Colenso's book and M. Renan's together, in her survey of the religious state of Europe, as facts of the same order, works, both of them, of "great importance," "great ability, power, and skill," Bishop Colenso's, perhaps, the most powerful; at least, Miss Cobbe gives special

---

[3] It has been said I make it "a crime against literary criticism and the higher culture to attempt to inform the ignorant."[5] Need I point out the the ignorant are not informed by being confirmed in a confusion?

[r] In his article, Arnold had made fun of Colenso's absurd attempt to discredit the literal reading of the Book of Leviticus by an arithmetical calculation about how many sacrificial pigeons it appeared to suggest that the priest would need to eat each day.

[5] [James Fitzjames Stephen], 'Mr Matthew Arnold and his Countrymen', *Saturday Review* (1864).

expression to her gratitude that to Bishop Colenso "has been given the strength to grasp, and the courage to teach, truths of such deep import."[1] In the same way, more than one popular writer has compared him to Luther. Now it is just this kind of false estimate which the critical spirit is, it seems to me, bound to resist. It is really the strongest possible proof of the low ebb at which, in England, the critical spirit is, that while the critical hit in the religious literature of Germany is Dr. Strauss's book, in that of France M. Renan's book, the book of Bishop Colenso is the critical hit in the religious literature of England.[ii] Bishop Colenso's book reposes on a total misconception of the essential elements of the religious problem, as that problem is now presented for solution. To criticism, therefore, which seeks to have the best that is known and thought on this problem, it is, however well meant, of no importance whatever. M. Renan's book attempts a new synthesis of the elements furnished to us by the Four Gospels. It attempts, in my opinion, a synthesis, perhaps premature, perhaps impossible, certainly not successful. Up to the present time, at any rate, we must acquiesce in Fleury's sentence on such recastings of the Gospel-story: *Quiconque s'imagine la pouvoir mieux écrire, ne l'entend pas.*[v] M. Renan had himself passed by anticipation a like sentence on his own work, when he said: "If a new presentation of the character of Jesus were offered to me, I would not have it; its very clearness would be, in my opinion, the best proof of its insufficiency." His friends may with perfect justice rejoin that at the sight of the Holy Land, and of the actual scene of the Gospel-story, all the current of M. Renan's thoughts may have naturally changed, and a new casting of that story irresistibly suggested itself to him; and that this is just a case for applying Cicero's maxim: Change of mind is not inconsistency—*nemo doctus unquam mutationem consilii inconstantiam dixit esse.* Nevertheless, for criticism, M. Renan's first thought must still be the truer one, as long as his new casting so fails more fully to commend itself, more fully (to use Coleridge's happy phrase about the

[1] Frances Power Cobbe, *Broken Lights: an Enquiry into the Present Condition and Future Prospects of Religious Faith* (1864); see also Arnold's reference at p. 46 to her *Religious Duty* (1864).

[ii] David Friedrich Strauss's *Das Leben Jesu* (1835) was published in an English translation by Marian Evans (who later wrote as 'George Eliot') in 1846; Ernest Renan's *La Vie de Jésus* was published in 1863. Both were serious works which Arnold greatly admired.

[v] 'Whoever imagines he can write it better does not understand it'; Claude Fleury, *Histoire Ecclésiastique* (1722).

Bible) to *find* us. Still M. Renan's attempt is, for criticism, of the most real interest and importance, since, with all its difficulty, a fresh synthesis of the New Testament *data*, — not a making war on them, in Voltaire's fashion, not a leaving them out of mind, in the world's fashion, but the putting a new construction upon them, the taking them from under the old, traditional, conventional point of view and placing them under a new one, — is the very essence of the religious problem, as now presented; and only by efforts in this direction can it receive a solution.

Again, in the same spirit in which she judges Bishop Colenso, Miss Cobbe, like so many earnest liberals of our practical race, both here and in America, herself sets vigorously about a positive reconstruction of religion, about making a religion of the future out of hand, or at least setting about making it. We must not rest, she and they are always thinking and saying, in negative criticism, we must be creative and constructive; hence we have such works as her recent *Religious Duty*, and works still more considerable, perhaps, by others, which will be in every one's mind. These works often have much ability; they often spring out of sincere convictions, and a sincere wish to do good; and they sometimes, perhaps, do good. Their fault is (if I may be permitted to say so) one which they have in common with the British College of Health, in the New Road.[w] Every one knows the British College of Health; it is that building with the lion and the statue of the Goddess Hygeia before it; at least I am sure about the lion, though I am not absolutely certain about the Goddess Hygeia. This building does credit, perhaps, to the resources of Dr. Morison and his disciples; but it falls a good deal short of one's idea of what a British College of Health ought to be. In England, where we hate public interference and love individual enterprise, we have a whole crop of places like the British College of Health; the grand name without the grand thing. Unluckily, creditable to individual enterprise as they are, they tend to impair our taste by making us forget what more grandiose, noble, or beautiful character properly belongs to a public institution. The same may be said of the religions of the future of Miss Cobbe and others. Creditable, like the British College of

---

[w] The British College of Health was the name given by James Morison (1770–1840), who styled himself 'the Hygeist', to the building in New Road (now King's Cross Road in central London) from which he distributed a patent medicine vegetable pill claimed to be of universal efficacy.

Health, to the resources of their authors, they yet tend to make us forget what more grandiose, noble, or beautiful character properly belongs to religious constructions. The historic religions, with all their faults, have had this; it certainly belongs to the religious sentiment, when it truly flowers, to have this; and we impoverish our spirit if we allow a religion of the future without it. What then is the duty of criticism here? To take the practical point of view, to applaud the liberal movement and all its works,—its New Road religions of the future into the bargain,—for their general utility's sake? By no means; but to be perpetually dissatisfied with these works, while they perpetually fall short of a high and perfect ideal.

For criticism, these are elementary laws; but they never can be popular, and in this country they have been very little followed, and one meets with immense obstacles in following them. That is a reason for asserting them again and again. Criticism must maintain its independence of the practical spirit and its aims. Even with well-meant efforts of the practical spirit it must express dissatisfaction, if in the sphere of the ideal they seem impoverishing and limiting. It must not hurry on to the goal because of its practical importance. It must be patient, and know how to wait; and flexible, and know how to attach itself to things and how to withdraw from them. It must be apt to study and praise elements that for the fulness of spiritual perfection are wanted, even though they belong to a power which in the practical sphere may be maleficent. It must be apt to discern the spiritual shortcomings or illusions of powers that in the practical sphere may be beneficent. And this without any notion of favouring or injuring, in the practical sphere, one power or the other; without any notion of playing off, in this sphere, one power against the other. When one looks, for instance, at the English Divorce Court,—an institution which perhaps has its practical conveniences, but which in the ideal sphere is so hideous; an institution which neither makes divorce impossible nor makes it decent, which allows a man to get rid of his wife, or a wife of her husband, but makes them drag one another first, for the public edification, through a mire of unutterable infamy,— when one looks at this charming institution, I say, with its crowded trials, its newspaper reports, and its money compensations, this institution in which the gross unregenerate British Philistine has indeed stamped an image of himself,—one may be permitted to find the marriage theory of Catholicism refreshing and elevating. Or when

Protestantism, in virtue of its supposed rational and intellectual
origin, gives the law to criticism too magisterially, criticism may and
must remind it that its pretensions, in this respect, are illusive and do
it harm; that the Reformation was a moral rather than an intellectual
event; that Luther's theory of grace no more exactly reflects the mind
of the spirit than Bossuet's philosophy of history reflects it; and that
there is no more antecedent probability of the Bishop of Durham's
stock of ideas being agreeable to perfect reason than of Pope Pius the
Ninth's.[x] But criticism will not on that account forget the achievements of Protestantism in the practical and moral sphere; nor that,
even in the intellectual sphere, Protestantism, though in a blind and
stumbling manner, carried forward the Renascence, while Catholicism threw itself violently across its path.

I lately heard a man of thought and energy contrasting the want of
ardour and movement which he now found amongst young men in
this country with what he remembered in his own youth, twenty years
ago. "What reformers we were then!" he exclaimed; "what a zeal we
had! how we canvassed every institution in Church and State, and
were prepared to remodel them all on first principles!" He was
inclined to regret, as a spiritual flagging, the lull which he saw. I am
disposed rather to regard it as a pause in which the turn to a new
mode of spiritual progress is being accomplished. Everything was long
seen, by the young and ardent amongst us, in inseparable connection
with politics and practical life. We have pretty well exhausted the
benefits of seeing things in this connection, we have got all that can be
got by so seeing them. Let us try a more disinterested mode of seeing
them; let us betake ourselves more to the serener life of the mind and
spirit. This life, too, may have its excesses and dangers; but they are
not for us at present. Let us think of quietly enlarging our stock of
true and fresh ideas, and not, as soon as we get an idea or half an idea,
be running out with it into the street, and trying to make it rule there.
Our ideas will, in the end, shape the world all the better for maturing
a little. Perhaps in fifty years' time it will in the English House of
Commons be an objection to an institution that it is an anomaly, and
my friend the Member of Parliament will shudder in his grave. But let
us in the meanwhile rather endeavour that in twenty years' time it

---

[x] Arnold is here balancing a Catholic against a Protestant claim in each case: J.-B. Bossuet
(1627–1704) was a French Catholic theologian and philosopher of history; the Bishop of
Durham, C.T. Baring (1807–79), was a strong evangelical.

may, in English literature, be an objection to a proposition that it is absurd. That will be a change so vast, that the imagination almost fails to grasp it. *Ab integro saeclorum nascitur ordo.*[y]

If I have insisted so much on the course which criticism must take where politics and religion are concerned, it is because, where these burning matters are in question, it is most likely to go astray. I have wished, above all, to insist on the attitude which criticism should adopt towards things in general; on its right tone and temper of mind. But then comes another question as to the subject-matter which literary criticism should most seek. Here, in general, its course is determined for it by the idea which is the law of its being; the idea of a disinterested endeavour to learn and propagate the best that is known and thought in the world, and thus to establish a current of fresh and true ideas. By the very nature of things, as England is not all the world, much of the best that is known and thought in the world cannot be of English growth, must be foreign; by the nature of things, again, it is just this that we are least likely to know, while English thought is streaming in upon us from all sides, and takes excellent care that we shall not be ignorant of its existence. The English critic of literature, therefore, must dwell much on foreign thought, and with particular heed on any part of it, which, while significant and fruitful in itself, is for any reason specially likely to escape him. Again, judging is often spoken of as the critic's one business, and so in some sense it is; but the judgment which almost insensibly forms itself in a fair and clear mind, along with fresh knowledge, is the valuable one; and thus knowledge, and ever fresh knowledge, must be the critic's great concern for himself. And it is by communicating fresh knowledge, and letting his own judgment pass along with it,—but insensibly, and in the second place, not the first, as a sort of companion and clue, not as an abstract law-giver,—that the critic will generally do most good to his readers. Sometimes, no doubt, for the sake of establishing an author's place in literature, and his relation to a central standard (and if this is not done, how are we to get at our *best in the world?*) criticism may have to deal with a subject-matter so familiar that fresh knowledge is out of the question, and then it must be all judgment; an enunciation and detailed application of principles. Here the great safeguard is never to let oneself become abstract, always to retain an

---

[y] 'The order of the ages is born anew'; Virgil, *Eclogues* IV, 5.

intimate and lively consciousness of the truth of what one is saying, and, the moment this fails us, to be sure that something is wrong. Still, under all circumstances, this mere judgment and application of principles is, in itself, not the most satisfactory work to the critic; like mathematics, it is tautological, and cannot well give us, like fresh learning, the sense of creative activity.

But stop, some one will say; all this talk is of no practical use to us whatever; this criticism of yours is not what we have in our minds when we speak of criticism; when we speak of critics and criticism, we mean critics and criticism of the current English literature of the day; when you offer to tell criticism its function, it is to this criticism that we expect you to address yourself. I am sorry for it, for I am afraid I must disappoint these expectations. I am bound by my own definition of criticism: *a disinterested endeavour to learn and propagate the best that is known and thought in the world.* How much of current English literature comes into this "best that is known and thought in the world?" Not very much, I fear; certainly less, at this moment, than of the current literature of France or Germany. Well, then, am I to alter my definition of criticism, in order to meet the requirements of a number of practising English critics, who, after all, are free in their choice of a business? That would be making criticism lend itself just to one of those alien practical considerations, which, I have said, are so fatal to it. One may say, indeed, to those who have to deal with the mass—so much better disregarded—of current English literature, that they may at all events endeavour, in dealing with this, to try it, so far as they can, by the standard of the best that is known and thought in the world; one may say, that to get anywhere near this standard, every critic should try and possess one great literature, at least, besides his own; and the more unlike his own, the better. But, after all, the criticism I am really concerned with,—the criticism which alone can much help us for the future, the criticism which, throughout Europe, is at the present day meant, when so much stress is laid on the importance of criticism and the critical spirit,—is a criticism which regards Europe as being, for intellectual and spiritual purposes, one great confederation, bound to a joint action and working to a common result; and whose members have, for their proper outfit, a knowledge of Greek, Roman, and Eastern antiquity, and of one another. Special, local, and temporary advantages being put out of account, that modern nation will in the intellectual and spiritual sphere make most progress, which most thoroughly carries out this programme. And what is that but saying that we too, all of us, as individuals, the more thoroughly we carry it out, shall make the more progress?

There is so much inviting us!—what are we to take? what will nourish us in growth towards perfection? That is the question which, with the immense field of life and of literature lying before him, the critic has to answer; for himself first, and afterwards for others. In this idea of the critic's business the essays brought together in the following pages[z] have had their origin; in this idea, widely different as are their subjects, they have, perhaps, their unity.

I conclude with what I said at the beginning: to have the sense of creative activity is the great happiness and the great proof of being alive, and it is not denied to criticism to have it; but then criticism must be sincere, simple, flexible, ardent, ever widening its knowledge. Then it may have, in no contemptible measure, a joyful sense of creative activity; a sense which a man of insight and conscience will prefer to what he might derive from a poor, starved, fragmentary, inadequate creation. And at some epochs no other creation is possible.

Still, in full measure, the sense of creative activity belongs only to genuine creation; in literature we must never forget that. But what true man of letters ever can forget it? It is no such common matter for a gifted nature to come into possession of a current of true and living ideas, and to produce amidst the inspiration of them, that we are likely to underrate it. The epochs of Æschylus and Shakspeare make us feel their pre-eminence. In an epoch like those is, no doubt, the true life of literature; there is the promised land, towards which criticism can only beckon. That promised land it will not be ours to enter, and we shall die in the wilderness: but to have desired to enter it, to have saluted it from afar, is already, perhaps, the best distinction among contemporaries; it will certainly be the best title to esteem with posterity.

[z] i.e. in the rest of *Essays in Criticism*, in which this article appeared as the opening essay.

# Culture & Anarchy

*An Essay in*
*Political and Social Criticism*

*Estote ergo vos perfecti!*[a]

---

[a] 'Be ye therefore perfect'; Matthew 5:48 (Vulgate version).

# Introduction

In one of his speeches a short time ago, that fine speaker and famous Liberal, Mr. Bright, took occasion to have a fling at the friends and preachers of culture. "People who talk about what they call *culture!*" said he, contemptuously; "by which they mean a smattering of the two dead languages of Greek and Latin." And he went on to remark, in a strain with which modern speakers and writers have made us very familiar, how poor a thing this culture is, how little good it can do to the world, and how absurd it is for its possessors to set much store by it.[b] And the other day a younger Liberal than Mr. Bright, one of a school whose mission it is to bring into order and system that body of truth with which the earlier Liberals merely fumbled, a member of the University of Oxford, and a very clever writer, Mr. Frederic Harrison, developed, in the systematic and stringent manner of his school, the thesis which Mr. Bright had propounded in only general terms. "Perhaps the very silliest cant of the day," said Mr. Frederic Harrison, "is the cant about culture. Culture is a desirable quality in a critic of new books, and sits well on a professor of *belles-lettres*; but as applied to politics, it means simply a turn for small fault-finding, love of selfish ease, and indecision in action. The man of culture is in politics one of the poorest mortals alive. For simple pedantry and want of good sense no man is his equal. No assumption is too unreal, no end is too unpractical for him. But the active exercise of politics requires common sense, sympathy, trust, resolution, and enthusiasm, qualities which your man of culture has carefully rooted up, lest they

[b] John Bright (1811–89), Liberal MP for Birmingham and a leading spokesman of middle-class radicalism, in the debate on the Franchise Bill, May 1866.

55

damage the delicacy of his critical olfactories. Perhaps they are the only class of responsible beings in the community who cannot with safety be entrusted with power."[c]

Now for my part I do not wish to see men of culture asking to be entrusted with power; and, indeed, I have freely said, that in my opinion the speech most proper, at present, for a man of culture to make to a body of his fellow-countrymen who get him into a committee-room, is Socrates's: *Know thyself!* and this is not a speech to be made by men wanting to be entrusted with power. For this very indifference to direct political action I have been taken to task by the *Daily Telegraph*, coupled, by a strange perversity of fate, with just that very one of the Hebrew prophets whose style I admire the least, and called "an elegant Jeremiah."[d] It is because I say (to use the words which the *Daily Telegraph* puts in my mouth):—"You mustn't make a fuss because you have no vote,—that is vulgarity; you mustn't hold big meetings to agitate for reform bills and to repeal corn laws,—that is the very height of vulgarity,"—it is for this reason that I am called, sometimes an elegant Jeremiah, sometimes a spurious Jeremiah, a Jeremiah about the reality of whose mission the writer in the *Daily Telegraph* has his doubts. It is evident, therefore, that I have so taken my line as not to be exposed to the whole brunt of Mr. Frederic Harrison's censure. Still, I have often spoken in praise of culture, I have striven to make all my works and ways serve the interests of culture. I take culture to be something a great deal more than what Mr. Frederic Harrison and others call it: "a desirable quality in a critic of new books." Nay, even though to a certain extent I am disposed to agree with Mr. Frederic Harrison, that men of culture are just the class of responsible beings in this community of ours who cannot properly, at present, be entrusted with power, I am not sure that I do not think this the fault of our community rather than of the men of culture. In short, although, like Mr. Bright and Mr. Frederic Harrison, and the editor of the *Daily Telegraph*, and a large body of valued friends of mine, I am a Liberal, yet I am a Liberal tempered by experience, reflection, and renouncement, and I am, above all, a

[c] Frederic Harrison (1831–1923), a former Fellow of Wadham College, Oxford, and a disciple of Auguste Comte, founder of Positivism, in 'Our Venetian Constitution', *Fortnightly Review* (1867).

[d] Arnold had been criticized as an 'elegant Jeremiah' and 'the high-priest of the kid-gloved persuasion' in an article in the *Daily Telegraph* for 8 September 1866.

believer in culture. Therefore I propose now to try and inquire, in the simple unsystematic way which best suits both my taste and my powers, what culture really is, what good it can do, what is our own special need of it; and I shall seek to find some plain grounds on which a faith in culture, — both my own faith in it and the faith of others, — may rest securely.

# CHAPTER I

# Sweetness and Light

The disparagers of culture make its motive curiosity; sometimes, indeed, they make its motive mere exclusiveness and vanity. The culture which is supposed to plume itself on a smattering of Greek and Latin is a culture which is begotten by nothing so intellectual as curiosity; it is valued either out of sheer vanity and ignorance or else as an engine of social and class distinction, separating its holder, like a badge or title, from other people who have not got it. No serious man would call this *culture*, or attach any value to it, as culture, at all. To find the real ground for the very different estimate which serious people will set upon culture, we must find some motive for culture in the terms of which may lie a real ambiguity; and such a motive the word *curiosity* gives us.

I have before now pointed out that we English do not, like the foreigners, use this word in a good sense as well as in a bad sense.[a] With us the word is always used in a somewhat disapproving sense. A liberal and intelligent eagerness about the things of the mind may be meant by a foreigner when he speaks of curiosity, but with us the word always conveys a certain notion of frivolous and unedifying activity. In the *Quarterly Review*, some little time ago, was an estimate of the celebrated French critic, M. Sainte-Beuve,[b] and a very inadequate estimate it in my judgment was. And its inadequacy con-

---

[a] See above p. 35.

[b] [F.T. Marzials], 'M. Sainte-Beuve', *Quarterly Review* (1866). Charles-Augustin Sainte-Beuve (1804–69), French literary critic, was greatly admired by Arnold who wrote an essay on him in 1869 and contributed the article on him to the ninth edition of the *Encyclopaedia Britannica* (1886).

sisted chiefly in this: that in our English way it left out of sight the double sense really involved in the word *curiosity*, thinking enough was said to stamp M. Sainte-Beuve with blame if it was said that he was impelled in his operations as a critic by curiosity, and omitting either to perceive that M. Sainte-Beuve himself, and many other people with him, would consider that this was praiseworthy and not blame-worthy, or to point out why it ought really to be accounted worthy of blame and not of praise. For as there is a curiosity about intellectual matters which is futile, and merely a disease, so there is certainly a curiosity,—a desire after the things of the mind simply for their own sakes and for the pleasure of seeing them as they are,—which is, in an intelligent being, natural and laudable. Nay, and the very desire to see things as they are implies a balance and regulation of mind which is not often attained without fruitful effort, and which is the very opposite of the blind and diseased impulse of mind which is what we mean to blame when we blame curiosity. Montesquieu says: "The first motive which ought to impel us to study is the desire to augment the excellence of our nature, and to render an intelligent being yet more intelligent." This is the true ground to assign for the genuine scientific passion, however manifested, and for culture, viewed simply as a fruit of this passion; and it is a worthy ground, even though we let the term *curiosity* stand to describe it.

But there is of culture another view, in which not solely the scientific passion, the sheer desire to see things as they are, natural and proper in an intelligent being, appears as the ground of it. There is a view in which all the love of our neighbour, the impulses towards action, help, and beneficence, the desire for removing human error, clearing human confusion, and diminishing human misery, the noble aspiration to leave the world better and happier than we found it,— motives eminently such as are called social,—come in as part of the grounds of culture, and the main and pre-eminent part. Culture is then properly described not as having its origin in curiosity, but as having its origin in the love of perfection; it is *a study of perfection*. It moves by the force, not merely or primarily of the scientific passion for pure knowledge, but also of the moral and social passion for doing good. As, in the first view of it, we took for its worthy motto Montesquieu's words: "To render an intelligent being yet more intelligent!" so, in the second view of it, there is no better motto which it can have than these words of Bishop Wilson: "To make reason and the will of God prevail!"[c]

Only, whereas the passion for doing good is apt to be over-hasty in determining what reason and the will of God say, because its turn is for acting rather than thinking and it wants to be beginning to act; and whereas it is apt to take its own conceptions, which proceed from its own state of development and share in all the imperfections and immaturities of this, for a basis of action; what distinguishes culture is, that it is possessed by the scientific passion as well as by the passion of doing good; that it demands worthy notions of reason and the will of God, and does not readily suffer its own crude conceptions to substitute themselves for them. And knowing that no action or institution can be salutary and stable which is not based on reason and the will of God, it is not so bent on acting and instituting, even with the great aim of diminishing human error and misery ever before its thoughts, but that it can remember that acting and instituting are of little use, unless we know how and what we ought to act and to institute.

This culture is more interesting and more far-reaching than that other, which is founded solely on the scientific passion for knowing. But it needs times of faith and ardour, times when the intellectual horizon is opening and widening all round us, to flourish in. And is not the close and bounded intellectual horizon within which we have long lived and moved now lifting up, and are not new lights finding free passage to shine in upon us? For a long time there was no passage for them to make their way in upon us, and then it was of no use to think of adapting the world's action to them. Where was the hope of making reason and the will of God prevail among people who had a routine which they had christened reason and the will of God, in which they were inextricably bound, and beyond which they had no power of looking? But now the iron force of adhesion to the old routine,—social, political, religious,—has wonderfully yielded; the iron force of exclusion of all which is new has wonderfully yielded. The danger now is, not that people should obstinately refuse to allow anything but their old routine to pass for reason and the will of God,

[c] Thomas Wilson (1663–1755), Bishop of Sodor and Man; Arnold quoted him very frequently, especially his *Maxims of Piety and of Christianity*, but he was so little known that Arnold was accused of having invented him.

but either that they should allow some novelty or other to pass for these too easily, or else that they should underrate the importance of them altogether, and think it enough to follow action for its own sake, without troubling themselves to make reason and the will of God prevail therein. Now, then, is the moment for culture to be of service, culture which believes in making reason and the will of God prevail, believes in perfection, is the study and pursuit of perfection, and is no longer debarred, by a rigid invincible exclusion of whatever is new, from getting acceptance for its ideas, simply because they are new.

The moment this view of culture is seized, the moment it is regarded not solely as the endeavour to see things as they are, to draw towards a knowledge of the universal order which seems to be intended and aimed at in the world, and which it is a man's happiness to go along with or his misery to go counter to,—to learn, in short, the will of God,—the moment, I say, culture is considered not merely as the endeavour to *see* and *learn* this, but as the endeavour, also, to make it *prevail*, the moral, social, and beneficent character of culture becomes manifest. The mere endeavour to see and learn the truth for our own personal satisfaction is indeed a commencement for making it prevail, a preparing the way for this, which always serves this, and is wrongly, therefore, stamped with blame absolutely in itself and not only in its caricature and degeneration. But perhaps it has got stamped with blame, and disparaged with the dubious title of curiosity, because in comparison with this wider endeavour of such great and plain utility it looks selfish, petty, and unprofitable.

And religion, the greatest and most important of the efforts by which the human race has manifested its impulse to perfect itself,— religion, that voice of the deepest human experience,—does not only enjoin and sanction the aim which is the great aim of culture, the aim of setting ourselves to ascertain what perfection is and to make it prevail; but also, in determining generally in what human perfection consists, religion comes to a conclusion identical with that which culture,—culture seeking the determination of this question through *all* the voices of human experience which have been heard upon it, of art, science, poetry, philosophy, history, as well as of religion, in order to give a greater fulness and certainty to its solution,—likewise reaches. Religion says: *The kingdom of God is within you*; and culture, in like manner, places human perfection in an *internal* condition, in the growth and predominance of our humanity proper, as distinguished from our animality. It places it in the ever-increasing efficacy and in the general harmonious expansion of those gifts of thought and feeling, which make the peculiar dignity, wealth, and happiness of human nature. As I have said on a former occasion: "It is in making endless additions to itself, in the endless expansion of its powers, in endless growth in wisdom and beauty, that the spirit of the human race finds its ideal. To reach this ideal, culture is an indispensable aid, and that is the true value of culture."[d] Not a having and a resting, but a growing and a becoming, is the character of perfection as culture conceives it; and here, too, it coincides with religion.

And because men are all members of one great whole, and the sympathy which is in human nature will not allow one member to be indifferent to the rest or to have a perfect welfare independent of the rest, the expansion of our humanity, to suit the idea of perfection which culture forms, must be a *general* expansion. Perfection, as culture conceives it, is not possible while the individual remains isolated. The individual is required, under pain of being stunted and enfeebled in his own development if he disobeys, to carry others along with him in his march towards perfection, to be continually doing all he can to enlarge and increase the volume of the human stream sweeping thitherward. And here, once more, culture lays on us the same obligation as religion, which says, as Bishop Wilson has admirably put it, that "to promote the kingdom of God is to increase and hasten one's own happiness."

But, finally, perfection,—as culture from a thorough disinterested study of human nature and human experience learns to conceive it,— is a harmonious expansion of *all* the powers which make the beauty and worth of human nature, and is not consistent with the over-development of any one power at the expense of the rest. Here culture goes beyond religion, as religion is generally conceived by us.

If culture, then, is a study of perfection, and of harmonious perfection, general perfection, and perfection which consists in becoming something rather than in having something, in an inward condition of the mind and spirit, not in an outward set of circumstances,—it is clear that culture, instead of being the frivolous and useless thing

[d] Arnold is quoting from his *A French Eton* (1864).

which Mr. Bright, and Mr. Frederic Harrison, and many other Liberals are apt to call it, has a very important function to fulfil for mankind. And this function is particularly important in our modern world, of which the whole civilisation is, to a much greater degree than the civilisation of Greece and Rome, mechanical and external, and tends constantly to become more so. But above all in our own country has culture a weighty part to perform, because here that mechanical character, which civilisation tends to take everywhere, is shown in the most eminent degree. Indeed nearly all the characters of perfection, as culture teaches us to fix them, meet in this country with some powerful tendency which thwarts them and sets them at defiance. The idea of perfection as an *inward* condition of the mind and spirit is at variance with the mechanical and material civilisation in esteem with us, and nowhere, as I have said, so much in esteem as with us. The idea of perfection as a *general* expansion of the human family is at variance with our strong individualism, our hatred of all limits to the unrestrained swing of the individual's personality, our maxim of "every man for himself." Above all, the idea of perfection as a *harmonious* expansion of human nature is at variance with our want of flexibility, with our inaptitude for seeing more than one side of a thing, with our intense energetic absorption in the particular pursuit we happen to be following. So culture has a rough task to achieve in this country. Its preachers have, and are likely long to have, a hard time of it, and they will much oftener be regarded, for a great while to come, as elegant or spurious Jeremiahs than as friends and benefactors. That, however, will not prevent their doing in the end good service if they persevere. And, meanwhile, the mode of action they have to pursue, and the sort of habits they must fight against, ought to be made quite clear for every one to see, who may be willing to look at the matter attentively and dispassionately.

Faith in machinery is, I said, our besetting danger; often in machinery most absurdly disproportioned to the end which this machinery, if it is to do any good at all, is to serve; but always in machinery, as if it had a value in and for itself. What is freedom but machinery? what is population but machinery? what is coal but machinery? what are railroads but machinery? what is wealth but machinery? what are, even, religious organisations but machinery? Now almost every voice in England is accustomed to speak of these things as if they were precious ends in themselves, and therefore had some of the characters of perfection indissolubly joined to them. I have before now noticed Mr. Roebuck's stock argument for proving the greatness and happiness of England as she is, and for quite stopping the mouths of all gainsayers.[e] Mr. Roebuck is never weary of reiterating this argument of his, so I do not know why I should be weary of noticing it. 'May not every man in England say what he likes?'—Mr. Roebuck perpetually asks; and that, he thinks, is quite sufficient, and when every man may say what he likes, our aspirations ought to be satisfied. But the aspirations of culture, which is the study of perfection, are not satisfied, unless what men say, when they may say what they like, is worth saying,—has good in it, and more good than bad. In the same way the *Times*, replying to some foreign strictures on the dress, looks, and behaviour of the English abroad, urges that the English ideal is that every one should be free to do and to look just as he likes. But culture indefatigably tries, not to make what each raw person may like the rule by which he fashions himself; but to draw ever nearer to a sense of what is indeed beautiful, graceful, and becoming, and to get the raw person to like that.

And in the same way with respect to railroads and coal. Every one must have observed the strange language current during the late discussions as to the possible failure of our supplies of coal. Our coal, thousands of people were saying, is the real basis of our national greatness; if our coal runs short, there is an end of the greatness of England. But what *is* greatness?—culture makes us ask. Greatness is a spiritual condition worthy to excite love, interest, and admiration; and the outward proof of possessing greatness is that we excite love, interest, and admiration. If England were swallowed up by the sea tomorrow, which of the two, a hundred years hence, would most excite the love, interest, and admiration of mankind,—would most, therefore, show the evidences of having possessed greatness,—the England of the last twenty years, or the England of Elizabeth, of a time of splendid spiritual effort, but when our coal, and our industrial operations depending on coal, were very little developed? Well, then, what an unsound habit of mind it must be which makes us talk of things like coal or iron as constituting the greatness of England, and

[e] See above pp. 39–40.

how salutary a friend is culture, bent on seeing things as they are, and thus dissipating delusions of this kind and fixing standards of perfection that are real!

Wealth, again, that end to which our prodigious works for material advantage are directed,—the commonest of common-places tells us how men are always apt to regard wealth as a precious end in itself; and certainly they have never been so apt thus to regard it as they are in England at the present time. Never did people believe anything more firmly than nine Englishmen out of ten at the present day believe that our greatness and welfare are proved by our being so very rich. Now, the use of culture is that it helps us, by means of its spiritual standard of perfection, to regard wealth as but machinery, and not only to say as a matter of words that we regard wealth as but machinery, but really to perceive and feel that it is so. If it were not for this purging effect wrought upon our minds by culture, the whole world, the future as well as the present, would inevitably belong to the Philistines. The people who believe most that our greatness and welfare are proved by our being very rich, and who most give their lives and thoughts to becoming rich, are just the very people whom we call Philistines. Culture says: "Consider these people, then, their way of life, their habits, their manners, the very tones of their voice; look at them attentively; observe the literature they read, the things which give them pleasure, the words which come forth out of their mouths, the thoughts which make the furniture of their minds; would any amount of wealth be worth having with the condition that one was to become just like these people by having it?" And thus culture begets a dissatisfaction which is of the highest possible value in stemming the common tide of men's thoughts in a wealthy and industrial community, and which saves the future, as one may hope, from being vulgarised, even if it cannot save the present.

Population, again, and bodily health and vigour, are things which are nowhere treated in such an unintelligent, misleading, exaggerated way as in England. Both are really machinery; yet how many people all around us do we see rest in them and fail to look beyond them! Why, one has heard people, fresh from reading certain articles of the *Times* on the Registrar-General's returns of marriages and births in this country, who would talk of our large English families in quite a solemn strain, as if they had something in itself beautiful, elevating, and meritorious in them; as if the British Philistine would have only to present himself before the Great Judge with his twelve children, in order to be received among the sheep as a matter of right!

But bodily health and vigour, it may be said, are not to be classed with wealth and population as mere machinery; they have a more real and essential value. True; but only as they are more intimately connected with a perfect spiritual condition than wealth or population are. The moment we disjoin them from the idea of a perfect spiritual condition, and pursue them, as we do pursue them, for their own sake and as ends in themselves, our worship of them becomes as mere worship of machinery, as our worship of wealth or population, and as unintelligent and vulgarising a worship as that is. Every one with anything like an adequate idea of human perfection has distinctly marked this subordination to higher and spiritual ends of the cultivation of bodily vigour and activity. "Bodily exercise profiteth little; but godliness is profitable unto all things," says the author of the Epistle to Timothy. And the utilitarian Franklin says just as explicitly: — "Eat and drink such an exact quantity as suits the constitution of thy body, *in reference to the services of the mind*." But the point of view of culture, keeping the mark of human perfection simply and broadly in view, and not assigning to this perfection, as religion or utilitarianism assigns to it, a special and limited character, this point of view, I say, of culture is best given by these words of Epictetus: — "It is a sign of ἀφυΐα," says he, — that is, of a nature not finely tempered, — "to give yourselves up to things which relate to the body; to make, for instance, a great fuss about exercise, a great fuss about eating, a great fuss about drinking, a great fuss about walking, a great fuss about riding. All these things ought to be done merely by the way: the formation of the spirit and character must be our real concern." This is admirable; and, indeed, the Greek word εὐφυΐα, a finely tempered nature, gives exactly the notion of perfection as culture brings us to conceive it: a harmonious perfection, a perfection in which the characters of beauty and intelligence are both present, which unites "the two noblest of things," — as Swift, who of one of the two, at any rate, had himself all too little, most happily calls them in his *Battle of the Books*, — "the two noblest of things, *sweetness and light*." The εὐφυής is the man who tends towards sweetness and light; the ἀφυής, on the other hand, is our Philistine. The immense spiritual significance of the Greeks is due to their having been inspired with this central and happy idea of

the essential character of human perfection; and Mr Bright's misconception of culture, as a smattering of Greek and Latin, comes
itself, after all, from this wonderful significance of the Greeks having
affected the very machinery of our education, and is in itself a kind of
homage to it.

In thus making sweetness and light to be characters of perfection,
culture is of like spirit with poetry, follows one law with poetry. Far
more than on our freedom, our population, and our industrialism,
many amongst us rely upon our religious organisations to save us. I
have called religion a yet more important manifestation of human
nature than poetry, because it has worked on a broader scale for
perfection, and with greater masses of men. But the idea of beauty
and of a human nature perfect on all its sides, which is the dominant
idea of poetry, is a true and invaluable idea, though it has not yet had
the success that the idea of conquering the obvious faults of our
animality, and of a human nature perfect on the moral side, — which is
the dominant idea of religion, — has been enabled to have; and it is
destined, adding to itself the religious idea of a devout energy, to
transform and govern the other.

The best art and poetry of the Greeks, in which religion and poetry
are one, in which the idea of beauty and of a human nature perfect on
all sides adds to itself a religious and devout energy, and works in the
strength of that, is on this account of such surpassing interest and
instructiveness for us, though it was, — as, having regard to the human
race in general, and, indeed, having regard to the Greeks themselves,
we must own, — a premature attempt, an attempt which for success
needed the moral and religious fibre in humanity to be more braced
and developed than it had yet been. But Greece did not err in having
the idea of beauty, harmony, and complete human perfection, so
present and paramount. It is impossible to have this idea too present
and paramount; only, the moral fibre must be braced too. And we,
because we have braced the moral fibre, are not on that account in the
right way, if at the same time the idea of beauty, harmony, and
complete human perfection, is wanting or misapprehended amongst
us; and evidently it *is* wanting or misapprehended at present. And
when we rely as we do on our religious organisations, which in
themselves do not and cannot give us this idea, and think we have
done enough if we make them spread and prevail, then I say, we fall
into our common fault of overvaluing machinery.

Nothing is more common than for people to confound the inward peace and satisfaction which follows the subduing of the obvious faults of our animality with what I may call absolute inward peace and satisfaction,—the peace and satisfaction which are reached as we draw near to complete spiritual perfection, and not merely to moral perfection, or rather to relative moral perfection. No people in the world have done more and struggled more to attain this relative moral perfection than our English race has. For no people in the world has the command to *resist the devil*, to *overcome the wicked one*, in the nearest and most obvious sense of those words, had such a pressing force and reality. And we have had our reward, not only in the great worldly prosperity which our obedience to this command has brought us, but also, and far more, in great inward peace and satisfaction. But to me few things are more pathetic than to see people, on the strength of the inward peace and satisfaction which their rudimentary efforts towards perfection have brought them, employ, concerning their incomplete perfection and the religious organisations within which they have found it, language which properly applies only to complete perfection, and is a far-off echo of the human soul's prophecy of it. Religion itself, I need hardly say, supplies them in abundance with this grand language. And very freely do they use it; yet it is really the severest possible criticism of such an incomplete perfection as alone we have yet reached through our religious organisations.

The impulse of the English race towards moral development and self-conquest has nowhere so powerfully manifested itself as in Puritanism. Nowhere has Puritanism found so adequate an expression as in the religious organisation of the Independents.[f] The modern Independents have a newspaper, the *Nonconformist*, written with great sincerity and ability. The motto, the standard, the profession of faith which this organ of theirs carries aloft, is: "The Dissidence of Dissent and the Protestantism of the Protestant religion." There is sweetness and light, and an ideal of complete harmonious human perfection! One need not go to culture and poetry to find language to judge it. Religion, with its instinct for perfection, supplies language to judge it, language, too, which is in our mouths every day. "Finally, be of one mind, united in feeling," says St. Peter.

---

[f] The Independents, who insisted on the autonomy of each congregation, had played an important part in the Puritan opposition to Charles I; by the nineteenth century they were more generally known as Congregationalists.

There is an ideal which judges the Puritan ideal: "The Dissidence of Dissent and the Protestantism of the Protestant religion!" And religious organisations like this are what people believe in, rest in, would give their lives for! Such, I say, is the wonderful virtue of even the beginnings of perfection, of having conquered even the plain faults of our animality, that the religious organisation which has helped us to do it can seem to us something precious, salutary, and to be propagated, even when it wears such a brand of imperfection on its forehead as this. And men have got such a habit of giving to the language of religion a special application, of making it a mere jargon, that for the condemnation which religion itself passes on the shortcomings of their religious organisations they have no ear; they are sure to cheat themselves and to explain this condemnation away. They can only be reached by the criticism which culture, like poetry, speaking a language not to be sophisticated, and resolutely testing these organisations by the ideal of a human perfection complete on all sides, applies to them.

But men of culture and poetry, it will be said, are again and again failing, and failing conspicuously, in the necessary first stage to a harmonious perfection, in the subduing of the great obvious faults of our animality, which it is the glory of these religious organisations to have helped us to subdue. True, they do often so fail. They have often been without the virtues as well as the faults of the Puritan; it has been one of their dangers that they so felt the Puritan's faults that they too much neglected the practice of his virtues. I will not, however, exculpate them at the Puritan's expense. They have often failed in morality, and morality is indispensable. And they have been punished for their failure, as the Puritan has been rewarded for his performance. They have been punished wherein they erred; but their ideal of beauty, of sweetness and light, and a human nature complete on all its sides, remains the true ideal of perfection still; just as the Puritan's ideal of perfection remains narrow and inadequate, although for what he did well he has been richly rewarded. Notwithstanding the mighty results of the Pilgrim Fathers' voyage, they and their standard of perfection are rightly judged when we figure to ourselves Shakspeare or Virgil,—souls in whom sweetness and light, and all that in human nature is most humane, were eminent,—accompanying them on their voyage, and think what intolerable company Shakspeare and Virgil would have found them! In the same way let us judge the religious organisations which we see all around us. Do not let us deny the good and the happiness which they have accomplished; but do not let us fail to see clearly that their idea of human perfection is narrow and inadequate, and that the Dissidence of Dissent and the Protestantism of the Protestant religion will never bring humanity to its true goal. As I said with regard to wealth: Let us look at the life of those who live in and for it, — so I say with regard to the religious organisations. Look at the life imaged in such a newspaper as the *Nonconformist*, — a life of jealousy of the Establishment, disputes, tea-meetings, openings of chapels, sermons; and then think of it as an ideal of a human life completing itself on all sides, and aspiring with all its organs after sweetness, light, and perfection!

Another newspaper, representing, like the *Nonconformist*, one of the religious organisations of this country, was a short time ago giving an account of the crowd at Epsom on the Derby day, and of all the vice and hideousness which was to be seen in that crowd; and then the writer turned suddenly round upon Professor Huxley, and asked him how he proposed to cure all this vice and hideousness without religion.[g] I confess I felt disposed to ask the asker this question: And how do you propose to cure it with such a religion as yours? How is the ideal of a life so unlovely, so unattractive, so incomplete, so narrow, so far removed from a true and satisfying ideal of human perfection, as is the life of your religious organisation as you yourself reflect it, to conquer and transform all this vice and hideousness? Indeed, the strongest plea for the study of perfection as pursued by culture, the clearest proof of the actual inadequacy of the idea of perfection held by the religious organisations, — expressing, as I have said, the most widespread effort which the human race has yet made after perfection, — is to be found in the state of our life and society with these in possession of it, and having been in possession of it I know not how many hundred years. We are all of us included in some religious organisation or other; we all call ourselves, in the sublime and aspiring language of religion which I have before noticed, *children of God*. Children of God; — it is an immense pretension! — and how are we to justify it? By the works which we do, and the words which we speak. And the work which we collective children of God do, our grand

---

[g] Thomas Henry Huxley (1825–95), known as 'Darwin's bulldog', was the most prominent, and most aggressive, spokesman for a scientific rather than a religious view of the world.

centre of life, our *city* which we have builded for us to dwell in, is London! London, with its unutterable external hideousness, and with its internal canker of *publicè egestas, privatim opulentia,*[h] — to use the words which Sallust puts into Cato's mouth about Rome, — unequalled in the world! The word, again, which we children of God speak, the voice which most hits our collective thought, the newspaper with the largest circulation in England, nay, with the largest circulation in the whole world, is the *Daily Telegraph!* I say that when our religious organisations, — which I admit to express the most considerable effort after perfection that our race has yet made, — land us in no better result than this, it is high time to examine carefully their idea of perfection, to see whether it does not leave out of account sides and forces of human nature which we might turn to great use; whether it would not be more operative if it were more complete. And I say that the English reliance on our religious organisations and on their ideas of human perfection just as they stand, is like our reliance on freedom, on muscular Christianity, on population, on coal, on wealth, — mere belief in machinery, and unfruitful; and that it is wholesomely counteracted by culture, bent on seeing things as they are, and on drawing the human race onwards to a more complete, a harmonious perfection.

Culture, however, shows its single-minded love of perfection, its desire simply to make reason and the will of God prevail, its freedom from fanaticism, by its attitude towards all this machinery, even while it insists that it *is* machinery. Fanatics, seeing the mischief men do themselves by their blind belief in some machinery or other, — whether it is wealth and industrialism, or whether it is the cultivation of bodily strength and activity, or whether it is a political organisation, or whether it is a religious organisation, — oppose with might and main the tendency to this or that political and religious organisation, or to games and athletic exercises, or to wealth and industrialism, and try violently to stop it. But the flexibility which sweetness and light give, and which is one of the rewards of culture pursued in good faith, enables a man to see that a tendency may be necessary, and even, as a preparation for something in the future, salutary, and yet that the generations or individuals who obey this tendency are sacrificed to it, that they fall short of the hope of perfection by following it; and that

[h] 'Public poverty and private opulence'.

its mischiefs are to be criticised, lest it should take too firm a hold and last after it has served its purpose.

Mr. Gladstone well pointed out, in a speech at Paris,—and others have pointed out the same thing,—how necessary is the present great movement towards wealth and industrialism, in order to lay broad foundations of material well-being for the society of the future. The worst of these justifications is, that they are generally addressed to the very people engaged, body and soul, in the movement in question; at all events, that they are always seized with the greatest avidity by these people, and taken by them as quite justifying their life; and that thus they tend to harden them in their sins. Now, culture admits the necessity of the movement towards fortune-making and exaggerated industrialism, readily allows that the future may derive benefit from it; but insists, at the same time, that the passing generations of industrialists,—forming, for the most part, the stout main body of Philistinism,—are sacrificed to it. In the same way, the result of all the games and sports which occupy the passing generation of boys and young men may be the establishment of a better and sounder physical type for the future to work with. Culture does not set itself against the games and sports; it congratulates the future, and hopes it will make a good use of its improved physical basis; but it points out that our passing generation of boys and young men is, meantime, sacrificed. Puritanism was perhaps necessary to develop the moral fibre of the English race, Nonconformity to break the yoke of ecclesiastical domination over men's minds and to prepare the way for freedom of thought in the distant future; still, culture points out that the harmonious perfection of generations of Puritans and Nonconformists have been, in consequence, sacrificed. Freedom of speech may be necessary for the society of the future, but the young lions of the *Daily Telegraph* in the meanwhile are sacrificed. A voice for every man in his country's government may be necessary for the society of the future, but meanwhile Mr. Beales and Mr. Bradlaugh are sacrificed.[i]

Oxford, the Oxford of the past, has many faults; and she has heavily paid for them in defeat, in isolation, in want of hold upon the modern world. Yet we in Oxford, brought up amidst the beauty and sweetness of that beautiful place, have not failed to seize one truth,—the truth

---

[i] Edmond Beales (1803–81) and Charles Bradlaugh (1833–91) were leading members of the Reform League which campaigned for the extension of the franchise during the 1860s.

that beauty and sweetness are essential characters of a complete human perfection. When I insist on this, I am all in the faith and tradition of Oxford. I say boldly that this our sentiment for beauty and sweetness, our sentiment against hideousness and rawness, has been at the bottom of our attachment to so many beaten causes, of our opposition to so many triumphant movements. And the sentiment is true, and has never been wholly defeated, and has shown its power even in its defeat. We have not won our political battles, we have not carried our main points, we have not stopped our adversaries' advance, we have not marched victoriously with the modern world; but we have told silently upon the mind of the country, we have prepared currents of feeling which sap our adversaries' position when it seems gained, we have kept up our own communications with the future. Look at the course of the great movement which shook Oxford to its centre some thirty years ago! It was directed, as any one who reads Dr Newman's *Apology* may see, against what in one word may be called "Liberalism."[j] Liberalism prevailed; it was the appointed force to do the work of the hour; it was necessary, it was inevitable that it should prevail. The Oxford movement was broken, it failed; our wrecks are scattered on every shore: —

Quæ regio in terris nostri non plena laboris?[k]

But what was it, this liberalism, as Dr. Newman saw it, and as it really broke the Oxford movement? It was the great middle-class liberalism, which had for the cardinal points of its belief the Reform Bill of 1832, and local self-government, in politics; in the social sphere, free-trade, unrestricted competition, and the making of large industrial fortunes; in the religious sphere, the Dissidence of Dissent and the Protestantism of the Protestant religion. I do not say that other and more intelligent forces than this were not opposed to the Oxford movement: but this was the force which really beat it; this was the force which Dr. Newman felt himself fighting with; this was the force which till only the other day seemed to be the paramount force in this country, and to be in possession of the future; this was the force

---

[j] The Oxford Movement, which flourished in the 1830s and early 1840s, expressed a 'Catholic' or High Church tendency within Anglicanism. Its leader, John Henry Newman (1801–90), who converted to Roman Catholicism in 1845, published his *Apologia Pro Vita Sua* in 1864.

[k] 'What part of the earth is not full of our toils?' (Virgil, *Aeneid* I, 460).

whose achievements fill Mr. Lowe with such inexpressible admiration, and whose rule he was so horror-struck to see threatened.[1] And where is this great force of Philistinism now? It is thrust into the second rank, it is become a power of yesterday, it has lost the future. A new power has suddenly appeared, a power which it is impossible yet to judge fully, but which is certainly a wholly different force from middle-class liberalism; different in its cardinal points of belief, different in its tendencies in every sphere. It loves and admires neither the legislation of middle-class Parliaments, nor the local self-government of middle-class vestries, nor the unrestricted competition of middle-class industrialists, nor the dissidence of middle-class Dissent and the Protestantism of middle-class Protestant religion. I am not now praising this new force, or saying that its own ideals are better; all I say is, that they are wholly different. And who will estimate how much the currents of feeling created by Dr. Newman's movement, the keen desire for beauty and sweetness which it nourished, the deep aversion it manifested to the hardness and vulgarity of middle-class liberalism, the strong light it turned on the hideous and grotesque illusions of middle-class Protestantism,—who will estimate how much all these contributed to swell the tide of secret dissatisfaction which has mined the ground under the self-confident liberalism of the last thirty years, and has prepared the way for its sudden collapse and supersession? It is in this manner that the sentiment of Oxford for beauty and sweetness conquers, and in this manner long may it continue to conquer!

In this manner it works to the same end as culture, and there is plenty of work for it yet to do. I have said that the new and more democratic force which is now superseding our old middle-class liberalism cannot yet be rightly judged. It has its main tendencies still to form. We hear promises of its giving us administrative reform, law reform, reform of education, and I know not what; but those promises come rather from its advocates, wishing to make a good plea for it and to justify it for superseding middle-class liberalism, than from clear tendencies which it has itself yet developed. But meanwhile it has

---

[1] Robert Lowe (1811–92), Liberal MP for Calne and, from 1868, Chancellor of the Exchequer; Lowe had been a particular bugbear of Arnold's ever since he had introduced the penny-pinching 'payment by results' method of apportioning state aid to the schools which Arnold inspected. In one of his earlier articles Arnold had quoted Lowe's speech, in May 1865, against extending the franchise, which he alludes to here.

plenty of well-intentioned friends against whom culture may with advantage continue to uphold steadily its ideal of human perfection; that this is *an inward spiritual activity, having for its characters increased sweetness, increased light, increased life, increased sympathy.* Mr. Bright, who has a foot in both worlds, the world of middle-class liberalism and the world of democracy, but who brings most of his ideas from the world of middle-class liberalism in which he was bred, always inclines to inculcate that faith in machinery to which, as we have seen, Englishmen are so prone, and which has been the bane of middle-class liberalism. He complains with a sorrowful indignation of people who "appear to have no proper estimate of the value of the franchise;" he leads his disciples to believe,—what the Englishman is always too ready to believe,—that the having a vote, like the having a large family, or a large business, or large muscles, has in itself some edifying and perfecting effect upon human nature. Or else he cries out to the democracy,—"the men," as he calls them, "upon whose shoulders the greatness of England rests,"—he cries out to them: "See what you have done! I look over this country and see the cities you have built, the railroads you have made, the manufactures you have produced, the cargoes which freight the ships of the greatest mercantile navy the world has ever seen! I see that you have converted by your labours what was once a wilderness, these islands, into a fruitful garden; I know that you have created this wealth, and are a nation whose name is a word of power throughout all the world." Why, this is just the very style of laudation with which Mr. Roebuck or Mr. Lowe debauches the minds of the middle classes, and makes such Philistines of them. It is the same fashion of teaching a man to value himself not on what he *is*, not on his progress in sweetness and light, but on the number of the railroads he has constructed, or the bigness of the tabernacle he has built. Only the middle classes are told they have done it all with their energy, self-reliance, and capital, and the democracy are told they have done it all with their hands and sinews. But teaching the democracy to put its trust in achievements of this kind is merely training them to be Philistines to take the place of the Philistines whom they are superseding; and they too, like the middle class, will be encouraged to sit down at the banquet of the future without having on a wedding garment, and nothing excellent can then come from them. Those who know their besetting faults, those who have watched them and listened to them, or those who will read the instructive account recently given of them by one of themselves, the *Journeyman Engineer*,[m] will agree that the idea which culture sets before us of perfection,—an increased spiritual activity, having for its characters increased sweetness, increased light, increased life, increased sympathy,—is an idea which the new democracy needs far more than the idea of the blessedness of the franchise, or the wonderfulness of its own industrial performances.

Other well-meaning friends of this new power are for leading it, not in the old ruts of middle-class Philistinism, but in ways which are naturally alluring to the feet of democracy, though in this country they are novel and untried ways. I may call them the ways of Jacobinism. Violent indignation with the past, abstract systems of renovation applied wholesale, a new doctrine drawn up in black and white for elaborating down to the very smallest details a rational society for the future,—these are the ways of Jacobinism. Mr. Frederic Harrison and other disciples of Comte,—one of them, Mr. Congreve, is an old friend of mine, and I am glad to have an opportunity of publicly expressing my respect for his talents and character,—are among the friends of democracy who are for leading it in paths of this kind.[n] Mr. Frederic Harrison is very hostile to culture, and from a natural enough motive; for culture is the eternal opponent of the two things which are the signal marks of Jacobinism,—its fierceness, and its addiction to an abstract system. Culture is always assigning to system-makers and systems a smaller share in the bent of human destiny than their friends like. A current in people's minds sets towards new ideas; people are dissatisfied with their old narrow stock of Philistine ideas, Anglo-Saxon ideas, or any other; and some man, some Bentham or Comte, who has the real merit of having early and strongly felt and helped the new current, but who brings plenty of narrowness and mistakes of his own into his feeling and help of it, is credited with being the author of the whole current, the fit person to be entrusted with its regulation and to guide the human race.

The excellent German historian of the mythology of Rome, Preller, relating the introduction at Rome under the Tarquins of the worship of Apollo, the god of light, healing, and reconciliation, will have us

---

[m] [Thomas Wright], *Some Habits and Customs of the Working Classes*, by 'the Journeyman Engineer' (1867).

[n] For Harrison, see above p. 56; Richard Congreve (1818–99), Tutor at Wadham College, Oxford and disciple of Comte.

observe that it was not so much the Tarquins who brought to Rome the new worship of Apollo, as a current in the mind of the Roman people which set powerfully at that time towards a new worship of this kind, and away from the old run of Latin and Sabine religious ideas. In a similar way, culture directs our attention to the natural current there is in human affairs, and to its continual working, and will not let us rivet our faith upon any one man and his doings. It makes us see not only his good side, but also how much in him was of necessity limited and transient; nay, it even feels a pleasure, a sense of an increased freedom and of an ampler future, in so doing.

I remember, when I was under the influence of a mind to which I feel the greatest obligations, the mind of a man who was the very incarnation of sanity and clear sense, a man the most considerable, it seems to me, whom America has yet produced,—Benjamin Franklin,—I remember the relief with which, after long feeling the sway of Franklin's imperturbable common-sense, I came upon a project of his for a new version of the Book of Job, to replace the old version, the style of which, says Franklin, has become obsolete, and thence less agreeable. "I give," he continues, "a few verses, which may serve as a sample of the kind of version I would recommend." We all recollect the famous verse in our translation: "Then Satan answered the Lord and said: 'Doth Job fear God for nought?' " Franklin makes this: "Does your Majesty imagine that Job's good conduct is the effect of mere personal attachment and affection?" I well remember how, when first I read that, I drew a deep breath of relief, and said to myself: "After all, there is a stretch of humanity beyond Franklin's victorious good sense!" So, after hearing Bentham cried loudly up as the renovator of modern society, and Bentham's mind and ideas proposed as the rulers of our future, I open the *Deontology*. There I read: "While Xenophon was writing his history and Euclid teaching geometry, Socrates and Plato were talking nonsense under pretence of teaching wisdom and morality. This morality of theirs consisted in words; this wisdom of theirs was the denial of matters known to every man's experience." From the moment of reading that, I am delivered from the bondage of Bentham! the fanaticism of his adherents can touch me no longer. I feel the inadequacy of his mind and ideas for supplying the rule of human society, for perfection.

Culture tends always thus to deal with the men of a system, of disciples, of a school; with men like Comte, or the late Mr. Buckle,⁰ or Mr. Mill. However much it may find to admire in these personages, or in some of them, it nevertheless remembers the text: "Be not ye called Rabbi!" and it soon passes on from any Rabbi. But Jacobinism loves a Rabbi; it does not want to pass on from its Rabbi in pursuit of a future and still unreached perfection; it wants its Rabbi and his ideas to stand for perfection, that they may with the more authority recast the world; and for Jacobinism, therefore, culture,—eternally passing onwards and seeking,—is an impertinence and an offence. But culture, just because it resists this tendency of Jacobinism to impose on us a man with limitations and errors of his own along with the true ideas of which he is the organ, really does the world and Jacobinism itself a service.

So, too, Jacobinism, in its fierce hatred of the past and of those whom it makes liable for the sins of the past, cannot away with the inexhaustible indulgence proper to culture, the consideration of circumstances, the severe judgment of actions joined to the merciful judgment of persons. "The man of culture is in politics," cries Mr. Frederic Harrison, "one of the poorest mortals alive!" Mr. Frederic Harrison wants to be doing business, and he complains that the man of culture stops him with a "turn for small fault-finding, love of selfish ease, and indecision in action." Of what use is culture, he asks, except for "a critic of new books or a professor of *belles-lettres?*" Why, it is of use because, in presence of the fierce exasperation which breathes, or rather, I may say, hisses through the whole production in which Mr. Frederic Harrison asks that question, it reminds us that the perfection of human nature is sweetness and light. It is of use because, like religion,—that other effort after perfection,—it testifies that, where bitter envying and strife are, there is confusion and every evil work.

The pursuit of perfection, then, is the pursuit of sweetness and light. He who works for sweetness and light, works to make reason and the will of God prevail. He who works for machinery, he who works for hatred, works only for confusion. Culture looks beyond machinery, culture hates hatred; culture has one great passion, the passion for sweetness and light. It has one even yet greater!—the passion for making them *prevail*. It is not satisfied till we *all* come to a

⁰ Henry Thomas Buckle (1821–62), author of *The History of Civilization in England* (1857–61), an attempt to apply 'scientific principles' to the study of history. The 'systems' associated with Comte and Mill were Positivism and Utilitarianism respectively.

perfect man; it knows that the sweetness and light of the few must be imperfect until the raw and unkindled masses of humanity are touched with sweetness and light. If I have not shrunk from saying that we must work for sweetness and light, so neither have I shrunk from saying that we must have a broad basis, must have sweetness and light for as many as possible. Again and again I have insisted how those are the happy moments of humanity, how those are the marking epochs of a people's life, how those are the flowering times for literature and art and all the creative power of genius, when there is a *national* glow of life and thought, when the whole of society is in the fullest measure permeated by thought, sensible to beauty, intelligent and alive. Only it must be *real* thought and *real* beauty; *real* sweetness and *real* light. Plenty of people will try to give the masses, as they call them, an intellectual food prepared and adapted in the way they think proper for the actual condition of the masses. The ordinary popular literature is an example of this way of working on the masses. Plenty of people will try to indoctrinate the masses with the set of ideas and judgments constituting the creed of their own profession or party. Our religious and political organisations give an example of this way of working on the masses. I condemn neither way; but culture works differently. It does not try to teach down to the level of inferior classes; it does not try to win them for this or that sect of its own, with ready-made judgments and watchwords. It seeks to do away with classes; to make the best that has been thought and known in the world current everywhere; to make all men live in an atmosphere of sweetness and light, where they may use ideas, as it uses them itself, freely,—nourished, and not bound by them.

This is the *social idea*; and the men of culture are the true apostles of equality. The great men of culture are those who have had a passion for diffusing, for making prevail, for carrying from one end of society to the other, the best knowledge, the best ideas of their time; who have laboured to divest knowledge of all that was harsh, uncouth, difficult, abstract, professional, exclusive; to humanise it, to make it efficient outside the clique of the cultivated and learned, yet still remaining the *best* knowledge and thought of the time, and a true source, therefore, of sweetness and light. Such a man was Abelard in the Middle Ages, in spite of all his imperfections; and thence the boundless emotion and enthusiasm which Abelard excited. Such were Lessing and Herder in Germany, at the end of the last century; and their services to Germany were in this way inestimably precious. Generations will pass, and literary monuments will accumulate, and works far more perfect than the works of Lessing and Herder will be produced in Germany; and yet the names of these two men will fill a German with a reverence and enthusiasm such as the names of the most gifted masters will hardly awaken. And why? Because they *humanised* knowledge; because they broadened the basis of life and intelligence; because they worked powerfully to diffuse sweetness and light, to make reason and the will of God prevail. With Saint Augustine they said: "Let us not leave thee alone to make in the secret of thy knowledge, as thou didst before the creation of the firmament, the division of light from darkness; let the children of thy spirit, placed in their firmament, make their light shine upon the earth, mark the division of night and day, and announce the revolution of the times; for the old order is passed, and the new arises; the night is spent, the day is come forth; and thou shalt crown the year with thy blessing, when thou shalt send forth labourers into thy harvest sown by other hands than theirs; when thou shalt send forth new labourers to new seed-times, whereof the harvest shall be not yet."

# CHAPTER II

# Doing as One Likes

I have been trying to show that culture is, or ought to be, the study and pursuit of perfection; and that of perfection as pursued by culture, beauty and intelligence, or, in other words, sweetness and light, are the main characters. But hitherto I have been insisting chiefly on beauty, or sweetness, as a character of perfection. To complete rightly my design, it evidently remains to speak also of intelligence, or light, as a character of perfection.

First, however, I ought perhaps to notice that, both here and on the other side of the Atlantic, all sorts of objections are raised against the "religion of culture," as the objectors mockingly call it, which I am supposed to be promulgating. It is said to be a religion proposing parmaceti, or some scented salve or other, as a cure for human miseries; a religion breathing a spirit of cultivated inaction, making its believer refuse to lend a hand at uprooting the definite evils on all sides of us, and filling him with antipathy against the reforms and reformers which try to extirpate them. In general, it is summed up as being not practical, or, — as some critics familiarly put it, — all moonshine. That Alcibiades, the editor of the *Morning Star*, taunts me, as its promulgator, with living out of the world and knowing nothing of life and men. That great austere toiler, the editor of the *Daily Telegraph*, upbraids me, — but kindly, and more in sorrow than in anger, — for trifling with aesthetics and poetical fancies, while he himself, in that arsenal of his in Fleet Street, is bearing the burden and heat of the day. An intelligent American newspaper, the *Nation*, says that it is very easy to sit in one's study and find fault with the course of modern society, but the thing is to propose practical improvements for it. While, finally, Mr. Frederic Harrison, in a very good-tempered and witty satire, which makes me quite understand his having apparently achieved such a conquest of my young Prussian friend, Arminius, at last gets moved to an almost stern moral impatience, to behold, as he says, "Death, sin, cruelty stalk among us, filling their maws with innocence and youth," and me, in the midst of the general tribulation, handing out my pouncet-box.[a]

It is impossible that all these remonstrances and reproofs should not affect me, and I shall try my very best, in completing my design and in speaking of light as one of the characters of perfection, and of culture as giving us light, to profit by the objections I have heard and read, and to drive at practice as much as I can, by showing the communications and passages into practical life from the doctrine which I am inculcating.

It is said that a man with my theories of sweetness and light is full of antipathy against the rougher or coarser movements going on around him, that he will not lend a hand to the humble operation of uprooting evil by their means, and that therefore the believers in action grow impatient with him. But what if rough and coarse action, ill-calculated action, action with insufficient light, is, and has for a long time been, our bane? What if our urgent want now is, not to act at any price, but rather to lay in a stock of light for our difficulties? In that case, to refuse to lend a hand to the rougher and coarser movements going on round us, to make the primary need, both for oneself and others, to consist in enlightening ourselves and qualifying ourselves to act less at random, is surely the best and in real truth the most practical line our endeavours can take. So that if I can show what my opponents call rough or coarse action, but what I would rather call random and ill-regulated action,—action with insufficient light, action pursued because we like to be doing something and doing it as we please, and do not like the trouble of thinking and the severe constraint of any kind of rule,—if I can show this to be, at the present moment, a practical mischief and dangerous to us, then I have found a practical

---

[a] There were several responses to the publication of Arnold's first chapter as a periodical article in 1867; in this paragraph he takes some phrases from one of them, Frederic Harrison's 'Culture: a Dialogue', *Fortnightly Review* (1867). 'Arminius' was a fictitious character from Arnold's own *Friendship's Garland*, which started to appear in the *Pall Mall Gazette* in 1866. Several of Arnold's critics had pursued the parallel between him and the delicate lord who approached Hotspur immediately after the battle in *Henry IV*, I, holding 'a pouncet-box' (i.e. small perfume box with perforated lid).

use for light in correcting this state of things, and have only to exemplify how, in cases which fall under everybody's observation, it may deal with it.

When I began to speak of culture, I insisted on our bondage to machinery, on our proneness to value machinery as an end in itself, without looking beyond it to the end for which alone, in truth, it is valuable. Freedom, I said, was one of those things which we thus worshipped in itself, without enough regarding the ends for which freedom is to be desired. In our common notions and talk about freedom, we eminently show our idolatry of machinery. Our prevalent notion is,—and I quoted a number of instances to prove it,—that it is a most happy and important thing for a man merely to be able to do as he likes. On what he is to do when he is thus free to do as he likes, we do not lay so much stress. Our familiar praise of the British Constitution under which we live, is that it is a system of checks,—a system which stops and paralyses any power in interfering with the free action of individuals. To this effect Mr. Bright, who loves to walk in the old ways of the Constitution, said forcibly in one of his great speeches, what many other people are every day saying less forcibly, that the central idea of English life and politics is *the assertion of personal liberty*. Evidently this is so; but evidently, also, as feudalism, which with its ideas and habits of subordination was for many centuries silently behind the British Constitution, dies out, and we are left with nothing but our system of checks, and our notion of its being the great right and happiness of an Englishman to do as far as possible what he likes, we are in danger of drifting towards anarchy. We have not the notion, so familiar on the Continent and to antiquity, of *the State*,—the nation in its collective and corporate character, entrusted with stringent powers for the general advantage, and controlling individual wills in the name of an interest wider than that of individuals. We say, what is very true, that this notion is often made instrumental to tyranny; we say that a State is in reality made up of the individuals who compose it, and that every individual is the best judge of his own interests. Our leading class is an aristocracy, and no aristocracy likes the notion of a State-authority greater than itself, with a stringent administrative machinery superseding the decorative inutilities of lord-lieutenancy, deputy-lieutenancy, and the *posse comitatus*, which are all in its own hands. Our middle class, the great representative of trade and Dissent, with its maxims of every man for

83

himself in business, every man for himself in religion, dreads a powerful administration which might somehow interfere with it; and besides, it has its own decorative inutilities of vestrymanship and guardianship, which are to this class what lord-lieutenancy and the county magistracy are to the aristocratic class, and a stringent administration might either take these functions out of its hands, or prevent its exercising them in its own comfortable, independent manner, as at present.

Then as to our working class. This class, pressed constantly by the hard daily compulsion of material wants, is naturally the very centre and stronghold of our national idea, that it is man's ideal right and felicity to do as he likes. I think I have somewhere related how M. Michelet said to me of the people of France, that it was "a nation of barbarians civilised by the conscription."[b] He meant that through their military service the idea of public duty and of discipline was brought to the mind of these masses, in other respects so raw and uncultivated. Our masses are quite as raw and uncultivated as the French; and so far from their having the idea of public duty and of discipline, superior to the individual's self-will, brought to their mind by a universal obligation of military service, such as that of the conscription,—so far from their having this, the very idea of a conscription is so at variance with our English notion of the prime right and blessedness of doing as one likes, that I remember the manager of the Clay Cross works in Derbyshire told me during the Crimean war, when our want of soldiers was much felt and some people were talking of a conscription, that sooner than submit to a conscription the population of that district would flee to the mines, and lead a sort of Robin Hood life under ground.

For a long time, as I have said, the strong feudal habits of subordination and deference continued to tell upon the working class. The modern spirit has now almost entirely dissolved those habits, and the anarchical tendency of our worship of freedom in and for itself, of our superstitious faith, as I say, in machinery, is becoming very manifest. More and more, because of this our blind faith in machinery, because of our want of light to enable us to look beyond machinery to the end for which machinery is valuable, this and that

[b] Arnold had first quoted this remark in his *The Popular Education of France* (1861). He had met Jules Michelet (1798–1874), the most famous French historian of his day, during his 1859 visit to France.

man, and this and that body of men, all over the country, are beginning to assert and put in practice an Englishman's right to do what he
likes; his right to march where he likes, meet where he likes, enter
where he likes, hoot as he likes, threaten as he likes, smash as he
likes.[c] All this, I say, tends to anarchy; and though a number of
excellent people, and particularly my friends of the Liberal or progressive party, as they call themselves, are kind enough to reassure us
by saying that these are trifles, that a few transient outbreaks of
rowdyism signify nothing, that our system of liberty is one which itself
cures all the evils which it works, that the educated and intelligent
classes stand in overwhelming strength and majestic repose, ready,
like our military force in riots, to act at a moment's notice,—yet one
finds that one's Liberal friends generally say this because they have
such faith in themselves and their nostrums, when they shall return,
as the public welfare requires, to place and power. But this faith of
theirs one cannot exactly share, when one has so long had them and
their nostrums at work, and sees that they have not prevented our
coming to our present embarrassed condition. And one finds, also,
that the outbreaks of rowdyism tend to become less and less of trifles,
to become more frequent rather than less frequent; and that meanwhile our educated and intelligent classes remain in their majestic
repose, and somehow or other, whatever happens, their overwhelming strength, like our military force in riots, never does act.

How, indeed, *should* their overwhelming strength act, when the
man who gives an inflammatory lecture, or breaks down the park
railings, or invades a Secretary of State's office,[d] is only following an
Englishman's impulse to do as he likes; and our own conscience tells
us that we ourselves have always regarded this impulse as something
primary and sacred? Mr. Murphy lectures at Birmingham, and
showers on the Catholic population of that town "words," says the
Home Secretary, "only fit to be addressed to thieves or murderers."[e]

[c] This and the following sentences chiefly refer to the so-called 'Hyde Park riots' of July
1866 when a large crowd attending a meeting of the Reform League got out of hand and
broke down the iron railings surrounding Hyde Park.

[d] In September 1867 a policeman was killed when a group of Fenians (see below)
attempted to rescue two of their number from arrest; the alleged murderers were caught
and sentenced to death, but in November a mob of English sympathizers, fearing that
innocent men had been convicted, broke into the Home Secretary's office and demanded they be pardoned.

[e] William Murphy, of the 'London Protestant Electoral Union', gave a series of inflammatory anti-Catholic lectures in Birmingham in June 1867.

What then? Mr. Murphy has his own reasons of several kinds. He suspects the Roman Catholic Church of designs upon Mrs. Murphy; and he says if mayors and magistrates do not care for their wives and daughters, he does. But, above all, he is doing as he likes; or, in worthier language, asserting his personal liberty. "I will carry out my lectures if they walk over my body as a dead corpse; and I say to the Mayor of Birmingham that he is my servant while I am in Birmingham, and as my servant he must do his duty and protect me." Touching and beautiful words, which find a sympathetic chord in every British bosom! The moment it is plainly put before us that a man is asserting his personal liberty, we are half disarmed; because we are believers in freedom, and not in some dream of a right reason to which the assertion of our freedom is to be subordinated. Accordingly, the Secretary of State had to say that although the lecturer's language was "only fit to be addressed to thieves or murderers," yet, "I do not think he is to be deprived, I do not think that anything I have said could justify the inference that he is to be deprived, of the right of protection in a place built by him for the purpose of these lectures; because the language was not language which afforded grounds for a criminal prosecution." No, nor to be silenced by Mayor, or Home Secretary, or any administrative authority on earth, simply on their notion of what is discreet and reasonable! This is in perfect consonance with our public opinion, and with our national love for the assertion of personal liberty.

In quite another department of affairs, an experienced and distinguished Chancery Judge relates an incident which is just to the same effect as this of Mr. Murphy. A testator bequeathed £300 a year, to be for ever applied as a pension to some person who had been unsuccessful in literature, and whose duty should be to support and diffuse, by his writings, the testator's own views, as enforced in the testator's publications. The views were not worth a straw, and the bequest was appealed against in the Court of Chancery on the ground of its absurdity; but, being only absurd, it was upheld, and the so-called charity was established. Having, I say, at the bottom of our English hearts a very strong belief in freedom, and a very weak belief in right reason, we are soon silenced when a man pleads the prime right to do as he likes, because this is the prime right for ourselves too; and even if we attempt now and then to mumble something about reason, yet we have ourselves thought so little about this and so much about liberty, that we are in conscience forced, when our brother Philistine with whom we are meddling turns boldly round upon us and asks: *Have you any light?*—to shake our heads ruefully, and to let him go his own way after all.

There are many things to be said on behalf of this exclusive attention of ours to liberty, and of the relaxed habits of government which it has engendered. It is very easy to mistake or to exaggerate the sort of anarchy from which we are in danger through them. We are not in danger from Fenianism, fierce and turbulent as it may show itself;[f] for against this our conscience is free enough to let us act resolutely and put forth our overwhelming strength the moment there is any real need for it. In the first place, it never was any part of our creed that the great right and blessedness of an Irishman, or, indeed, of anybody on earth except an Englishman, is to do as he likes; and we can have no scruple at all about abridging, if necessary, a non-Englishman's assertion of personal liberty. The British Constitution, its checks, and its prime virtues, are for Englishmen. We may extend them to others out of love and kindness; but we find no real divine law written on our hearts constraining us so to extend them. And then the difference between an Irish Fenian and an English rough is so immense, and the case, in dealing with the Fenian, so much more clear! He is so evidently desperate and dangerous, a man of a conquered race, a Papist, with centuries of ill-usage to inflame him against us, with an alien religion established in his country by us at his expense, with no admiration of our institutions, no love of our virtues, no talents for our business, no turn for our comfort! Show him our symbolical Truss Manufactory on the finest site in Europe,[g] and tell him that British industrialism and individualism can bring a man to that, and he remains cold! Evidently, if we deal tenderly with a sentimentalist like this, it is out of pure philanthropy.

But with the Hyde Park rioter how different! He is our own flesh and blood; he is a Protestant; he is framed by nature to do as we do, hate what we hate, love what we love; he is capable of feeling the symbolical force of the Truss Manufactory; the question of questions,

---

[f] The Fenians were an Irish–American revolutionary society who committed several spectacular terrorist outrages in England and Ireland in the 1860s.

[g] Coles's Truss Manufactory was prominently advertised near Trafalgar Square, which Sir Robert Peel had called 'the finest site in Europe'; Arnold had already made fun of this juxtaposition in *Friendship's Garland*.

for him, is a wages question. That beautiful sentence Sir Daniel
Gooch quoted to the Swindon workmen, and which I treasure as Mrs.
Gooch's Golden Rule, or the Divine Injunction "Be ye Perfect" done
into British,—the sentence Sir Daniel Gooch's mother repeated to
him every morning when he was a boy going to work:—"*Ever remember, my dear Dan, that you should look forward to being some day manager
of that concern!*"[h]—this fruitful maxim is perfectly fitted to shine forth
in the heart of the Hyde Park rough also, and to be his guiding-star
through life. He has no visionary schemes of revolution and transformation, though of course he would like his class to rule, as the
aristocratic class like their class to rule, and the middle class theirs.
But meanwhile our social machine is a little out of order; there are a
good many people in our paradisiacal centres of industrialism and
individualism taking the bread out of one another's mouths. The
rough has not yet quite found his groove and settled down to his work,
and so he is just asserting his personal liberty a little, going where he
likes, assembling where he likes, bawling as he likes, hustling as he
likes. Just as the rest of us,—as the country squires in the aristocratic
class, as the political dissenters in the middle class,—he has no idea of
a *State*, of the nation in its collective and corporate character controlling, as government, the free swing of this or that one of its members
in the name of the higher reason of all of them, his own as well as that
of others. He sees the rich, the aristocratic class, in occupation of the
executive government, and so if he is stopped from making Hyde Park
a bear-garden or the streets impassable, he says he is being butchered
by the aristocracy.

His apparition is somewhat embarrassing, because too many cooks
spoil the broth; because, while the aristocratic and middle classes
have long been doing as they like with great vigour, he has been too
undeveloped and submissive hitherto to join in the game; and now,
when he does come, he comes in immense numbers, and is rather raw
and rough. But he does not break many laws, or not many at one time;
and, as our laws were made for very different circumstances from our
present (but always with an eye to Englishmen doing as they like), and
as the clear letter of the law must be against our Englishman who does
as he likes and not only the spirit of the law and public policy, and as
Government must neither have any discretionary power nor act

---

[h] Sir Daniel Gooch (1816–89), was Chairman of the Great Western Railway, which had
its headquarters at Swindon.

resolutely on its own interpretation of the law if any one disputes it, it is evident our laws give our playful giant, in doing as he likes, considerable advantage. Besides, even if he can be clearly proved to commit an illegality in doing as he likes, there is always the resource of not putting the law in force, or of abolishing it. So he has his way, and if he has his way he is soon satisfied for the time. However, he falls into the habit of taking it oftener and oftener, and at last begins to create by his operations a confusion of which mischievous people can take advantage, and which, at any rate, by troubling the common course of business throughout the country, tends to cause distress, and so to increase the sort of anarchy and social disintegration which had previously commenced. And thus that profound sense of settled order and security, without which a society like ours cannot live and grow at all, sometimes seems to be beginning to threaten us with taking its departure.

Now, if culture, which simply means trying to perfect oneself, and one's mind as part of oneself, brings us light, and if light shows us that there is nothing so very blessed in merely doing as one likes, that the worship of the mere freedom to do as one likes is worship of machinery, that the really blessed thing is to like what right reason ordains, and to follow her authority, then we have got a practical benefit out of culture. We have got a much wanted principle, a principle of authority, to counteract the tendency to anarchy which seems to be threatening us.

But how to organise this authority, or to what hands to entrust the wielding of it? How to get your *State*, summing up the right reason of the community, and giving effect to it, as circumstances may require, with vigour? And here I think I see my enemies waiting for me with a hungry joy in their eyes. But I shall elude them.

The *State*, the power most representing the right reason of the nation, and most worthy, therefore, of ruling,—of exercising, when circumstances require it, authority over us all,—is for Mr. Carlyle the aristocracy. For Mr. Lowe, it is the middle class with its incomparable Parliament. For the Reform League, it is the working class, the class with "the brightest powers of sympathy and readiest powers of action." Now culture, with its disinterested pursuit of perfection, culture, simply trying to see things as they are in order to seize on the best and to make it prevail, is surely well fitted to help us to judge rightly, by all the aids of observing, reading, and thinking, the qualifications and titles to our confidence of these three candidates for authority, and can thus render us a practical service of no mean value.

So when Mr. Carlyle, a man of genius to whom we have all at one time or other been indebted for refreshment and stimulus, says we should give rule to the aristocracy, mainly because of its dignity and politeness,[i] surely culture is useful in reminding us, that in our idea of perfection the characters of beauty and intelligence are both of them present, and sweetness and light, the two noblest of things, are united. Allowing, therefore, with Mr. Carlyle, the aristocratic class to possess sweetness, culture insists on the necessity of light also, and shows us that aristocracies, being by the very nature of things inaccessible to ideas, unapt to see how the world is going, must be somewhat wanting in light, and must therefore be, at a moment when light is our great requisite, inadequate to our needs. Aristocracies, those children of the established fact, are for epochs of concentration. In epochs of expansion, epochs such as that in which we now live, epochs when always the warning voice is again heard: *Now is the judgment of this world,*—in such epochs aristocracies with their natural clinging to the established fact, their want of sense for the flux of things, for the inevitable transitoriness of all human institutions, are bewildered and helpless. Their serenity, their high spirit, their power of haughty resistance,—the great qualities of an aristocracy, and the secret of its distinguished manners and dignity,—these very qualities, in an epoch of expansion, turn against their possessors. Again and again I have said how the refinement of an aristocracy may be precious and educative to a raw nation as a kind of shadow of true refinement; how its serenity and dignified freedom from petty cares may serve as a useful foil to set off the vulgarity and hideousness of that type of life which a hard middle class tends to establish, and to help people to see this vulgarity and hideousness in their true colours.[j] But the true grace and serenity is that of which Greece and Greek art suggest the admirable ideals of perfection,—a serenity which comes from having made order among ideas and harmonised them; whereas the serenity of aristocracies, at least the peculiar serenity of aristocracies of Teutonic origin, appears to come from their never having had any

[i] Carlyle had most recently expressed his high opinion of the aristocracy in 'Shooting Niagara: and After?', *Macmillan's Magazine* (1867).
[j] See above pp. 3–4, 10–11.

ideas to trouble them. And so, in a time of expansion like the present, a time for ideas, one gets perhaps, in regarding an aristocracy, even more than the idea of serenity, the idea of futility and sterility.

One has often wondered whether upon the whole earth there is anything so unintelligent, so unapt to perceive how the world is really going, as an ordinary young Englishman of our upper class. Ideas he has not, and neither has he that seriousness of our middle class which is, as I have often said, the great strength of this class, and may become its salvation. Why, a man may hear a young Dives of the aristocratic class, when the whim takes him to sing the praises of wealth and material comfort, sing them with a cynicism from which the conscience of the veriest Philistine of our industrial middle class would recoil in affright. And when, with the natural sympathy of aristocracies for firm dealing with the multitude, and his uneasiness at our feeble dealing with it at home, an unvarnished young Englishman of our aristocratic class applauds the absolute rulers on the Continent, he in general manages completely to miss the grounds of reason and intelligence which alone can give any colour of justification, any possibility of existence, to those rulers, and applauds them on grounds which it would make their own hair stand on end to listen to.

And all this time we are in an epoch of expansion; and the essence of an epoch of expansion is a movement of ideas, and the one salvation of an epoch of expansion is a harmony of ideas. The very principle of the authority which we are seeking as a defence against anarchy is right reason, ideas, light. The more, therefore, an aristocracy calls to its aid its innate forces,—its impenetrability, its high spirit, its power of haughty resistance,—to deal with an epoch of expansion, the graver is the danger, the greater the certainty of explosion, the surer the aristocracy's defeat; for it is trying to do violence to nature instead of working along with it. The best powers shown by the best men of an aristocracy at such an epoch are, it will be observed, non-aristocratical powers, powers of industry, powers of intelligence; and these powers thus exhibited, tend really not to strengthen the aristocracy, but to take their owners out of it, to expose them to the dissolving agencies of thought and change, to make them men of the modern spirit and of the future. If, as sometimes happens, they add to their non-aristocratical qualities of labour and thought, a strong dose of aristocratical qualities also,—of pride, defiance, turn for resistance,—this truly aristocratical side of them, so far from adding any strength to them, really neutralises their force and makes them impracticable and ineffective.

Knowing myself to be indeed sadly to seek, as one of my many critics says, in "a philosophy with coherent, interdependent, subordinate, and derivative principles," I continually have recourse to a plain man's expedient of trying to make what few simple notions I have, clearer and more intelligible to myself by means of example and illustration. And having been brought up at Oxford in the bad old times, when we were stuffed with Greek and Aristotle, and thought nothing of preparing ourselves by the study of modern languages, — as after Mr. Lowe's great speech at Edinburgh we shall do,[k] — to fight the battle of life with the waiters in foreign hotels, my head is still full of a lumber of phrases we learnt at Oxford from Aristotle, about virtue being in a mean, and about excess and defect, and so on. Once when I had had the advantage of listening to the Reform debates in the House of Commons, having heard a number of interesting speakers, and among them a well-known lord and a well-known baronet, I remember it struck me, applying Aristotle's machinery of the mean to my ideas about our aristocracy, that the lord was exactly the perfection, or happy mean, or virtue, of aristocracy, and the baronet the excess. And I fancied that by observing these two we might see both the inadequacy of aristocracy to supply the principle of authority needful for our present wants, and the danger of its trying to supply it when it was not really competent for the business. On the one hand, in the brilliant lord, showing plenty of high spirit, but remarkable, far above and beyond his gift of high spirit, for the fine tempering of his high spirit, for ease, serenity, politeness, — the great virtues, as Mr. Carlyle says, of aristocracy, — in this beautiful and virtuous mean, there seemed evidently some insufficiency of light; while, on the other hand, the worthy baronet, in whom the high spirit of aristocracy, its impenetrability, defiant courage, and pride of resistance, were developed even in excess, was manifestly capable, if he had his way given him, of causing us great danger, and, indeed, of throwing the whole commonwealth into confusion. Then I reverted to that old fundamental notion of mine about the grand merit of our race being really our

---

[k] In a speech at Edinburgh in November 1867, Robert Lowe had argued against the traditional educational supremacy of the classics and in favour of (among other subjects) modern languages. Arnold seizes on Lowe's light-hearted remark that this would enable an Englishman to order a meal in Paris without becoming a laughing-stock.

honesty. And the very helplessness of our aristocratic or governing class in dealing with our perturbed social condition, their jealousy of entrusting too much power to the State as it now actually exists—that is to themselves—gave me a sort of pride and satisfaction; because I saw they were, as a whole, too honest to try and manage a business for which they did not feel themselves capable.

Surely, now, it is no inconsiderable boon which culture confers upon us, if in embarrassed times like the present it enables us to look at the ins and the outs of things in this way, without hatred and without partiality, and with a disposition to see the good in everybody all round. And I try to follow just the same course with our middle class as with our aristocracy. Mr. Lowe talks to us of this strong middle part of the nation, of the unrivalled deeds of our Liberal middle-class Parliament, of the noble, the heroic work it has performed in the last thirty years; and I begin to ask myself if we shall not, then, find in our middle class the principle of authority we want, and if we had not better take administration as well as legislation away from the weak extreme which now administers for us, and commit both to the strong middle part. I observe, too, that the heroes of middle-class liberalism, such as we have hitherto known it, speak with a kind of prophetic anticipation of the great destiny which awaits them, and as if the future was clearly theirs. The advanced party, the progressive party, the party in alliance with the future, are the names they like to give themselves. "The principles which will obtain recognition in the future," says Mr. Miall, a personage of deserved eminence among the political Dissenters, as they are called, who have been the backbone of middle-class liberalism,[1]—"the principles which will obtain recognition in the future are the principles for which I have long and zealously laboured. I qualified myself for joining in the work of harvest by doing to the best of my ability the duties of seedtime." These duties, if one is to gather them from the works of the great Liberal party in the last thirty years, are, as I have elsewhere summed them up, the advocacy of free trade, of Parliamentary reform, of abolition of church-rates, of voluntaryism in religion and education, of non-interference of the State between employers and employed, and of marriage with one's deceased wife's sister.

Now I know, when I object that all this is machinery, the great

---

[1] Edward Miall (1809–81), leading Dissenter and editor of *The Nonconformist*, who campaigned against the educational and other privileges of the Established Church.

Liberal middle class has by this time grown cunning enough to answer that it always meant more by these things than meets the eye; that it has had that within which passes show, and that we are soon going to see, in a Free Church and all manner of good things, what it was. But I have learned from Bishop Wilson (if Mr. Frederic Harrison will forgive my again quoting that poor old hierophant of a decayed superstition): "If we would really know our heart let us impartially view our actions;" and I cannot help thinking that if our Liberals had had so much sweetness and light in their inner minds as they allege, more of it must have come out in their sayings and doings.

An American friend of the English Liberals says, indeed, that their Dissidence of Dissent has been a mere instrument of the political Dissenters for making reason and the will of God prevail (and no doubt he would say the same of marriage with one's deceased wife's sister); and that the abolition of a State Church is merely the Dissenter's means to this end, just as culture is mine. Another American defender of theirs says just the same of their industrialism and free trade; indeed, this gentleman, taking the bull by the horns, proposes that we should for the future call industrialism culture, and the industrialists the men of culture, and then of course there can be no longer any misapprehension about their true character; and besides the pleasure of being wealthy and comfortable, they will have authentic recognition as vessels of sweetness and light.

All this is undoubtedly specious; but I must remark that the culture of which I talked was an endeavour to come at reason and the will of God by means of reading, observing, and thinking; and that whoever calls anything else culture, may, indeed, call it so if he likes, but then he talks of something quite different from what I talked of. And, again, as culture's way of working for reason and the will of God is by directly trying to know more about them, while the Dissidence of Dissent is evidently in itself no effort of this kind, nor is its Free Church, in fact, a church with worthier conceptions of God and the ordering of the world than the State Church professes, but with mainly the same conceptions of these as the State Church has, only that every man is to comport himself as he likes in professing them,— this being so, I cannot at once accept the Nonconformity any more than the industrialism and the other great works of our Liberal middle class as proof positive that this class is in possession of light, and that here is the true seat of authority for which we are in search; but I must try a little further, and seek for other indications which may enable me to make up my mind.

Why should we not do with the middle class as we have done with the aristocratic class,—find in it some representative men who may stand for the virtuous mean of this class, for the perfection of its present qualities and mode of being, and also for the excess of them. Such men must clearly not be men of genius like Mr. Bright; for, as I have formerly said, so far as a man has genius he tends to take himself out of the category of class altogether, and to become simply a man. Some more ordinary man would be more to the purpose,—would sum up better in himself, without disturbing influences, the general liberal force of the middle class, the force by which it has done its great works of free trade, Parliamentary reform, voluntaryism, and so on, and the spirit in which it has done them. Now it happens that a typical middle-class man, the member for one of our chief industrial cities, has given us a famous sentence which bears directly on the resolution of our present question: whether there is light enough in our middle class to make it the proper seat of the authority we wish to establish. When there was a talk some little while ago about the state of middle-class education, our friend, as the representative of that class, spoke some memorable words:—"There had been a cry that middle-class education ought to receive more attention. He confessed himself very much surprised by the clamour that was raised. He did not think that class need excite the sympathy either of the legislature or the public."[m] Now this satisfaction of our middle-class member of Parliament with the mental state of the middle class was truly representative, and makes good his claim to stand as the beautiful and virtuous mean of that class. But it is obviously at variance with our definition of culture, or the pursuit of light and perfection, which made light and perfection consist, not in resting and being, but in growing and becoming, in a perpetual advance in beauty and wisdom. So the middle class is by its essence, as one may say, by its incomparable self-satisfaction decisively expressed through its beautiful and virtuous mean, self-excluded from wielding an authority of which light is to be the very soul.

Clear as this is, it will be made clearer still if we take some representative man as the excess of the middle class, and remember

[m] Sir Thomas Bazley (1797–1885), a rich manufacturer and MP for Manchester, in a speech in November 1864.

that the middle class, in general, is to be conceived as a body swaying between the qualities of its mean and of its excess, and on the whole, of course, as human nature is constituted, inclining rather towards the excess than the mean. Of its excess no better representative can possibly be imagined than a Dissenting minister from Walsall, who came before the public in connection with the proceedings at Birmingham of Mr. Murphy, already mentioned. Speaking in the midst of an irritated population of Catholics, this Walsall gentleman exclaimed: "I say, then, away with the Mass! It is from the bottomless pit; and in the bottomless pit shall all liars have their part, in the lake that burneth with fire and brimstone." And again: "When all the praties were black in Ireland, why didn't the priests say the hocus-pocus over them, and make them all good again?" He shared, too, Mr. Murphy's fears of some invasion of his domestic happiness: "What I wish to say to you as Protestant husbands is, *Take care of your wives!*" And finally, in the true vein of an Englishman doing as he likes, a vein of which I have at some length pointed out the present dangers, he recommended for imitation the example of some church-wardens at Dublin, among whom, said he, "there was a Luther and also a Melanchthon," who had made very short work with some ritualist or other, hauled him down from his pulpit, and kicked him out of church. Now it is manifest, as I said in the case of our aristocratical baronet, that if we let this excess of the sturdy English middle class, this conscientious Protestant Dissenter, so strong, so self-reliant, so fully persuaded in his own mind, have his way, he would be capable, with his want of light,—or, to use the language of the religious world, with his zeal without knowledge,—of stirring up strife which neither he nor any one else could easily compose.

And then comes in, as it did also with the aristocracy, the honesty of our race, and by the voice of another middle-class man, Alderman of the City of London and Colonel of the City of London Militia, proclaims that it has twinges of conscience, and that it will not attempt to cope with our social disorders, and to deal with a business which it feels to be too high for it.[n] Every one remembers how this virtuous Alderman-Colonel, or Colonel-Alderman, led his militia through the

[n] In June 1867 the City of London Militia, led by their Colonel, Alderman Samuel Wilson, paraded through the streets of London. The parade attracted numerous roughs and pickpockets who robbed and attacked members of the crowd, but Wilson declined to intervene, saying that it was a matter for the police not the army.

London streets; how the bystanders gathered to see him pass; how the London roughs, asserting an Englishman's best and most blissful right of doing what he likes, robbed and beat the bystanders; and how the blameless warrior-magistrate refused to let his troops interfere. "The crowd," he touchingly said afterwards, "was mostly composed of fine healthy strong men, bent on mischief; if he had allowed his soldiers to interfere they might have been overpowered, their rifles taken from them and used against them by the mob; a riot, in fact, might have ensued, and been attended with bloodshed, compared with which the assaults and loss of property that actually occurred would have been as nothing." Honest and affecting testimony of the English middle class to its own inadequacy for the authoritative part one's admiration would sometimes incline one to assign to it! "Who are we," they say by the voice of their Alderman-Colonel, "that we should not be overpowered if we attempt to cope with social anarchy, our rifles taken from us and used against us by the mob, and we, perhaps, robbed and beaten ourselves? Or what light have we, beyond a free-born Englishman's impulse to do as he likes, which could justify us in preventing, at the cost of bloodshed, other free-born Englishmen from doing as they like, and robbing and beating us as much as they please?"

This distrust of themselves as an adequate centre of authority does not mark the working class, as was shown by their readiness the other day in Hyde Park to take upon themselves all the functions of government. But this comes from the working class being, as I have often said, still an embryo, of which no one can yet quite foresee the final development; and from its not having the same experience and self-knowledge as the aristocratic and middle classes. Honesty it no doubt has, just like the other classes of Englishmen, but honesty in an inchoate and untrained state; and meanwhile its powers of action, which are, as Mr. Frederic Harrison says, exceedingly ready, easily run away with it. That it cannot at present have a sufficiency of light which comes by culture,—that is, by reading, observing, and thinking,—is clear from the very nature of its condition; and, indeed, we saw that Mr. Frederic Harrison, in seeking to make a free stage for its bright powers of sympathy and ready powers of action, had to begin by throwing overboard culture, and flouting it as only fit for a professor of *belles-lettres*. Still, to make it perfectly manifest that no more in the working class than in the aristocratic and middle classes can one find an adequate centre of authority,—that is, as culture teaches us to conceive our required authority, of light,—let us again follow, with this class, the method we have followed with the aristocratic and middle classes, and try to bring before our minds representative men, who may figure to us its virtue and its excess.

We must not take, of course, men like the chiefs of the Hyde Park demonstration, Colonel Dickson⁰ or Mr. Beales; because Colonel Dickson, by his martial profession and dashing exterior, seems to belong properly, like Julius Caesar and Mirabeau and other great popular leaders, to the aristocratic class, and to be carried into the popular ranks only by his ambition or his genius; while Mr. Beales belongs to our solid middle class, and, perhaps, if he had not been a great popular leader, would have been a Philistine. But Mr. Odger, whose speeches we have all read, and of whom his friends relate, besides, much that is favourable, may very well stand for the beautiful and virtuous mean of our present working class; and I think everybody will admit that in Mr. Odger there is manifestly, with all his good points, some insufficiency of light.ᵖ The excess of the working class, in its present state of development, is perhaps best shown in Mr. Bradlaugh, the iconoclast, who seems to be almost for baptizing us all in blood and fire into his new social dispensation, and to whose reflections, now that I have once been set going on Bishop Wilson's track, I cannot forbear commending this maxim of the good old man: "Intemperance in talk makes a dreadful havoc in the heart." Mr. Bradlaugh, like our types of excess in the aristocratic and middle classes, is evidently capable, if he had his head given him, of running us all into great dangers and confusion. I conclude, therefore,—what indeed, few of those who do me the honour to read this disquisition are likely to dispute,—that we can as little find in the working class as in the aristocratic or in the middle class our much-wanted source of authority, as culture suggests it to us.

Well, then, what if we tried to rise above the idea of class to the idea of the whole community, *the State*, and to find our centre of light and authority there? Every one of us has the idea of country, as a sentiment; hardly any one of us has the idea of *the State*, as a working

⁰ Lt-Colonel Lothian Sheffield Dickson was also one of the leaders of the Reform League.

ᵖ George Odger (1820–77) was Secretary of the London Trades Council as well as an active figure in the Reform League.

98

power. And why? Because we habitually live in our ordinary selves, which do not carry us beyond the ideas and wishes of the class to which we happen to belong. And we are all afraid of giving to the State too much power, because we only conceive of the State as something equivalent to the class in occupation of the executive government, and are afraid of that class abusing power to its own purposes. If we strengthen the State with the aristocratic class in occupation of the executive government, we imagine we are delivering ourselves up captive to the ideas and wishes of our fierce aristocratical baronet; if with the middle class in occupation of the executive government, to those of our truculent middle-class Dissenting minister; if with the working class, to those of its notorious tribune, Mr. Bradlaugh. And with much justice; owing to the exaggerated notion which we English, as I have said, entertain of the right and blessedness of the mere doing as one likes, of the affirming oneself, and oneself just as it is. People of the aristocratic class want to affirm their ordinary selves, their likings and dislikings; people of the middle class the same, people of the working class the same. By our everyday selves, however, we are separate, personal, at war; we are only safe from one another's tyranny when no one has any power; and this safety, in its turn, cannot save us from anarchy. And when, therefore, anarchy presents itself as a danger to us, we know not where to turn.

But by our *best self* we are united, impersonal, at harmony. We are in no peril from giving authority to this, because it is the truest friend we all of us can have; and when anarchy is a danger to us, to this authority we may turn with sure trust. Well, and this is the very self which culture, or the study of perfection, seeks to develop in us; at the expense of our old untransformed self, taking pleasure only in doing what it likes or is used to do, and exposing us to the risk of clashing with every one else who is doing the same! So that our poor culture, which is flouted as so unpractical, leads us to the very ideas capable of meeting the great want of our present embarrassed times! We want an authority, and we find nothing but jealous classes, checks, and a dead-lock; culture suggests the idea of *the State*. We find no basis for a firm State-power in our ordinary selves; culture suggests one to us in our *best self*.

It cannot but acutely try a tender conscience to be accused, in a practical country like ours, of keeping aloof from the work and hope of a multitude of earnest-hearted men, and of merely toying with poetry and aesthetics. So it is with no little sense of relief that I find myself thus in the position of one who makes a contribution in aid of the practical necessities of our times. The great thing, it will be observed, is to find our *best* self, and to seek to affirm nothing but that; not, —as we English with our over-value for merely being free and busy have been so accustomed to do, —resting satisfied with a self which comes uppermost long before our best self, and affirming that with blind energy. In short, —to go back yet once more to Bishop Wilson, —of these two excellent rules of Bishop Wilson's for a man's guidance: "Firstly, never go against the best light you have; secondly, take care that your light be not darkness," we English have followed with praiseworthy zeal the first rule, but we have not given so much heed to the second. We have gone manfully according to the best light we have; but we have not taken enough care that this should be really the best light possible for us, that it should not be darkness. And, our honesty being very great, conscience has whispered to us that the light we were following, our ordinary self, was, indeed, perhaps, only an inferior self, only darkness; and that it would not do to impose this seriously on all the world.

But our best self inspires faith, and is capable of affording a serious principle of authority. For example. We are on our way to what the late Duke of Wellington, with his strong sagacity, foresaw and admirably described as "a revolution by due course of law." This is undoubtedly, —if we are still to live and grow, and this famous nation is not to stagnate and dwindle away on the one hand, or, on the other, to perish miserably in mere anarchy and confusion, —what we are on the way to. Great changes there must be, for a revolution cannot accomplish itself without great changes; yet order there must be, for without order a revolution cannot accomplish itself by due course of law. So whatever brings risk of tumult and disorder, multitudinous processions in the streets of our crowded towns, multitudinous meetings in their public places and parks, —demonstrations perfectly unnecessary in the present course of our affairs, —our best self, or right reason, plainly enjoins us to set our faces against. It enjoins us to encourage and uphold the occupants of the executive power, whoever they may be, in firmly prohibiting them. But it does this clearly and resolutely, and is thus a real principle of authority, because it does it with a free conscience; because in thus provisionally strengthening the executive power, it knows that it is not doing this merely to enable our aristocratical baronet to affirm himself as against our working-men's tribune, or our middle-class Dissenter to affirm himself as against both. It knows that it is stablishing *the State*, or organ of our collective best self, of our national right reason. And it has the testimony of conscience that it is stablishing the State on behalf of whatever great changes are needed, just as much as on behalf of order; stablishing it to deal just as stringently, when the time comes, with our baronet's aristocratical prejudices, or with the fanaticism of our middle-class Dissenter, as it deals with Mr. Bradlaugh's street-processions.

CHAPTER III

# Barbarians, Philistines, Populace

From a man without a philosophy no one can expect philosophical completeness. Therefore I may observe without shame, that in trying to get a distinct notion of our aristocratic, our middle, and our working class, with a view of testing the claims of each of these classes to become a centre of authority, I have omitted, I find, to complete the old-fashioned analysis which I had the fancy of applying, and have not shown in these classes, as well as the virtuous mean and the excess, the defect also. I do not know that the omission very much matters. Still, as clearness is the one merit which a plain, unsystematic writer, without a philosophy, can hope to have, and as our notion of the three great English classes may perhaps be made clearer if we see their distinctive qualities in the defect, as well as in the excess and in the mean, let us try, before proceeding further, to remedy this omission.

It is manifest, if the perfect and virtuous mean of that fine spirit which is the distinctive quality of aristocracies, is to be found in a high, chivalrous style, and its excess in a fierce turn for resistance, that its defect must lie in a spirit not bold and high enough, and in an excessive and pusillanimous unaptness for resistance. If, again, the perfect and virtuous mean of that force by which our middle class has done its great works, and of that self-reliance with which it contemplates itself and them, is to be seen in the performances and speeches of our commercial member of Parliament, and the excess of that force and of that self-reliance in the performances and speeches of our fanatical Dissenting minister, then it is manifest that their defect must lie in a helpless inaptitude for the great works of the middle class, and in a poor and despicable lack of its self-satisfaction.

To be chosen to exemplify the happy mean of a good quality, or set of good qualities, is evidently a praise to a man; nay, to be chosen to exemplify even their excess, is a kind of praise. Therefore I could have no hesitation in taking actual personages to exemplify, respectively, the mean and the excess of aristocratic and middle-class qualities. But perhaps there might be a want of urbanity in singling out this or that personage as the representative of defect. Therefore I shall leave the defect of aristocracy unillustrated by any representative man. But with oneself one may always, without impropriety, deal quite freely; and, indeed, this sort of plain-dealing with oneself has in it, as all the moralists tell us, something very wholesome. So I will venture to humbly offer myself as an illustration of defect in those forces and qualities which make our middle class what it is. The too well-founded reproaches of my opponents declare how little I have lent a hand to the great works of the middle class; for it is evidently these works, and my slackness at them, which are meant, when I am said to "refuse to lend a hand to the humble operation of uprooting certain definite evils" (such as church-rates and others), and that therefore "the believers in action grow impatient" with me. The line, again, of a still unsatisfied seeker which I have followed, the idea of self-trans-formation, of growing towards some measure of sweetness and light not yet reached, is evidently at clean variance with the perfect self-satisfaction current in my class, the middle class, and may serve to indicate in me, therefore, the extreme defect of this feeling. But these confessions, though salutary, are bitter and unpleasant.

To pass, then, to the working class. The defect of this class would be the falling short in what Mr. Frederic Harrison calls those "bright powers of sympathy and ready powers of action," of which we saw in Mr. Odger the virtuous mean, and in Mr. Bradlaugh the excess. The working class is so fast growing and rising at the present time, that instances of this defect cannot well be now very common. Perhaps Canning's "Needy Knife-Grinder" (who is dead, and therefore cannot be pained at my taking him for an illustration) may serve to give us the notion of defect in the essential quality of a working class;[a] or I might even cite (since, though he is alive in the flesh, he is dead to all heed of criticism) my poor old poaching friend, Zephaniah Diggs, who, between his hare-snaring and his gin-drinking, has got his

---

[a] 'The Friend of Humanity and the Knife-Grinder' was a poetical skit on Robert Southey by George Canning, published in the *Anti-Jacobin* in November 1797.

powers of sympathy quite dulled and his powers of action in any great movement of his class hopelessly impaired.[b] But examples of this defect belong, as I have said, to a bygone age rather than to the present.

The same desire for clearness, which has led me thus to extend a little my first analysis of the three great classes of English society, prompts me also to improve my nomenclature for them a little, with a view to making it thereby more manageable. It is awkward and tiresome to be always saying the aristocratic class, the middle class, the working class. For the middle class, for that great body which, as we know, "has done all the great things that have been done in all departments," and which is to be conceived as moving between its two cardinal points of our commercial member of Parliament and our fanatical Protestant Dissenter,—for this class we have a designation which now has become pretty well known, and which we may as well still keep for them, the designation of Philistines. What this term means I have so often explained that I need not repeat it here. For the aristocratic class, conceived mainly as a body moving between the two cardinal points of our chivalrous lord and our defiant baronet, we have as yet got no special designation. Almost all my attention has naturally been concentrated on my own class, the middle class, with which I am in closest sympathy, and which has been, besides, the great power of our day, and has had its praises sung by all speakers and newspapers.

Still the aristocratic class is so important in itself, and the weighty functions which Mr. Carlyle proposes at the present critical time to commit to it, must add so much to its importance, that it seems neglectful, and a strong instance of that want of coherent philosophic method for which Mr. Frederic Harrison blames me, to leave the aristocratic class so much without notice and denomination. It may be thought that the characteristic which I have occasionally mentioned as proper to aristocracies,—their natural inaccessibility, as children of the established fact, to ideas,—points to our extending to this class also the designation of Philistines; the Philistine being, as is well known, the enemy of the children of light or servants of the idea. Nevertheless, there seems to be an inconvenience in thus giving one and the same designation to two very different classes; and besides, if

[b] 'Zephaniah Diggs' was a low-life character Arnold had created in *Friendship's Garland*.

we look into the thing closely, we shall find that the term Philistine conveys a sense which makes it more peculiarly appropriate to our middle class than to our aristocratic. For *Philistine* gives the notion of something particularly stiff-necked and perverse in the resistance to light and its children; and therein it specially suits our middle class, who not only do not pursue sweetness and light, but who even prefer to them that sort of machinery of business, chapels, tea-meetings, and addresses from Mr. Murphy, which makes up the dismal and illiberal life on which I have so often touched. But the aristocratic class has actually, as we have seen, in its well-known politeness, a kind of image or shadow of sweetness; and as for light, if it does not pursue light, it is not that it perversely cherishes some dismal and illiberal existence in preference to light, but it is lured off from following light by those mighty and eternal seducers of our race which weave for this class their most irresistible charms, — by worldly splendour, security, power, and pleasure. These seducers are exterior goods, but in a way they are goods; and he who is hindered by them from caring for light and ideas, is not so much doing what is perverse as what is too natural.

Keeping this in view, I have in my own mind often indulged myself with the fancy of employing, in order to designate our aristocratic class, the name of *the Barbarians*. The Barbarians, to whom we all owe so much, and who reinvigorated and renewed our worn-out Europe, had, as is well known, eminent merits; and in this country, where we are for the most part sprung from the Barbarians, we have never had the prejudice against them which prevails among the races of Latin origin. The Barbarians brought with them that staunch individualism, as the modern phrase is, and that passion for doing as one likes, for the assertion of personal liberty, which appears to Mr. Bright the central idea of English life, and of which we have, at any rate, a very rich supply. The stronghold and natural seat of this passion was in the nobles of whom our aristocratic class are the inheritors; and this class, accordingly, have signally manifested it, and have done much by their example to recommend it to the body of the nation, who already, indeed, had it in their blood. The Barbarians, again, had the passion for field-sports; and they have handed it on to our aristocratic class, who of this passion too, as of the passion for asserting one's personal liberty, are the great natural stronghold. The care of the Barbarians for the body, and for all manly exercises; the vigour, good looks, and fine complexion which they acquired and perpetuated in their families by these means,—all this may be observed still in our aristocratic class. The chivalry of the Barbarians, with its characteristics of high spirit, choice manners, and distinguished bearing,—what is this but the attractive commencement of the politeness of our aristocratic class? In some Barbarian noble, no doubt, one would have admired, if one could have been then alive to see it, the rudiments of our politest peer. Only, all this culture (to call it by that name) of the Barbarians was an exterior culture mainly. It consisted principally in outward gifts and graces, in looks, manners, accomplishments, prowess. The chief inward gifts which had part in it were the most exterior, so to speak, of inward gifts, those which come nearest to outward ones; they were courage, a high spirit, self-confidence. Far within, and unawakened, lay a whole range of powers of thought and feeling, to which these interesting productions of nature had, from the circumstances of their life, no access. Making allowances for the difference of the times, surely we can observe precisely the same thing now in our aristocratic class. In general its culture is exterior chiefly; all the exterior graces and accomplishments, and the more external of the inward virtues, seem to be principally its portion. It now, of course, cannot but be often in contact with those studies by which, from the world of thought and feeling, true culture teaches us to fetch sweetness and light; but its hold upon these very studies appears remarkably external, and unable to exert any deep power upon its spirit. Therefore the one insufficiency which we noted in the perfect mean of this class was an insufficiency of light. And owing to the same causes, does not a subtle criticism lead us to make, even on the good looks and politeness of our aristocratic class, and of even the most fascinating half of that class, the feminine half, the one qualifying remark, that in these charming gifts there should perhaps be, for ideal perfection, a shade more *soul?*

I often, therefore, when I want to distinguish clearly the aristocratic class from the Philistines proper, or middle class, name the former, in my own mind, *the Barbarians.* And when I go through the country, and see this and that beautiful and imposing seat of theirs crowning the landscape, "There," I say to myself, "is a great fortified post of the Barbarians."

It is obvious that that part of the working class which, working diligently by the light of Mrs. Gooch's Golden Rule, looks forward to the happy day when it will sit on thrones with commercial members of

Parliament and other middle-class potentates, to survey, as Mr. Bright beautifully says, "the cities it has built, the railroads it has made, the manufactures it has produced, the cargoes which freight the ships of the greatest mercantile navy the world has ever seen,"—it is obvious, I say, that this part of the working class is, or is in a fair way to be, one in spirit with the industrial middle class. It is notorious that our middle-class Liberals have long looked forward to this consummation, when the working class shall join forces with them, aid them heartily to carry forward their great works, go in a body to their tea-meetings, and, in short, enable them to bring about their millennium. That part of the working class, therefore, which does really seem to lend itself to these great aims, may, with propriety, be numbered by us among the Philistines. That part of it, again, which so much occupies the attention of philanthropists at present,—the part which gives all its energies to organising itself, through trades' unions and other means, so as to constitute, first, a great working-class power independent of the middle and aristocratic classes, and then, by dint of numbers, give the law to them and itself reign absolutely,—this lively and promising part must also, according to our definition, go with the Philistines; because it is its class and its class instinct which it seeks to affirm—its ordinary self, not its best self; and it is a machinery, an industrial machinery, and power and pre-eminence and other external goods, which fill its thoughts, and not an inward perfection. It is wholly occupied, according to Plato's subtle expression, with the things of itself and not its real self, with the things of the State and not the real State. But that vast portion, lastly, of the working class which, raw and half-developed, has long lain half-hidden amidst its poverty and squalor, and is now issuing from its hiding-place to assert an Englishman's heaven-born privilege of doing as he likes, and is beginning to perplex us by marching where it likes, meeting where it likes, bawling what it likes, breaking what it likes,—to this vast residuum we may with great propriety give the name of *Populace*.

Thus we have got three distinct terms, *Barbarians, Philistines, Populace*, to denote roughly the three great classes into which our society is divided; and though this humble attempt at a scientific nomenclature falls, no doubt, very far short in precision of what might be required from a writer equipped with a complete and coherent philosophy, yet, from a notoriously unsystematic and unpretending writer, it will, I trust, be accepted as sufficient.

But in using this new, and, I hope, convenient division of English society, two things are to be borne in mind. The first is, that since, under all our class divisions, there is a common basis of human nature, therefore, in every one of us, whether we be properly Barbarians, Philistines, or Populace, there exist, sometimes only in germ and potentially, sometimes more or less developed, the same tendencies and passions which have made our fellow-citizens of other classes what they are. This consideration is very important, because it has great influence in begetting that spirit of indulgence which is a necessary part of sweetness, and which, indeed, when our culture is complete, is, as I have said, inexhaustible. Thus, an English Barbarian who examines himself will, in general, find himself to be not so entirely a Barbarian but that he has in him, also, something of the Philistine, and even something of the Populace as well. And the same with Englishmen of the two other classes.

This is an experience which we may all verify every day. For instance, I myself (I again take myself as a sort of *corpus vile* to serve for illustration in a matter where serving for illustration may not by every one be thought agreeable), I myself am properly a Philistine, — Mr. Swinburne would add, the son of a Philistine.[c] And although, through circumstances which will perhaps one day be known if ever the affecting history of my conversion comes to be written, I have, for the most part, broken with the ideas and the tea-meetings of my own class, yet I have not, on that account, been brought much the nearer to the ideas and works of the Barbarians or of the Populace. Nevertheless, I never take a gun or a fishing-rod in my hands without feeling that I have in the ground of my nature the self-same seeds which, fostered by circumstances, do so much to make the Barbarian; and that, with the Barbarian's advantages, I might have rivalled him. Place me in one of his great fortified posts, with these seeds of a love for field-sports sown in my nature, with all the means of developing them, with all pleasures at my command, with most whom I met deferring to me, every one I met smiling on me, and with every appearance of permanence and security before me and behind me, — then I too might have grown, I feel, into a very passable child of the

[c] The poet A.C. Swinburne (1837–1909), in an article on Arnold's poetry in the *Fortnightly Review* (1867), expressed mock surprise that 'the son of his father' (or 'David, the son of Goliath') should have been the author of such a thoroughgoing critique of philistinism.

established fact, of commendable spirit and politeness, and, at the same time, a little inaccessible to ideas and light; not, of course, with either the eminent fine spirit of our type of aristocratic perfection, or the eminent turn for resistance of our type of aristocratic excess, but, according to the measure of the common run of mankind, something between the two. And as to the Populace, who, whether he be Barbarian or Philistine, can look at them without sympathy, when he remembers how often,—every time that we snatch up a vehement opinion in ignorance and passion, every time that we long to crush an adversary by sheer violence, every time that we are envious, every time that we are brutal, every time that we adore mere power or success, every time that we add our voice to swell a blind clamour against some unpopular personage, every time that we trample savagely on the fallen,—he has found in his own bosom the eternal spirit of the Populace, and that there needs only a little help from circumstances to make it triumph in him untamably.

The second thing to be borne in mind I have indicated several times already. It is this. All of us, so far as we are Barbarians, Philistines, or Populace, imagine happiness to consist in doing what one's ordinary self likes. What one's ordinary self likes differs according to the class to which one belongs, and has its severer and its lighter side; always, however, remaining machinery, and nothing more. The graver self of the Barbarian likes honours and consideration; his more relaxed self, field-sports and pleasure. The graver self of one kind of Philistine likes fanaticism, business, and money-making; his more relaxed self, comfort and tea-meetings. Of another kind of Philistine, the graver self likes rattening;[d] the relaxed self, deputations, or hearing Mr. Odger speak. The sterner self of the Populace likes bawling, hustling, and smashing; the lighter self, beer. But in each class there are born a certain number of natures with a curiosity about their best self, with a bent for seeing things as they are, for disentangling themselves from machinery, for simply concerning themselves with reason and the will of God, and doing their best to make these prevail;—for the pursuit, in a word, of perfection. To certain manifestations of this love for perfection mankind have accustomed themselves to give the name of genius; implying, by this name, something original and heaven-bestowed in the passion. But

[d] 'The act or practice of abstracting tools, destroying machinery or appliances, etc., as a means of enforcing compliance with the rules of a trade-union' (*OED*).

the passion is to be found far beyond those manifestations of it to which the world usually gives the name of genius, and in which there is, for the most part, a *talent* of some kind or other, a special and striking faculty of execution, informed by the heaven-bestowed ardour, or genius. It is to be found in many manifestations besides these, and may best be called, as we have called it, the love and pursuit of perfection; culture being the true nurse of the pursuing love, and sweetness and light the true character of the pursued perfection. Natures with this bent emerge in all classes,—among the Barbarians, among the Philistines, among the Populace. And this bent always tends to take them out of their class, and to make their distinguishing characteristic not their Barbarianism or their Philistinism, but their *humanity*. They have, in general, a rough time of it in their lives; but they are sown more abundantly than one might think, they appear where and when one least expects it, they set up a fire which enfilades, so to speak, the class with which they are ranked; and, in general, by the extrication of their best self as the self to develop, and by the simplicity of the ends fixed by them as paramount, they hinder the unchecked predominance of that class-life which is the affirmation of our ordinary self, and seasonably disconcert mankind in their worship of machinery.

Therefore, when we speak of ourselves as divided into Barbarians, Philistines, and Populace, we must be understood always to imply that within each of these classes there are a certain number of *aliens*, if we may so call them,—persons who are mainly led, not by their class spirit, but by a general *humane* spirit, by the love of human perfection; and that this number is capable of being diminished or augmented. I mean, the number of those who will succeed in developing this happy instinct will be greater or smaller, in proportion both to the force of the original instinct within them, and to the hindrance or encouragement which it meets with from without. In almost all who have it, it is mixed with some infusion of the spirit of an ordinary self, some quantity of class-instinct, and even, as has been shown, of more than one class-instinct at the same time; so that, in general, the extrication of the best self, the predominance of the *humane* instinct, will very much depend upon its meeting, or not, with what is fitted to help and elicit it. At a moment, therefore, when it is agreed that we want a source of authority, and when it seems probable that the right source is our best self, it becomes of vast importance to see whether or not the things around us are, in general, such as to help and elicit our best self, and if they are not, to see why they are not, and the most promising way of mending them.

Now, it is clear that the very absence of any powerful authority amongst us, and the prevalent doctrine of the duty and happiness of doing as one likes, and asserting our personal liberty, must tend to prevent the erection of any very strict standard of excellence, the belief in any very paramount authority of right reason, the recognition of our best self as anything very recondite and hard to come at. It may be, as I have said, a proof of our honesty that we do not attempt to give to our ordinary self, as we have it in action, predominant authority, and to impose its rule upon other people. But it is evident, also, that it is not easy, with our style of proceeding, to get beyond the notion of an ordinary self at all, or to get the paramount authority of a commanding best self, or right reason, recognised. The learned Martinus Scriblerus well says: — "The taste of the bathos is implanted by nature itself in the soul of man; till, perverted by custom or example, he is taught, or rather compelled, to relish the sublime."[e] But with us everything seems directed to prevent any such perversion of us by custom or example as might compel us to relish the sublime; by all means we are encouraged to keep our natural taste for the bathos unimpaired.

I have formerly pointed out how in literature the absence of any authoritative centre, like an Academy, tends to do this. Each section of the public has its own literary organ, and the mass of the public is without any suspicion that the value of these organs is relative to their being nearer a certain ideal centre of correct information, taste, and intelligence, or farther away from it. I have said that within certain limits, which any one who is likely to read this will have no difficulty in drawing for himself, my old adversary, the *Saturday Review*, may, on matters of literature and taste, be fairly enough regarded, relatively to the mass of newspapers which treat these matters, as a kind of organ of reason. But I remember once conversing with a company of Nonconformist admirers of some lecturer who had let off a great firework, which the *Saturday Review* said was all noise and false lights, and feeling my way as tenderly as I could about the effect of this unfavourable judgment upon those with whom I was conversing.

[e] *The Memoirs of Martinus Scriblerus* (1741) by John Arbuthnot was a satire on 'all the false tastes in learning'.

"Oh," said one who was their spokesman, with the most tranquil air of conviction, "it is true the *Saturday Review* abuses the lecture, but the *British Banner*"[f] (I am not quite sure it was the *British Banner*, but it was some newspaper of that stamp) "says that the *Saturday Review* is quite wrong." The speaker had evidently no notion that there was a scale of value for judgments on these topics, and that the judgments of the *Saturday Review* ranked high on this scale, and those of the *British Banner* low; the taste of the bathos implanted by nature in the literary judgments of man had never, in my friend's case, encountered any let or hindrance.

Just the same in religion as in literature. We have most of us little idea of a high standard to choose our guides by, of a great and profound spirit which is an authority while inferior spirits are none. It is enough to give importance to things that this or that person says them decisively, and has a large following of some strong kind when he says them. This habit of ours is very well shown in that able and interesting work of Mr. Hepworth Dixon's, which we were all reading lately, *The Mormons, by One of Themselves.*[g] Here, again, I am not quite sure that my memory serves me as to the exact title, but I mean the well-known book in which Mr. Hepworth Dixon described the Mormons, and other similar religious bodies in America, with so much detail and such warm sympathy. In this work it seems enough for Mr. Dixon that this or that doctrine has its Rabbi, who talks big to him, has a staunch body of disciples, and, above all, has plenty of rifles. That there are any further stricter tests to be applied to a doctrine, before it is pronounced important, never seems to occur to him. "It is easy to say," he writes of the Mormons, "that these saints are dupes and fanatics, to laugh at Joe Smith and his church, but what then? *The great facts remain.* Young and his people are at Utah; a church of 200,000 souls; an army of 20,000 rifles." But if the followers of a doctrine are really dupes, or worse, and its promulgators are really fanatics, or worse, it gives the doctrine no seriousness or authority the more that there should be found 200,000 souls, — 200,000 of the innumerable multitude with a natural taste for the bathos, — to hold it, and 20,000 rifles to defend it. And again, of another religious

[f] The *British Banner* (1847–58) was a somewhat sensationalist, poor-quality weekly newspaper of the Evangelical Nonconformists.

[g] William Hepworth Dixon (1821–79), journalist and travel-writer, author of *New America* (1867) and *Spiritual Wives* (1868).

organisation in America: "A fair and open field is not to be refused when hosts so mighty throw down wager of battle on behalf of what they hold to be true, however strange their faith may seem." A fair and open field is not to be refused to any speaker; but this solemn way of heralding him is quite out of place, unless he has, for the best reason and spirit of man, some significance. "Well, but," says Mr. Hepworth Dixon, "a theory which has been accepted by men like Judge Edmonds, Dr. Hare, Elder Frederick, and Professor Bush!" And again: "Such are, in brief, the bases of what Newman Weeks, Sarah Horton, Deborah Butler, and the associated brethren, proclaimed in Pratt's Hall as the new covenant!" If he was summing up an account of the doctrine of Plato, or of St. Paul, and of its followers, Mr. Hepworth Dixon could not be more earnestly reverential. But the question is, Have personages like Judge Edmonds, and Newman Weeks, and Elderess Polly, and Elderess Antoinette, and the rest of Mr. Hepworth Dixon's heroes and heroines, anything of the weight and significance for the best reason and spirit of man that Plato and St. Paul have? Evidently they, at present, have not; and a very small taste of them and their doctrines ought to have convinced Mr. Hepworth Dixon that they never could have. "But," says he, "the magnetic power which Shakerism is exercising on American thought would of itself compel us,"—and so on. Now, so far as real thought is concerned,—thought which affects the best reason and spirit of man, the scientific or the imaginative thought of the world, the only thought which deserves speaking of in this solemn way,—America has up to the present time been hardly more than a province of England, and even now would not herself claim to be more than abreast of England; and of this only real human thought, English thought itself is not just now, as we must all admit, the most significant factor. Neither, then, can American thought be; and the magnetic power which Shakerism exercises on American thought is about as important, for the best reason and spirit of man, as the magnetic power which Mr. Murphy exercises on Birmingham Protestantism. And as we shall never get rid of our natural taste for the bathos in religion,—never get access to a best self and right reason which may stand as a serious authority,—by treating Mr. Murphy as his own disciples treat him, seriously, and as if he was as much an authority as any one else: so we shall never get rid of it while our able and popular writers treat their Joe Smiths and Deborah Butlers, with their so many thousand souls and so many thousand rifles, in the like exaggerated and misleading manner, and so do their best to confirm us in a bad mental habit to which we are already too prone.

If our habits make it hard for us to come at the idea of a high best self, of a paramount authority, in literature or religion, how much more do they make this hard in the sphere of politics! In other countries the governors, not depending so immediately on the favour of the governed, have everything to urge them, if they know anything of right reason (and it is at least supposed that governors should know more of this than the mass of the governed), to set it authoritatively before the community. But our whole scheme of government being representative, every one of our governors has all possible temptation, instead of setting up before the governed who elect him, and on whose favour he depends, a high standard of right reason, to accommodate himself as much as possible to their natural taste for the bathos; and even if he tries to go counter to it, to proceed in this with so much flattering and coaxing, that they shall not suspect their ignorance and prejudices to be anything very unlike right reason, or their natural taste for the bathos to differ much from a relish for the sublime. Every one is thus in every possible way encouraged to trust in his own heart; but, "He that trusteth in his own heart," says the Wise Man, "is a fool;" and at any rate this, which Bishop Wilson says, is undeniably true: "The number of those who need to be awakened is far greater than that of those who need comfort."

But in our political system everybody is comforted. Our guides and governors who have to be elected by the influence of the Barbarians, and who depend on their favour, sing the praises of the Barbarians, and say all the smooth things that can be said of them. With Mr. Tennyson, they celebrate "the great broad-shouldered genial Englishman," with his "sense of duty," his "reverence for the laws," and his "patient force," who saves us from the "revolts, republics, revolutions, most no graver than a schoolboy's barring out," which upset other and less broad-shouldered nations.[h] Our guides who are chosen by the Philistines and who have to look to their favour, tell the Philistines how "all the world knows that the great middle class of this country supplies the mind, the will, and the power requisite for all the great and good things that have to be done," and congratulate them

[h] Alfred, Lord Tennyson, *The Princess* (1847).

on their "earnest good sense, which penetrates through sophisms, ignores commonplaces, and gives to conventional illusions their true value." Our guides who look to the favour of the Populace, tell them that "theirs are the brightest powers of sympathy, and the readiest powers of action."

Harsh things are said too, no doubt, against all the great classes of the community; but these things so evidently come from a hostile class, and are so manifestly dictated by the passions and prepossessions of a hostile class, and not by right reason, that they make no serious impression on those at whom they are launched, but slide easily off their minds. For instance, when the Reform League orators inveigh against our cruel and bloated aristocracy, these invectives so evidently show the passions and point of view of the Populace, that they do not sink into the minds of those at whom they are addressed, or awaken any thought or self-examination in them. Again, when our aristocratical baronet describes the Philistines and the Populace as influenced with a kind of hideous mania for emasculating the aristocracy, that reproach so clearly comes from the wrath and excited imagination of the Barbarians, that it does not much set the Philistines and the Populace thinking. Or when Mr. Lowe calls the Populace drunken and venal,[i] he so evidently calls them this in an agony of apprehension for his Philistine or middle-class Parliament, which has done so many great and heroic works, and is now threatened with mixture and debasement, that the Populace do not lay his words seriously to heart.

So the voice which makes a permanent impression on each of our classes is the voice of its friends, and this is from the nature of things, as I have said, a comforting voice. The Barbarians remain in the belief that the great broad-shouldered genial Englishman may be well satisfied with himself; the Philistines remain in the belief that the great middle class of this country, with its earnest common-sense penetrating through sophisms and ignoring commonplaces, may be well satisfied with itself; the Populace, that the working man with his bright powers of sympathy and ready powers of action, may be well satisfied with himself. What hope, at this rate, of extinguishing the taste of the bathos implanted by nature itself in the soul of man, or of inculcating the belief that excellence dwells among high and steep

---

[i] Robert Lowe had used these words to characterize the working class in the Reform Bill Debates of March 1866; they were widely quoted against him (see also below p. 165).

rocks, and can only be reached by those who sweat blood to reach her?

But it will be said, perhaps, that candidates for political influence and leadership, who thus caress the self-love of those whose suffrages they desire, know quite well that they are not saying the sheer truth as reason sees it, but that they are using a sort of conventional language, or what we call clap-trap, which is essential to the working of representative institutions. And therefore, I suppose, we ought rather to say with Figaro: *Qui est-ce qu'on trompe ici?* Now, I admit that often, but not always, when our governors say smooth things to the self-love of the class whose political support they want, they know very well that they are overstepping, by a long stride, the bounds of truth and soberness; and while they talk, they in a manner, no doubt, put their tongue in their cheek. Not always; because, when a Barbarian appeals to his own class to make him their representative and give him political power, he, when he pleases their self-love by extolling broad-shouldered genial Englishmen with their sense of duty, reverence for the laws, and patient force, pleases his own self-love and extols himself, and is, therefore, himself ensnared by his own smooth words. And so, too, when a Philistine wants to be sent to Parliament by his brother Philistines, and extols the earnest good sense which characterises Manchester and supplies the mind, the will, and the power, as the *Daily News* eloquently says, requisite for all the great and good things that have to be done, he intoxicates and deludes himself as well as his brother Philistines who hear him.

But it is true that a Barbarian often wants the political support of the Philistines; and he unquestionably, when he flatters the self-love of Philistinism, and extols, in the approved fashion, its energy, enterprise, and self-reliance, knows that he is talking clap-trap, and so to say, puts his tongue in his cheek. On all matters where Nonconformity and its catchwords are concerned, this insincerity of Barbarians needing Nonconformist support, and, therefore, flattering the self-love of Nonconformity and repeating its catchwords without the least real belief in them, is very noticeable. When the Nonconformists, in a transport of blind zeal, threw out Sir James Graham's useful Education Clauses in 1843, one-half of their Parliamentary advocates, no doubt, who cried aloud against "trampling on the religious liberty of the Dissenters by taking the money of Dissenters to teach the tenets of the Church of England," put their tongue in their cheek while they so cried out.[j] And perhaps there is even a sort of motion of Mr. Frederic Harrison's tongue towards his cheek when he talks of "the shriek of superstition," and tells the working class that "theirs are the brightest powers of sympathy and the readiest powers of action."[k] But the point on which I would insist is, that this involuntary tribute to truth and soberness on the part of certain of our governors and guides never reaches at all the mass of us governed, to serve as a lesson to us, to abate our self-love, and to awaken in us a suspicion that our favourite prejudices may be, to a higher reason, all nonsense. Whatever by-play goes on among the more intelligent of our leaders, we do not see it; and we are left to believe that, not only in our own eyes, but in the eyes of our representative and ruling men, there is nothing more admirable than our ordinary self, whatever our ordinary self happens to be, Barbarian, Philistine, or Populace.

Thus everything in our political life tends to hide from us that there is anything wiser than our ordinary selves, and to prevent our getting the notion of a paramount right reason. Royalty itself, in its idea the expression of the collective nation, and a sort of constituted witness to its best mind, we try to turn into a kind of grand advertising van, meant to give publicity and credit to the inventions, sound or unsound, of the ordinary self of individuals.

I remember, when I was in North Germany, having this very strongly brought to my mind in the matter of schools and their institution. In Prussia, the best schools are Crown patronage schools, as they are called: schools which have been established and endowed (and new ones are to this day being established and endowed) by the Sovereign himself out of his own revenues, to be under the direct control and management of him or of those representing him, and to serve as types of what schools should be. The Sovereign, as his position raises him above many prejudices and littlenesses, and as he can always have at his disposal the best advice, has evident advantages over private founders in well planning and directing a school; while at the same time his great means and his great influence secure, to a well-planned school of his, credit and authority. This is what, in North Germany, the governors do in the matter of education for the

---

[j] The Dissenters had opposed clauses in the Factory Act of 1843 which would have allowed children working in factories to receive religious instruction according to the doctrines of the Church of England.

[k] In the article cited on p. 56, n. c above.

governed; and one may say that they thus give the governed a lesson, and draw out in them the idea of a right reason higher than the suggestions of an ordinary man's ordinary self.

But in England how different is the part which in this matter our governors are accustomed to play! The Licensed Victuallers or the Commercial Travellers propose to make a school for their children; and I suppose, in the matter of schools, one may call the Licensed Victuallers or the Commercial Travellers ordinary men, with their natural taste for the bathos still strong; and a Sovereign with the advice of men like Wilhelm von Humboldt or Schleiermacher may, in this matter, be a better judge, and nearer to right reason.[1] And it will be allowed, probably, that right reason would suggest that, to have a sheer school of Licensed Victuallers' children, or a sheer school of Commercial Travellers' children, and to bring them all up, not only at home but at school too, in a kind of odour of licensed victualism or of bagmanism, is not a wise training to give to these children. And in Germany, I have said, the action of the national guides or governors is to suggest and provide a better. But, in England, the action of the national guides or governors is, for a Royal Prince or a great Minister to go down to the opening of the Licensed Victuallers' or of the Commercial Travellers' school, to take the chair, to extol the energy and self-reliance of the Licensed Victuallers or the Commercial Travellers, to be all of their way of thinking, to predict full success to their schools, and never so much as to hint to them that they are probably doing a very foolish thing, and that the right way to go to work with their children's education is quite different. And it is the same in almost every department of affairs. While, on the Continent, the idea prevails that it is the business of the heads and representatives of the nation, by virtue of their superior means, power, and information, to set an example and to provide suggestions of right reason, among us the idea is that the business of the heads and representatives of the nation is to do nothing of the kind, but to applaud the natural taste for the bathos showing itself vigorously in any part of the community, and to encourage its works.

Now I do not say that the political system of foreign countries has not inconveniences which may outweigh the inconveniences of our

[1] Wilhelm von Humboldt (1767–1835), the first Prussian Minister of Education, founded the University of Berlin, in which he was aided by his friend, the theologian Friedrich Schleiermacher (1768–1834). See also the note on p. 123 below.

own political system; nor am I the least proposing to get rid of our own political system and to adopt theirs. But a sound centre of authority being what, in this disquisition, we have been led to seek, and right reason, or our best self, appearing alone to offer such a sound centre of authority, it is necessary to take note of the chief impediments which hinder, in this country, the extrication or recognition of this right reason as a paramount authority, with a view to afterwards trying in what way they can best be removed.

This being borne in mind, I proceed to remark how not only do we get no suggestions of right reason, and no rebukes of our ordinary self, from our governors, but a kind of philosophical theory is widely spread among us to the effect that there is no such thing at all as a best self and a right reason having claim to paramount authority, or, at any rate, no such thing ascertainable and capable of being made use of; and that there is nothing but an infinite number of ideas and works of our ordinary selves, and suggestions of our natural taste for the bathos, pretty nearly equal in value, which are doomed either to an irreconcilable conflict, or else to a perpetual give and take; and that wisdom consists in choosing the give and take rather than the conflict, and in sticking to our choice with patience and good humour.

And, on the other hand, we have another philosophical theory rife among us, to the effect that without the labour of perverting ourselves by custom or example to relish right reason, but by continuing all of us to follow freely our natural taste for the bathos, we shall, by the mercy of Providence, and by a kind of natural tendency of things, come in due time to relish and follow right reason.

The great promoters of these philosophical theories are our newspapers, which, no less than our Parliamentary representatives, may be said to act the part of guides and governors to us; and these favourite doctrines of theirs I call,—or should call, if the doctrines were not preached by authorities I so much respect,—the first, a peculiarly British form of Atheism, the second, a peculiarly British form of Quietism. The first-named melancholy doctrine is preached in the *Times* with great clearness and force of style; indeed, it is well known, from the example of the poet Lucretius and others, what great masters of style the atheistic doctrine has always counted among its promulgators. "It is of no use," says the *Times*, "for us to attempt to force upon our neighbours our several likings and dislikings. We must take things as they are. Everybody has his own little vision of religious or civil perfection. Under the evident impossibility of satisfying everybody, we agree to take our stand on equal laws and on a system as open and liberal as is possible. The result is that everybody has more liberty of action and of speaking here than anywhere else in the Old World." We come again here upon Mr. Roebuck's celebrated definition of happiness, on which I have so often commented: "I look around me and ask what is the state of England? Is not every man able to say what he likes? I ask you whether the world over, or in past history, there is anything like it? Nothing. I pray that our unrivalled happiness may last." This is the old story of our system of checks and every Englishman doing as he likes, which we have already seen to have been convenient enough so long as there were only the Barbarians and the Philistines to do what they liked, but to be getting inconvenient, and productive of anarchy, now that the Populace wants to do what it likes too.

But for all that, I will not at once dismiss this famous doctrine, but will first quote another passage from the *Times*, applying the doctrine to a matter of which we have just been speaking, —education. "The difficulty here" (in providing a national system of education), says the *Times*, "does not reside in any removable arrangements. It is inherent and native in the actual and inveterate state of things in this country. All these powers and personages, all these conflicting influences and varieties of character, exist, and have long existed among us; they are fighting it out, and will long continue to fight it out, without coming to that happy consummation when some one element of the British character is to destroy or to absorb all the rest." There it is! the various promptings of the natural taste for the bathos in this man and that amongst us are fighting it out; and the day will never come (and, indeed, why should we wish it to come?) when one man's particular sort of taste for the bathos shall tyrannise over another man's; nor when right reason (if that may be called an element of the British character) shall absorb and rule them all. "The whole system of this country, like the constitution we boast to inherit, and are glad to uphold, is made up of established facts, prescriptive authorities, existing usages, powers that be, persons in possession, and communities or classes that have won dominion for themselves, and will hold it against all comers." Every force in the world, evidently, except the one reconciling force, right reason! Barbarian here, Philistine there, Mr. Bradlaugh and Populace striking in!—pull devil, pull baker!

Really, presented with the mastery of style of our leading journal, the sad picture, as one gazes upon it, assumes the iron and inexorable solemnity of tragic Destiny.

After this, the milder doctrine of our other philosophical teacher, the *Daily News*, has, at first, something very attractive and assuaging. The *Daily News* begins, indeed, in appearance, to weave the iron web of necessity round us like the *Times*. "The alternative is between a man's doing what he likes and his doing what some one else, probably not one whit wiser than himself, likes." This points to the tacit compact, mentioned in my last paper, between the Barbarians and the Philistines, and into which it is hoped that the Populace will one day enter; the compact, so creditable to English honesty, that since each class has only the ideas and aims of its ordinary self to give effect to, none of them shall, if it exercise power, treat its ordinary self too seriously, or attempt to impose it on others; but shall let these others,—the fanatical Protestant, for instance, in his Papist-baiting, and the popular tribune in his Hyde Park anarchy-mongering,—have their fling. But then the *Daily News* suddenly lights up the gloom of necessitarianism with bright beams of hope. "No doubt," it says, "the common reason of society ought to check the aberrations of individual eccentricity." This common reason of society looks very like our best self or right reason, to which we want to give authority, by making the action of the *State*, or nation in its collective character, the expression of it. But of this project of ours, the *Daily News*, with its subtle dialectics, makes havoc. "Make the State the organ of the common reason?"—it says. "You may make it the organ of something or other, but how can you be certain that reason will be the quality which will be embodied in it?" You cannot be certain of it, undoubtedly, if you never try to bring the thing about; but the question is, the action of the State being the action of the collective nation, and the action of the collective nation carrying naturally great publicity, weight, and force of example with it, whether we should not try to put into the action of the State as much as possible of right reason or our best self, which may, in this manner, come back to us with new force and authority; may have visibility, form, and influence; and help to confirm us, in the many moments when we are tempted to be our ordinary selves merely, in resisting our natural taste of the bathos rather than in giving way to it?

But no! says our teacher: "It is better there should be an infinite variety of experiments in human action; the common reason of society will in the main check the aberrations of individual eccentricity well enough, if left to its natural operation." This is what I call the specially British form of Quietism, or a devout, but excessive, reliance on an over-ruling Providence. Providence, as the moralists are careful to tell us, generally works in human affairs by human means; so, when we want to make right reason act on individual inclination, our best self on our ordinary self, we seek to give it more power of doing so by giving it public recognition and authority, and embodying it, so far as we can, in the State. It seems too much to ask of Providence, that while we, on our part, leave our congenital taste for the bathos to its natural operation and its infinite variety of experiments, Providence should mysteriously guide it into the true track, and compel it to relish the sublime. At any rate, great men and great institutions have hitherto seemed necessary for producing any considerable effect of this kind. No doubt we have an infinite variety of experiments and an ever-multiplying multitude of explorers. Even in these few chapters I have enumerated many: the *British Banner*, Judge Edmonds, Newman Weeks, Deborah Butler, Elderess Polly, Brother Noyes, Mr. Murphy, the Licensed Victuallers, the Commercial Travellers, and I know not how many more; and the numbers of the noble army are swelling every day. But what a depth of Quietism, or rather, what an over-bold call on the direct interposition of Providence, to believe that these interesting explorers will discover the true track, or at any rate, "will do so in the main well enough" (whatever that may mean) if left to their natural operation; that is, by going on as they are! Philosophers say, indeed, that we learn virtue by performing acts of virtue; but to say that we shall learn virtue by performing any acts to which our natural taste for the bathos carries us, that the fanatical Protestant comes at his best self by Papist-baiting, or Newman Weeks and Deborah Butler at right reason by following their noses, this certainly does appear over-sanguine.

It is true, what we want is to make right reason act on individual reason, the reason of individuals; all our search for authority has that for its end and aim. The *Daily News* says, I observe, that all my argument for authority "has a non-intellectual root;" and from what I know of my own mind and its poverty I think this so probable, that I should be inclined easily to admit it, if it were not that, in the first place, nothing of this kind, perhaps, should be admitted without examination; and, in the second, a way of accounting for the charge being made, in this particular instance, without good grounds, appears to present itself. What seems to me to account here, perhaps, for the charge, is the want of flexibility of our race, on which I have so often remarked. I mean, it being admitted that the conformity of the individual reason of the fanatical Protestant or the popular rioter with right reason is our true object, and not the mere restraining them, by the strong arm of the State, from Papist-baiting, or railing-breaking,—admitting this, we English have so little flexibility that we cannot readily perceive that the State's restraining them from these indulgences may yet fix clearly in their minds that, to the collective nation, these indulgences appear irrational and unallowable, may make them pause and reflect, and may contribute to bringing, with time, their individual reason into harmony with right reason. But in no country, owing to the want of intellectual flexibility above mentioned, is the leaning which is our natural one, and, therefore, needs no recommending to us, so sedulously recommended, and the leaning which is not our natural one, and, therefore, does not need dispraising to us, so sedulously dispraised, as in ours. To rely on the individual being, with us, the natural leaning, we will hear of nothing but the good of relying on the individual; to act through the collective nation on the individual being not our natural leaning, we will hear nothing in recommendation of it. But the wise know that we often need to hear most of that to which we are least inclined, and even to learn to employ, in certain circumstances, that which is capable, if employed amiss, of being a danger to us.

Elsewhere this is certainly better understood than here. In a recent number of the *Westminster Review*, an able writer, but with precisely our national want of flexibility of which I have been speaking, has unearthed, I see, for our present needs, an English translation, published some years ago, of Wilhelm von Humboldt's book, *The Sphere and Duties of Government*.[m] Humboldt's object in this book is to show that the operation of government ought to be severely limited to what directly and immediately relates to the security of person and property. Wilhelm von Humboldt, one of the most beautiful souls that

---

[m] [Anon], 'Dangers of Democracy', *Westminster Review* (1868), discussed Carlyle's 'Shooting Niagara: and After?' and particularly Humboldt's *The Sphere and Duties of Government*, originally written (in German) in 1792 and published in English in 1854; the epigraph for J.S. Mill's *On Liberty* (1859) was taken from the English translation.

have ever existed, used to say that one's business in life was first to perfect one's self by all the means in one's power, and secondly, to try and create in the world around one an aristocracy, the most numerous that one possibly could, of talents and characters. He saw, of course, that, in the end, everything comes to this, — that the individual must act for himself, and must be perfect in himself; and he lived in a country, Germany, where people were disposed to act too little for themselves, and to rely too much on the Government. But even thus, such was his flexibility, so little was he in bondage to a mere abstract maxim, that he saw very well that for his purpose itself, of enabling the individual to stand perfect on his own foundations and to do without the State, the action of the State would for long, long years be necessary. And soon after he wrote his book on *The Sphere and Duties of Government*, Wilhelm von Humboldt became Minister of Education in Prussia; and from his ministry all the great reforms which give the control of Prussian education to the State, — the transference of the management of public schools from their old boards of trustees to the State, the obligatory State-examination for schoolmasters, and the foundation of the great State-University of Berlin, — take their origin. This his English reviewer says not a word of. But, writing for a people whose dangers lie, as we have seen, on the side of their unchecked and unguided individual action, whose dangers none of them lie on the side of an over-reliance on the State, he quotes just so much of Wilhelm von Humboldt's example as can flatter them in their propensities, and do them no good; and just what might make them think, and be of use to them, he leaves on one side. This precisely recalls the manner, it will be observed, in which we have seen that our royal and noble personages proceed with the Licensed Victuallers.

In France the action of the State on individuals is yet more preponderant than in Germany; and the need which friends of human perfection feel for what may enable the individual to stand perfect on his own foundations is all the stronger. But what says one of the staunchest of these friends, M. Renan, on State action; and even State action in that very sphere where in France it is most excessive, the sphere of education? Here are his words: — "A Liberal believes in liberty, and liberty signifies the non-intervention of the State. *But such an ideal is still a long way off from us, and the very means to remove it to an indefinite distance would be precisely the State's withdrawing its action too soon.*"[n] And this, he adds, is even truer of education than of any other department of public affairs.

We see, then, how indispensable to that human perfection which we seek is, in the opinion of good judges, some public recognition and establishment of our best self, or right reason. We see how our habits and practice oppose themselves to such a recognition, and the many inconveniences which we therefore suffer. But now let us try to go a little deeper, and to find, beneath our actual habits and practice, the very ground and cause out of which they spring.

---

[n] For Renan, see above pp. 44–5. The quotation is from 'L'Instruction supérieure en France', *Questions contemporaines* (1868).

# CHAPTER IV

# Hebraism and Hellenism

This fundamental ground is our preference of doing to thinking. Now this preference is a main element in our nature, and as we study it we find ourselves opening up a number of large questions on every side.

Let me go back for a moment to Bishop Wilson, who says: "First, never go against the best light you have; secondly, take care that your light be not darkness." We show, as a nation, laudable energy and persistence in walking according to the best light we have, but are not quite careful enough, perhaps, to see that our light be not darkness. This is only another version of the old story that energy is our strong point and favourable characteristic, rather than intelligence. But we may give to this idea a more general form still, in which it will have a yet larger range of application. We may regard this energy driving at practice, this paramount sense of the obligation of duty, self-control, and work, this earnestness in going manfully with the best light we have, as one force. And we may regard the intelligence driving at those ideas which are, after all, the basis of right practice, the ardent sense for all the new and changing combinations of them which man's development brings with it, the indomitable impulse to know and adjust them perfectly, as another force. And these two forces we may regard as in some sense rivals,—rivals not by the necessity of their own nature, but as exhibited in man and his history,—and rivals dividing the empire of the world between them. And to give these forces names from the two races of men who have supplied the most signal and splendid manifestations of them, we may call them respectively the forces of Hebraism and Hellenism. Hebraism and Hellenism,—between these two points of influence moves our world. At one time it feels more powerfully the attraction of one of them, at another time of the other; and it ought to be, though it never is, evenly and happily balanced between them.

The final aim of both Hellenism and Hebraism, as of all great spiritual disciplines, is no doubt the same: man's perfection or salvation. The very language which they both of them use in schooling us to reach this aim is often identical. Even when their language indicates by variation, —sometimes a broad variation, often a but slight and subtle variation, —the different courses of thought which are uppermost in each discipline, even then the unity of the final end and aim is still apparent. To employ the actual words of that discipline with which we ourselves are all of us most familiar, and the words of which, therefore, come most home to us, that final end and aim is "that we might be partakers of the divine nature." These are the words of a Hebrew apostle, but of Hellenism and Hebraism alike this is, I say, the aim. When the two are confronted, as they very often are confronted, it is nearly always with what I may call a rhetorical purpose; the speaker's whole design is to exalt and enthrone one of the two, and he uses the other only as a foil and to enable him the better to give effect to his purpose. Obviously, with us, it is usually Hellenism which is thus reduced to minister to the triumph of Hebraism. There is a sermon on Greece and the Greek spirit by a man never to be mentioned without interest and respect, Frederick Robertson, in which this rhetorical use of Greece and the Greek spirit, and the inadequate exhibition of them necessarily consequent upon this, is almost ludicrous, and would be censurable if it were not to be explained by the exigencies of a sermon.[a] On the other hand, Heinrich Heine, and other writers of his sort, give us the spectacle of the tables completely turned, and of Hebraism brought in just as a foil and contrast to Hellenism, and to make the superiority of Hellenism more manifest. In both these cases there is injustice and misrepresentation. The aim and end of both Hebraism and Hellenism is, as I have said, one and the same, and this aim and end is august and admirable.

Still, they pursue this aim by very different courses. The uppermost idea with Hellenism is to see things as they really are; the uppermost idea with Hebraism is conduct and obedience. Nothing can do away with this ineffaceable difference. The Greek quarrel with the body

---

[a] Frederick Robertson (1816–53), a popular preacher at Trinity Chapel, Brighton, whose sermons Arnold had been reading with admiration.

and its desires is, that they hinder right thinking; the Hebrew quarrel with them is, that they hinder right acting. "He that keepeth the law, happy is he;" "Blessed is the man that feareth the Eternal, that delighteth greatly in his commandments;"—that is the Hebrew notion of felicity; and, pursued with passion and tenacity, this notion would not let the Hebrew rest till, as is well known, he had at last got out of the law a network of prescriptions to enwrap his whole life, to govern every moment of it, every impulse, every action. The Greek notion of felicity, on the other hand, is perfectly conveyed in these words of a great French moralist: *"C'est le bonheur des hommes,"*— when? when they abhor that which is evil?— no; when they exercise themselves in the law of the Lord day and night?—no; when they die daily?—no; when they walk about the New Jerusalem with palms in their hands?—no; but when they think aright, when their thought hits: *"quand ils pensent juste."*[b] At the bottom of both the Greek and the Hebrew notion is the desire, native in man, for reason and the will of God, the feeling after the universal order,—in a word, the love of God. But, while Hebraism seizes upon certain plain, capital intimations of the universal order, and rivets itself, one may say, with unequalled grandeur of earnestness and intensity on the study and observance of them, the bent of Hellenism is to follow, with flexible activity, the whole play of the universal order, to be apprehensive of missing any part of it, of sacrificing one part to another, to slip away from resting in this or that intimation of it, however capital. An unclouded clearness of mind, an unimpeded play of thought, is what this bent drives at. The governing idea of Hellenism is *spontaneity of consciousness*; that of Hebraism, *strictness of conscience*.

Christianity changed nothing in this essential bent of Hebraism to set doing above knowing. Self-conquest, self-devotion, the following not our own individual will, but the will of God, *obedience*, is the fundamental idea of this form, also, of the discipline to which we have attached the general name of Hebraism. Only, as the old law and the network of prescriptions with which it enveloped human life were evidently a motive-power not driving and searching enough to produce the result aimed at,—patient continuance in well-doing, self-conquest,— Christianity substituted for them boundless devotion to that inspiring and affecting pattern of self-conquest offered by Jesus

[b] Arnold is quoting from Sainte-Beuve (see above p. 58), *Causeries du lundi* (1862).

Christ; and by the new motive-power, of which the essence was this, though the love and admiration of Christian churches have for centuries been employed in varying, amplifying, and adorning the plain description of it, Christianity, as St. Paul truly says, "establishes the law," and in the strength of the ampler power which she has thus supplied to fulfil it, has accomplished the miracles, which we all see, of her history.

So long as we do not forget that both Hellenism and Hebraism are profound and admirable manifestations of man's life, tendencies, and powers, and that both of them aim at a like final result, we can hardly insist too strongly on the divergence of line and of operation with which they proceed. It is a divergence so great that it most truly, as the prophet Zechariah says, "has raised up thy sons, O Zion, against thy sons, O Greece!" The difference whether it is by doing or by knowing that we set most store, and the practical consequences which follow from this difference, leave their mark on all the history of our race and of its development. Language may be abundantly quoted from both Hellenism and Hebraism to make it seem that one follows the same current as the other towards the same goal. They are, truly, borne towards the same goal; but the currents which bear them are infinitely different. It is true, Solomon will praise knowing: "Understanding is a well-spring of life unto him that hath it." And in the New Testament, again, Jesus Christ is a "light," and "truth makes us free." It is true, Aristotle will undervalue knowing: "In what concerns virtue," says he, "three things are necessary—knowledge, deliberate will, and perseverance; but, whereas the two last are all-important, the first is a matter of little importance." It is true that with the same impatience with which St. James enjoins a man to be not a forgetful hearer, but a *doer of the word*, Epictetus exhorts us to *do* what we have demonstrated to ourselves we ought to do; or he taunts us with futility, for being armed at all points to prove that lying is wrong, yet all the time continuing to lie. It is true, Plato, in words which are almost the words of the New Testament or the Imitation,ᶜ calls life a learning to die. But underneath the superficial agreement the fundamental divergence still subsists. The understanding of Solomon is "the walking in the way of the commandments;" this is "the way of peace," and

---

ᶜ Thomas à Kempis, *The Imitation of Christ* (probably completed in 1424), a frequently reprinted work of late-medieval mysticism about whose authorship there had long been dispute: see Arnold's further references on pp. 132, 174, 189–90.

it is of this that blessedness comes. In the New Testament, the truth which gives us the peace of God and makes us free, is the love of Christ constraining us to crucify, as he did, and with a like purpose of moral regeneration, the flesh with its affections and lusts, and thus establishing, as we have seen, the law. The moral virtues, on the other hand, are with Aristotle but the porch and access to the intellectual, and with these last is blessedness. That partaking of the divine life, which both Hellenism and Hebraism, as we have said, fix as their crowning aim, Plato expressly denies to the man of practical virtue merely, of self-conquest with any other motive than that of perfect intellectual vision. He reserves it for the lover of pure knowledge, of seeing things as they really are, — the φιλομαθής.

Both Hellenism and Hebraism arise out of the wants of human nature, and address themselves to satisfying those wants. But their methods are so different, they lay stress on such different points, and call into being by their respective disciplines such different activities, that the face which human nature presents when it passes from the hands of one of them to those of the other, is no longer the same. To get rid of one's ignorance, to see things as they are, and by seeing them as they are to see them in their beauty, is the simple and attractive ideal which Hellenism holds out before human nature; and from the simplicity and charm of this ideal, Hellenism, and human life in the hands of Hellenism, is invested with a kind of aërial ease, clearness, and radiancy; they are full of what we call sweetness and light. Difficulties are kept out of view, and the beauty and rationalness of the ideal have all our thoughts. "The best man is he who most tries to perfect himself, and the happiest man is he who most feels that he *is* perfecting himself," — this account of the matter by Socrates, the true Socrates of the *Memorabilia*, has something so simple, spontaneous, and unsophisticated about it, that it seems to fill us with clearness and hope when we hear it. But there is a saying which I have heard attributed to Mr. Carlyle about Socrates, — a very happy saying, whether it is really Mr. Carlyle's or not, — which excellently marks the essential point in which Hebraism differs from Hellenism. "Socrates," this saying goes, "is terribly *at ease in Zion*." Hebraism, — and here is the source of its wonderful strength, — has always been severely preoccupied with an awful sense of the impossibility of being at ease in Zion; of the difficulties which oppose themselves to man's pursuit or attainment of that perfection of which Socrates talks so hopefully, and, as from this point of view one might almost say, so glibly. It is all very well to talk of getting rid of one's ignorance, of seeing things in their reality, seeing them in their beauty; but how is this to be done when there is something which thwarts and spoils all our efforts?

This something is *sin*; and the space which sin fills in Hebraism, as compared with Hellenism, is indeed prodigious. This obstacle to perfection fills the whole scene, and perfection appears remote and rising away from earth, in the background. Under the name of sin, the difficulties of knowing oneself and conquering oneself which impede man's passage to perfection, become, for Hebraism, a positive, active entity hostile to man, a mysterious power which I heard Dr. Pusey the other day, in one of his impressive sermons, compare to a hideous hunch-back seated on our shoulders, and which it is the main business of our lives to hate and oppose.[d] The discipline of the Old Testament may be summed up as a discipline teaching us to abhor and flee from sin; the discipline of the New Testament, as a discipline teaching us to die to it. As Hellenism speaks of thinking clearly, seeing things in their essence and beauty, as a grand and precious feat for man to achieve, so Hebraism speaks of becoming conscious of sin, of awakening to a sense of sin, as a feat of this kind. It is obvious to what wide divergence these differing tendencies, actively followed, must lead. As one passes and repasses from Hellenism to Hebraism, from Plato to St. Paul, one feels inclined to rub one's eyes and ask oneself whether man is indeed a gentle and simple being, showing the traces of a noble and divine nature; or an unhappy chained captive, labouring with groanings that cannot be uttered to free himself from the body of this death.

Apparently it was the Hellenic conception of human nature which was unsound, for the world could not live by it. Absolutely to call it unsound, however, is to fall into the common error of its Hebraising enemies; but it was unsound at that particular moment of man's development, it was premature. The indispensable basis of conduct and self-control, the platform upon which alone the perfection aimed at by Greece can come into bloom, was not to be reached by our race so easily; centuries of probation and discipline were needed to bring

[d] Edward Bouverie Pusey (1800–82), Regius Professor of Hebrew at Oxford, had been prominent in the Oxford Movement (see above p. 73), and remained one of the leaders of High-Church Anglicanism.

us to it. Therefore the bright promise of Hellenism faded, and Hebraism ruled the world. Then was seen that astonishing spectacle, so well marked by the often-quoted words of the prophet Zechariah, when men of all languages of the nations took hold of the skirt of him that was a Jew, saying:—"*We will go with you, for we have heard that God is with you.*" And the Hebraism which thus received and ruled a world all gone out of the way and altogether become unprofitable, was, and could not but be, the later, the more spiritual, the more attractive development of Hebraism. It was Christianity; that is to say, Hebraism aiming at self-conquest and rescue from the thrall of vile affections, not by obedience to the letter of a law, but by conformity to the image of a self-sacrificing example. To a world stricken with moral enervation Christianity offered its spectacle of an inspired self-sacrifice; to men who refused themselves nothing, it showed one who refused himself everything;—"*my Saviour banished joy!*" says George Herbert. When the *alma Venus*, the life-giving and joy-giving power of nature, so fondly cherished by the Pagan world, could not save her followers from self-dissatisfaction and ennui, the severe words of the apostle came bracingly and refreshingly: "Let no man deceive you with vain words, for because of these things cometh the wrath of God upon the children of disobedience." Through age after age and generation after generation, our race, or all that part of our race which was most living and progressive, was *baptized into a death*; and endeavoured, by suffering in the flesh, to cease from sin. Of this endeavour, the animating labours and afflictions of early Christianity, the touching asceticism of mediaeval Christianity, are the great historical manifestations. Literary monuments of it, each in its own way incomparable, remain in the Epistles of St. Paul, in St. Augustine's Confessions and in the two original and simplest books of the Imitation.[1]

Of two disciplines laying their main stress, the one, on clear intelligence, the other, on firm obedience; the one, on comprehensively knowing the grounds of one's duty, the other, on diligently practising it; the one, on taking all possible care (to use Bishop Wilson's words again) that the light we have be not darkness, the other, that according to the best light we have we diligently walk,—the priority naturally belongs to that discipline which braces all man's moral powers, and

---

[1] The two first books.

founds for him an indispensable basis of character. And, therefore, it is justly said of the Jewish people, who were charged with setting powerfully forth that side of the divine order to which the words *conscience* and *self-conquest* point, that they were "entrusted with the oracles of God;" as it is justly said of Christianity, which followed Judaism and which set forth this side with a much deeper effectiveness and a much wider influence, that the wisdom of the old Pagan world was foolishness compared to it. No words of devotion and admiration can be too strong to render thanks to these beneficent forces which have so borne forward humanity in its appointed work of coming to the knowledge and possession of itself; above all, in those great moments when their action was the wholesomest and the most necessary.

But the evolution of these forces, separately and in themselves, is not the whole evolution of humanity, — their single history is not the whole history of man; whereas their admirers are always apt to make it stand for the whole history. Hebraism and Hellenism are, neither of them, the *law* of human development, as their admirers are prone to make them; they are, each of them, *contributions* to human development, — august contributions, invaluable contributions; and each showing itself to us more august, more invaluable, more preponderant over the other, according to the moment in which we take them, and the relation in which we stand to them. The nations of our modern world, children of that immense and salutary movement which broke up the Pagan world, inevitably stand to Hellenism in a relation which dwarfs it, and to Hebraism in a relation which magnifies it. They are inevitably prone to take Hebraism as the law of human development, and not as simply a contribution to it, however precious. And yet the lesson must perforce be learned, that the human spirit is wider than the most priceless of the forces which bear it onward, and that to the whole development of man Hebraism itself is, like Hellenism, but a contribution.

Perhaps we may help ourselves to see this clearer by an illustration drawn from the treatment of a single great idea which has profoundly engaged the human spirit, and has given it eminent opportunities for showing its nobleness and energy. It surely must be perceived that the idea of immortality, as this idea rises in its generality before the human spirit, is something grander, truer, and more satisfying, than it is in the particular forms by which St. Paul, in the famous fifteenth chapter of the Epistle to the Corinthians, and Plato, in the *Phædo*, endeavour to develop and establish it. Surely we cannot but feel, that the argumentation with which the Hebrew apostle goes about to expound this great idea is, after all, confused and inconclusive; and that the reasoning, drawn from analogies of likeness and equality, which is employed upon it by the Greek philosopher, is over-subtle and sterile. Above and beyond the inadequate solutions which Hebraism and Hellenism here attempt, extends the immense and august problem itself, and the human spirit which gave birth to it. And this single illustration may suggest to us how the same thing happens in other cases also.

But meanwhile, by alternations of Hebraism and Hellenism, of a man's intellectual and moral impulses, of the effort to see things as they really are, and the effort to win peace by self-conquest, the human spirit proceeds; and each of these two forces has its appointed hours of culmination and seasons of rule. As the great movement of Christianity was a triumph of Hebraism and man's moral impulses, so the great movement which goes by the name of the Renascence[2] was an uprising and re-instatement of man's intellectual impulses and of Hellenism. We in England, the devoted children of Protestantism, chiefly know the Renascence by its subordinate and secondary side of the Reformation. The Reformation has been often called a Hebraising revival, a return to the ardour and sincereness of primitive Christianity. No one, however, can study the development of Protestantism and of Protestant churches without feeling that into the Reformation too, — Hebraising child of the Renascence and offspring of its fervour, rather than its intelligence, as it undoubtedly was, — the subtle Hellenic leaven of the Renascence found its way, and that the exact respective parts, in the Reformation, of Hebraism and of Hellenism, are not easy to separate. But what we may with truth say is, that all which Protestantism was to itself clearly conscious of, all which it succeeded in clearly setting forth in words, had the characters of Hebraism rather than of Hellenism. The Reformation was strong, in that it was an earnest return to the Bible and to doing from the heart the will of God as there written. It was weak, in that it never consciously grasped or applied the central idea of the Renascence, —

---

[2] I have ventured to give to the foreign word *Renaissance*, — destined to become of more common use amongst us as the movement which it denotes comes, as it will come, increasingly to interest us, — an English form.

the Hellenic idea of pursuing, in all lines of activity, the law and science, to use Plato's words, of things as they really are. Whatever direct superiority, therefore, Protestantism had over Catholicism was a moral superiority, a superiority arising out of its greater sincerity and earnestness, — at the moment of its apparition at any rate, — in dealing with the heart and conscience. Its pretensions to an intellectual superiority are in general quite illusory. For Hellenism, for the thinking side in man as distinguished from the acting side, the attitude of mind of Protestantism towards the Bible in no respect differs from the attitude of mind of Catholicism towards the Church. The mental habit of him who imagines that Balaam's ass spoke, in no respect differs from the mental habit of him who imagines that a Madonna of wood or stone winked; and the one, who says that God's Church makes him believe what he believes, and the other, who says that God's Word makes him believe what he believes, are for the philosopher perfectly alike in not really and truly knowing, when they say *God's Church* and *God's Word*, what it is they say, or whereof they affirm.

In the sixteenth century, therefore, Hellenism re-entered the world, and again stood in presence of Hebraism, — a Hebraism renewed and purged. Now, it has not been enough observed, how, in the seventeenth century, a fate befell Hellenism in some respects analogous to that which befell it at the commencement of our era. The Renascence, that great re-awakening of Hellenism, that irresistible return of humanity to nature and to seeing things as they are, which in art, in literature, and in physics, produced such splendid fruits, had, like the anterior Hellenism of the Pagan world, a side of moral weakness and of relaxation or insensibility of the moral fibre, which in Italy showed itself with the most startling plainness, but which in France, England, and other countries was very apparent too. Again this loss of spiritual balance, this exclusive preponderance given to man's perceiving and knowing side, this unnatural defect of his feeling and acting side, provoked a reaction. Let us trace that reaction where it most nearly concerns us.

Science has now made visible to everybody the great and pregnant elements of difference which lie in race, and in how signal a manner they make the genius and history of an Indo-European people vary from those of a Semitic people. Hellenism is of Indo-European growth, Hebraism is of Semitic growth; and we English, a nation of

Indo-European stock, seem to belong naturally to the movement of Hellenism. But nothing more strongly marks the essential unity of man, than the affinities we can perceive, in this point or that, between members of one family of peoples and members of another. And no affinity of this kind is more strongly marked than that likeness in the strength and prominence of the moral fibre, which, notwithstanding immense elements of difference, knits in some special sort the genius and history of us English, and our American descendants across the Atlantic, to the genius and history of the Hebrew people. Puritanism, which has been so great a power in the English nation, and in the strongest part of the English nation, was originally the reaction in the seventeenth century of the conscience and moral sense of our race, against the moral indifference and lax rule of conduct which in the sixteenth century came in with the Renascence. It was a reaction of Hebraism against Hellenism; and it powerfully manifested itself, as was natural, in a people with much of what we call a Hebraising turn, with a signal affinity for the bent which was the master-bent of Hebrew life. Eminently Indo-European by its *humour*, by the power it shows, through this gift, of imaginatively acknowledging the multiform aspects of the problem of life, and of thus getting itself unfixed from its own over-certainty, of smiling at its own over-tenacity, our race has yet (and a great part of its strength lies here), in matters of practical life and moral conduct, a strong share of the assuredness, the tenacity, the intensity of the Hebrews. This turn manifested itself in Puritanism, and has had a great part in shaping our history for the last two hundred years. Undoubtedly it checked and changed amongst us that movement of the Renascence which we see producing in the reign of Elizabeth such wonderful fruits. Undoubtedly it stopped the prominent rule and direct development of that order of ideas which we call by the name of Hellenism, and gave the first rank to a different order of ideas. Apparently, too, as we said of the former defeat of Hellenism, if Hellenism was defeated, this shows that Hellenism was imperfect, and that its ascendency at the moment would not have been for the world's good.

Yet there is a very important difference between the defeat inflicted on Hellenism by Christianity eighteen hundred years ago, and the check given to the Renascence by Puritanism. The greatness of the difference is well measured by the difference in force, beauty, significance, and usefulness, between primitive Christianity and Protestantism. Eighteen hundred years ago it was altogether the hour of Hebraism. Primitive Christianity was legitimately and truly the ascendant force in the world at that time, and the way of mankind's progress lay through its full development. Another hour in man's development began in the fifteenth century, and the main road of his progress then lay for a time through Hellenism. Puritanism was no longer the central current of the world's progress, it was a side stream crossing the central current and checking it. The cross and the check may have been necessary and salutary, but that does not do away with the essential difference between the main stream of man's advance and a cross or side stream. For more than two hundred years the main stream of man's advance has moved towards knowing himself and the world, seeing things as they are, spontaneity of consciousness; the main impulse of a great part, and that the strongest part, of our nation has been towards strictness of conscience. They have made the secondary the principal at the wrong moment, and the principal they have at the wrong moment treated as secondary. This contravention of the natural order has produced, as such contravention always must produce, a certain confusion and false movement, of which we are now beginning to feel, in almost every direction, the inconvenience. In all directions our habitual courses of action seem to be losing efficaciousness, credit, and control, both with others and even with ourselves. Everywhere we see the beginnings of confusion, and we want a clue to some sound order and authority. This we can only get by going back upon the actual instincts and forces which rule our life, seeing them as they really are, connecting them with other instincts and forces, and enlarging our whole view and rule of life.

# CHAPTER V

# Porro Unum Est Necessarium[a]

The matter here opened is so large, and the trains of thought to which it gives rise are so manifold, that we must be careful to limit ourselves scrupulously to what has a direct bearing upon our actual discussion. We have found that at the bottom of our present unsettled state, so full of the seeds of trouble, lies the notion of its being the prime right and happiness, for each of us, to affirm himself, and his ordinary self; to be doing, and to be doing freely and as he likes. We have found at the bottom of it the disbelief in right reason as a lawful authority. It was easy to show from our practice and current history that this is so; but it was impossible to show why it is so without taking a somewhat wider sweep and going into things a little more deeply. Why, in fact, should good, well-meaning, energetic, sensible people, like the bulk of our countrymen, come to have such light belief in right reason, and such an exaggerated value for their own independent doing, however crude? The answer is: because of an exclusive and excessive development in them, without due allowance for time, place and circumstance, of that side of human nature, and that group of human forces, to which we have given the general name of Hebraism. Because they have thought their real and only important homage was owed to a power concerned with their obedience rather than with their intelligence, a power interested in the moral side of their nature almost exclusively. Thus they have been led to regard in themselves, as the one thing needful, *strictness of conscience*, the staunch adherence to some fixed law of doing we have got already, instead of *spontaneity of*

---

[a] 'But one thing is needful'; Luke 10:42 (Vulgate version).

*consciousness*, which tends continually to enlarge our whole law of doing. They have fancied themselves to have in their religion a sufficient basis for the whole of their life fixed and certain for ever, a full law of conduct and a full law of thought, so far as thought is needed, as well; whereas what they really have is a law of conduct, a law of unexampled power for enabling them to war against the law of sin in their members and not to serve it in the lusts thereof. The book which contains this invaluable law they call the Word of God, and attribute to it, as I have said, and as, indeed, is perfectly well known, a reach and sufficiency co-extensive with all the wants of human nature.

This might, no doubt, be so, if humanity were not the composite thing it is, if it had only or in quite overpowering eminence, a moral side, and the group of instincts and powers which we call moral. But it has besides, and in notable eminence, an intellectual side, and the group of instincts and powers which we call intellectual. No doubt, mankind makes in general its progress in a fashion which gives at one time full swing to one of these groups of instincts, at another time to the other; and man's faculties are so intertwined, that when his moral side, and the current of force which we call Hebraism, is uppermost, this side will manage somehow to provide, or appear to provide, satisfaction for his intellectual needs; and when his intellectual side, and the current of force which we call Hellenism, is uppermost, this again will provide, or appear to provide, satisfaction for men's moral needs. But sooner or later it becomes manifest that when the two sides of humanity proceed in this fashion of alternate preponderance, and not of mutual understanding and balance, the side which is uppermost does not really provide in a satisfactory manner for the needs of the side which is undermost, and a state of confusion is, sooner or later, the result. The Hellenic half of our nature, bearing rule, makes a sort of provision for the Hebrew half, but it turns out to be an inadequate provision; and again the Hebrew half of our nature, bearing rule, makes a sort of provision for the Hellenic half, but this, too, turns out to be an inadequate provision. The true and smooth order of humanity's development is not reached in either way. And therefore, while we willingly admit with the Christian apostle that the world by wisdom, — that is, by the isolated preponderance of its intellectual impulses, — knew not God, or the true order of things, it is yet necessary, also, to set up a sort of converse to this proposition, and to say likewise (what is equally true) that the world by Puritanism knew not God. And it is on this converse of the apostle's proposition that it is particularly needful to insist in our own country just at present.

Here, indeed, is the answer to many criticisms which have been addressed to all that we have said in praise of sweetness and light. Sweetness and light evidently have to do with the bent or side in humanity which we call Hellenic. Greek intelligence has obviously for its essence the instinct for what Plato calls the true, firm, intelligible law of things; the law of light, of seeing things as they are. Even in the natural sciences, where the Greeks had not time and means adequately to apply this instinct, and where we have gone a great deal further than they did, it is this instinct which is the root of the whole matter and the ground of all our success; and this instinct the world has mainly learnt of the Greeks, inasmuch as they are humanity's most signal manifestation of it. Greek art, again, Greek beauty, have their root in the same impulse to see things as they really are, inasmuch as Greek art and beauty rest on fidelity to nature,—the *best* nature,—and on a delicate discrimination of what this best nature is. To say we work for sweetness and light, then, is only another way of saying that we work for Hellenism. But, oh! cry many people, sweetness and light are not enough; you must put strength or energy along with them, and make a kind of trinity of strength, sweetness and light, and then, perhaps, you may do some good. That is to say, we are to join Hebraism, strictness of the moral conscience, and manful walking by the best light we have, together with Hellenism, inculcate both, and rehearse the praises of both.

Or, rather, we may praise both in conjunction, but we must be careful to praise Hebraism most. "Culture," says an acute, though somewhat rigid critic, Mr. Sidgwick, "diffuses sweetness and light. I do not undervalue these blessings, but religion gives fire and strength, and the world wants fire and strength even more than sweetness and light."[b] By religion, let me explain, Mr. Sidgwick here means particularly that Puritanism on the insufficiency of which I have been commenting and to which he says I am unfair. Now, no doubt, it is possible to be a fanatical partisan of light and the instincts which push us to it, a fanatical enemy of strictness of moral conscience and the instincts which push us to it. A fanaticism of this sort deforms and

[b] Henry Sidgwick (1838–1900), 'The Prophet of Culture', *Macmillian's Magazine* (1867).

vulgarises the well-known work, in some respects so remarkable, of the late Mr. Buckle. Such a fanaticism carries its own mark with it, in lacking sweetness; and its own penalty, in that, lacking sweetness, it comes in the end to lack light too. And the Greeks,—the great exponents of humanity's bent for sweetness and light united, of its perception that the truth of things must be at the same time beauty,— singularly escaped the fanaticism which we moderns, whether we Hellenise or whether we Hebraise, are so apt to show. They arrived,—though failing, as has been said, to give adequate practical satisfaction to the claims of man's moral side,—at the idea of a comprehensive adjustment of the claims of both the sides in man, the moral as well as the intellectual, of a full estimate of both, and of a reconciliation of both; an idea which is philosophically of the greatest value, and the best of lessons for us moderns. So we ought to have no difficulty in conceding to Mr. Sidgwick that manful walking by the best light one has,— fire and strength as he calls it,—has its high value as well as culture, the endeavour to see things in their truth and beauty, the pursuit of sweetness and light. But whether at this or that time, and to this or that set of persons, one ought to insist most on the praises of fire and strength, or on the praises of sweetness and light, must depend, one would think, on the circumstances and needs of that particular time and those particular persons. And all that we have been saying, and indeed any glance at the world around us shows that with us, with the most respectable and strongest part of us, the ruling force is now, and long has been, a Puritan force,—the care for fire and strength, strictness of conscience, Hebraism, rather than the care for sweetness and light, spontaneity of consciousness, Hellenism.

Well, then, what is the good of our now rehearsing the praises of fire and strength to ourselves, who dwell too exclusively on them already? When Mr. Sidgwick says so broadly, that the world wants fire and strength even more than sweetness and light, is he not carried away by a turn for broad generalisation? does he not forget that the world is not all of one piece, and every piece with the same needs at the same time? It may be true that the Roman world at the beginning of our era, or Leo the Tenth's Court at the time of the Reformation, or French society in the eighteenth century, needed fire and strength even more than sweetness and light. But can it be said that the Barbarians who overran the empire needed fire and strength even more than sweetness and light; or that the Puritans needed them more; or that Mr. Murphy, the Birmingham lecturer, and his friends, need them more?

The Puritan's great danger is that he imagines himself in possession of a rule telling him the *unum necessarium*, or one thing needful, and that he then remains satisfied with a very crude conception of what this rule really is and what it tells him, thinks he has now knowledge and henceforth needs only to act, and, in this dangerous state of assurance and self-satisfaction, proceeds to give full swing to a number of the instincts of his ordinary self. Some of the instincts of his ordinary self he has, by the help of his rule of life, conquered; but others which he has not conquered by this help he is so far from perceiving to need subjugation, and to be instincts of an inferior self, that he even fancies it to be his right and duty, in virtue of having conquered a limited part of himself, to give unchecked swing to the remainder. He is, I say, a victim of Hebraism, of the tendency to cultivate strictness of conscience rather than spontaneity of consciousness. And what he wants is a larger conception of human nature, showing him the number of other points at which his nature must come to its best, besides the points which he himself knows and thinks of. There is no *unum necessarium*, or one thing needful, which can free human nature from the obligation of trying to come to its best at all these points. The real *unum necessarium* for us is to come to our best at all points. Instead of our "one thing needful," justifying in us vulgarity, hideousness, ignorance, violence, — our vulgarity, hideousness, ignorance, violence, are really so many touchstones which try our one thing needful, and which prove that in the state, at any rate, in which we ourselves have it, it is not all we want. And as the force which encourages us to stand staunch and fast by the rule and ground we have is Hebraism, so the force which encourages us to go back upon this rule, and to try the very ground on which we appear to stand, is Hellenism, — a turn for giving our consciousness free play and enlarging its range. And what I say is, not that Hellenism is always for everybody more wanted than Hebraism, but that for Mr. Murphy at this particular moment, and for the great majority of us his fellow-countrymen, it is more wanted.

Nothing is more striking than to observe in how many ways a limited conception of human nature, the notion of a one thing needful, a one side in us to be made uppermost, the disregard of a full and

harmonious development of ourselves, tells injuriously on our thinking and acting. In the first place, our hold upon the rule or standard,
to which we look for our one thing needful, tends to become less and
less near and vital, our conception of it more and more mechanical,
and more and more unlike the thing itself as it was conceived in the
mind where it originated. The dealings of Puritanism with the writings of St. Paul afford a noteworthy illustration of this. Nowhere so
much as in the writings of St. Paul, and in that great apostle's greatest
work, the Epistle to the Romans, has Puritanism found what seemed
to furnish it with the one thing needful, and to give it canons of truth
absolute and final. Now all writings, as has been already said, even the
most precious writings and the most fruitful, must inevitably, from the
very nature of things, be but contributions to human thought and
human development, which extend wider than they do. Indeed, St.
Paul, in the very Epistle of which we are speaking, shows, when he
asks, "Who hath known the mind of the Lord?"—who hath known,
that is, the true and divine order of things in its entirety,—that he
himself acknowledges this fully. And we have already pointed out in
another Epistle of St. Paul a great and vital idea of the human spirit,—
the idea of immortality,—transcending and overlapping, so to speak,
the expositor's power to give it adequate definition and expression.

But quite distinct from the question whether St. Paul's expression,
or any man's expression, can be a perfect and final expression of
truth, comes the question whether we rightly seize and understand his
expression as it exists. Now, perfectly to seize another man's meaning,
as it stood in his own mind, is not easy; especially when the man is
separated from us by such differences of race, training, time, and
circumstances as St. Paul. But there are degrees of nearness in getting at a man's meaning; and though we cannot arrive quite at what
St. Paul had in his mind, yet we may come near it. And who, that
comes thus near it, must not feel how terms which St. Paul employs,
in trying to follow with his analysis of such profound power and
originality some of the most delicate, intricate, obscure, and con-
tradictory workings and states of the human spirit, are detached and
employed by Puritanism, not in the connected and fluid way in which
St. Paul employs them, and for which alone words are really meant,
but in an isolated, fixed, mechanical way, as if they were talismans;
and how all trace and sense of St. Paul's true movement of ideas, and
sustained masterly analysis, is thus lost? Who, I say, that has watched

Puritanism,—the force which so strongly Hebraises, which so takes St. Paul's writings as something absolute and final, containing the one thing needful,—handle such terms as *grace, faith, election, righteousness,* but must feel, not only that these terms have for the mind of Puritanism a sense false and misleading, but also that this sense is the most monstrous and grotesque caricature of the sense of St. Paul, and that his true meaning is by these worshippers of his words altogether lost?

Or to take another eminent example, in which not Puritanism only, but, one may say, the whole religious world, by their mechanical use of St. Paul's writings, can be shown to miss or change his real meaning. The whole religious world, one may say, use now the word *resurrection,*—a word which is so often in their thoughts and on their lips, and which they find so often in St. Paul's writings,—in one sense only. They use it to mean a rising again after the physical death of the body. Now it is quite true that St. Paul speaks of resurrection in this sense, that he tries to describe and explain it, and that he condemns those who doubt and deny it. But it is true, also, that in nine cases out of ten when St. Paul thinks and speaks of resurrection, he thinks and speaks of it in a sense different from this;—in the sense of a rising to a new life before the physical death of the body, and not after it. The idea on which we have already touched, the profound idea of being baptized into the death of the great exemplar of self-devotion and self-annulment, of repeating in our own person, by virtue of identification with our exemplar, his course of self-devotion and self-annulment, and of thus coming, within the limits of our present life, to a new life, in which, as in the death going before it, we are identified with our exemplar,—this is the fruitful and original conception of being *risen with Christ* which possesses the mind of St. Paul, and this is the central point round which, with such incomparable emotion and eloquence, all his teaching moves. For him, the life after our physical death is really in the main but a consequence and continuation of the inexhaustible energy of the new life thus originated on this side the grave. This grand Pauline idea of Christian resurrection is worthily rehearsed in one of the noblest collects of the Prayer-Book, and is destined, no doubt, to fill a more and more important place in the Christianity of the future. But meanwhile, almost as signal as the essentialness of this characteristic idea in St. Paul's teaching, is the completeness with which the worshippers of St. Paul's words as an absolute final expression of saving truth have lost it, and have substituted for the apostle's living and near conception of a resurrection now, their mechanical and remote conception of a resurrection hereafter.

In short, so fatal is the notion of possessing, even in the most precious words or standards, the one thing needful, of having in them, once for all, a full and sufficient measure of light to guide us, and of there being no duty left for us except to make our practice square exactly with them, — so fatal, I say, is this notion to the right knowledge and comprehension of the very words or standards we thus adopt, and to such strange distortions and perversions of them does it inevitably lead, that whenever we hear that commonplace which Hebraism, if we venture to inquire what a man knows, is so apt to bring out against us, in disparagement of what we call culture, and in praise of a man's sticking to the one thing needful, — *he knows*, says Hebraism, *his Bible!* — whenever we hear this said, we may, without any elaborate defence of culture, content ourselves with answering simply: "No man, who knows nothing else, knows even his Bible."

Now the force which we have so much neglected, Hellenism, may be liable to fail in moral strength and earnestness, but by the law of its nature, — the very same law which makes it sometimes deficient in intensity when intensity is required, — it opposes itself to the notion of cutting our being in two, of attributing to one part the dignity of dealing with the one thing needful, and leaving the other part to take its chance, which is the bane of Hebraism. Essential in Hellenism is the impulse to the development of the whole man, to connecting and harmonising all parts of him, perfecting all, leaving none to take their chance.

The characteristic bent of Hellenism, as has been said, is to find the intelligible law of things, to see them in their true nature and as they really are. But many things are not seen in their true nature and as they really are, unless they are seen beautiful. Behaviour is not intelligible, does not account for itself to the mind and show the reason for its existing, unless it is beautiful. The same with discourse, the same with song, the same with worship, all of them modes in which man pours his activity and expresses himself. To think that when one produces in these what is mean, or vulgar, or hideous, one can be permitted to plead that one has that within which passes show; to suppose that the possession of what benefits and satisfies one part of our being can make allowable either discourse like Mr. Murphy's, or poetry like the hymns we all hear, or places of worship like the chapels we all see,—this it is abhorrent to the nature of Hellenism to concede. And to be, like our honoured and justly honoured Faraday, a great natural philosopher with one side of his being and a Sandemanian with the other, would to Archimedes have been impossible.[c]

It is evident to what a many-sided perfecting of man's powers and activities this demand of Hellenism for satisfaction to be given to the mind by everything which we do, is calculated to impel our race. It has its dangers, as has been fully granted. The notion of this sort of equipollency in man's modes of activity may lead to moral relaxation; what we do not make our one thing needful, we may come to treat not enough as if it were needful, though it is indeed very needful and at the same time very hard. Still, what side in us has not its dangers, and which of our impulses can be a talisman to give us perfection outright, and not merely a help to bring us towards it? Has not Hebraism, as we have shown, its dangers as well as Hellenism? Or have we used so excessively the tendencies in ourselves to which Hellenism makes appeal, that we are now suffering from it? Are we not, on the contrary, now suffering because we have not enough used these tendencies as a help towards perfection?

For we see whither it has brought us, the long exclusive predominance of Hebraism,—the insisting on perfection in one part of our nature and not in all; the singling out the moral side, the side of obedience and action, for such intent regard; making strictness of the moral conscience so far the principal thing, and putting off for hereafter and for another world the care for being complete at all points, the full and harmonious development of our humanity. Instead of watching and following on its ways the desire which, as Plato says, "for ever through all the universe tends towards that which is lovely," we think that the world has settled its accounts with this desire, knows what this desire wants of it, and that all the impulses of our ordinary self which do not conflict with the terms of this settlement, in our narrow view of it, we may follow unrestrainedly, under the sanction of some such text as "Not slothful in business," or, "Whatsoever thy hand findeth to do, do it with all thy might," or something else of the same kind. And to any of these impulses we soon come to give that

---

[c] Michael Faraday (1791–1867) was the most distinguished physicist of his day, but a lifelong member of the Sandemanians, a Presbyterian sect which believed in the literal interpretation of the Bible.

same character of a mechanical, absolute law, which we give to our religion; we regard it, as we do our religion, as an object for strictness of conscience, not for spontaneity of consciousness; for unremitting adherence on its own account, not for going back upon, viewing in its connection with other things, and adjusting to a number of changing circumstances. We treat it, in short, just as we treat our religion, —as machinery. It is in this way that the Barbarians treat their bodily exercises, the Philistines their business, Mr. Spurgeon his voluntary-ism, Mr. Bright the assertion of personal liberty, Mr. Beales the right of meeting in Hyde Park. In all those cases what is needed is a freer play of consciousness upon the object of pursuit; and in all of them Hebraism, the valuing staunchness and earnestness more than this free play, the entire subordination of thinking to doing, has led to a mistaken and misleading treatment of things.

The newspapers a short time ago contained an account of the suicide of a Mr. Smith, secretary to some insurance company, who, it was said, "laboured under the apprehension that he would come to poverty, and that he was eternally lost." And when I read these words, it occurred to me that the poor man who came to such a mournful end was, in truth, a kind of type, —by the selection of his two grand objects of concern, by their isolation from everything else, and their jux-taposition to one another, —of all the strongest, most respectable, and most representative part of our nation. "He laboured under the apprehension that he would come to poverty, and that he was eternally lost." The whole middle class have a conception of things, — a conception which makes us call them Philistines, —just like that of this poor man; though we are seldom, of course, shocked by seeing it take the distressing, violently morbid, and fatal turn, which it took with him. But how generally, with how many of us, are the main concerns of life limited to these two: the concern for making money, and the concern for saving our souls! And how entirely does the narrow and mechanical conception of our secular business proceed from a narrow and mechanical conception of our religious business! What havoc do the united conceptions make of our lives! It is because the second-named of these two master-concerns presents to us the one thing needful in so fixed, narrow, and mechanical a way, that so ignoble a fellow master-concern to it as the first-named becomes possible; and, having been once admitted, takes the same rigid and absolute character as the other.

Poor Mr. Smith had sincerely the nobler master-concern as well as the meaner,—the concern for saving his soul (according to the narrow and mechanical conception which Puritanism has of what the salvation of the soul is), as well as the concern for making money. But let us remark how many people there are especially outside the limits of the serious and conscientious middle class to which Mr. Smith belonged, who take up with a meaner master-concern,—whether it be pleasure, or field-sports, or bodily exercises, or business, or popular agitation,—who take up with one of these exclusively, and neglect Mr. Smith's nobler master-concern, because of the mechanical form which Hebraism has given to this noble master-concern. Hebraism makes it stand, as we have said, as something talismanic, isolated, and all-sufficient, justifying our giving our ordinary selves free play in bodily exercises, or business, or popular agitation, if we have made our accounts square with this master-concern; and, if we have not, rendering other things indifferent, and our ordinary self all we have to follow, and to follow with all the energy that is in us, till we do. Whereas the idea of perfection at all points, the encouraging in ourselves spontaneity of consciousness, and letting a free play of thought live and flow around all our activity, the indisposition to allow one side of our activity to stand as so all-important and all-sufficing that it makes other sides indifferent,—this bent of mind in us may not only check us in following unreservedly a mean master-concern of any kind, but may even, also, bring new life and movement into that side of us with which alone Hebraism concerns itself, and awaken a healthier and less mechanical activity there. Hellenism may thus actually serve to further the designs of Hebraism.

Undoubtedly it thus served in the first days of Christianity. Christianity, as has been said, occupied itself, like Hebraism, with the moral side of man exclusively, with his moral affections and moral conduct; and so far it was but a continuation of Hebraism. But it transformed and renewed Hebraism by criticising a fixed rule, which had become mechanical, and had thus lost its vital motive power; by letting the thought play freely around this old rule, and perceive its inadequacy; by developing a new motive power, which men's moral consciousness could take living hold of, and could move in sympathy with. What was this but an importation of Hellenism, as we have defined it, into Hebraism? St. Paul used the contradiction between the Jew's profession and practice, his shortcomings on that very side of moral affection and moral conduct which the Jew and St. Paul, both of them, regarded as all in all ("Thou that sayest a man should not steal, dost thou steal? thou that sayest a man should not commit adultery, dost thou commit adultery?"), for a proof of the inadequacy of the old rule of life in the Jew's mechanical conception of it; and tried to rescue him by making his consciousness play freely around this rule,—that is, by a so far Hellenic treatment of it. Even so we, too, when we hear so much said of the growth of commercial immorality in our serious middle class, of the melting away of habits of strict probity before the temptation to get quickly rich and to cut a figure in the world; when we see, at any rate, so much confusion of thought and of practice in this great representative class of our nation,—may we not be disposed to say, that this confusion shows that his new motive-power of grace and imputed righteousness has become to the Puritan as mechanical, and with as ineffective a hold upon his practice, as the old motive-power of the law was to the Jew? and that the remedy is the same as that which St. Paul employed,—an importation of what we have called Hellenism into his Hebraism, a making his consciousness flow freely round his petrified rule of life and renew it? Only with this difference: that whereas St. Paul imported Hellenism within the limits of our moral part only, this part being still treated by him as all in all; and whereas he well-nigh exhausted, one may say, and used to the very uttermost, the possibilities of fruitfully importing it on that side exclusively; we ought to try and import it,—guiding ourselves by the ideal of a human nature harmoniously perfect in all points,—into all the lines of our activity. Only by so doing can we rightly quicken, refresh, and renew those very instincts, now so much baffled, to which Hebraism makes appeal.

But if we will not be warned by the confusion visible enough at present in our thinking and acting, that we are on a false line in having developed our Hebrew side so exclusively, and our Hellenic side so feebly and at random, in loving fixed rules of action so much more than the intelligible law of things, let us listen to a remarkable testimony which the opinion of the world around us offers. All the world now sets great and increasing value on three objects which have long been very dear to us, and pursues them in its own way, or tries to pursue them. These three objects are industrial enterprise, bodily exercises, and freedom. Certainly we have, before and beyond our neighbours, given ourselves to these three things with ardent passion and with high success. And this our neighbours cannot but acknowledge; and they must needs, when they themselves turn to these things, have an eye to our example, and take something of our practice.

Now, generally, when people are interested in an object of pursuit, they cannot help feeling an enthusiasm for those who have already laboured successfully at it, and for their success. Not only do they study them, they also love and admire them. In this way a man who is interested in the art of war not only acquaints himself with the performance of great generals, but he has an admiration and enthusiasm for them. So, too, one who wants to be a painter or a poet cannot help loving and admiring the great painters or poets who have gone before him and shown him the way.

But it is strange with how little of love, admiration, or enthusiasm, the world regards us and our freedom, our bodily exercises, and our industrial prowess, much as these things themselves are beginning to interest it. And is not the reason because we follow each of these things in a mechanical manner, as an end in and for itself, and not in reference to a general end of human perfection; and this makes our pursuit of them uninteresting to humanity, and not what the world truly wants? It seems to them mere machinery that we can, knowingly, teach them to worship,—a mere fetish. British freedom, British industry, British muscularity, we work for each of these three things blindly, with no notion of giving each its due proportion and prominence, because we have no ideal of harmonious human perfection before our minds, to set our work in motion, and to guide it. So the rest of the world, desiring industry, or freedom, or bodily strength, yet desiring these not, as we do, absolutely, but as means to something else, imitate, indeed, of our practice what seems useful for them, but us, whose practice they imitate, they seem to entertain neither love nor admiration for.

Let us observe, on the other hand, the love and enthusiasm excited by others who have laboured for these very things. Perhaps of what we call industrial enterprise it is not easy to find examples in former times; but let us consider how Greek freedom and Greek gymnastics have attracted the love and praise of mankind, who give so little love and praise to ours. And what can be the reason of this difference? Surely because the Greeks pursued freedom and pursued gymnastics not mechanically, but with constant reference to some ideal of complete human perfection and happiness. And therefore, in spite of faults and failures, they interest and delight by their pursuit of them all the rest of mankind, who instinctively feel that only as things are pursued with reference to this ideal are they valuable.

Here again, therefore, as in the confusion into which the thought and action of even the steadiest class amongst us is beginning to fall, we seem to have an admonition that we have fostered our Hebraising instincts, our preference of earnestness of doing to delicacy and flexibility of thinking, too exclusively, and have been landed by them in a mechanical and unfruitful routine. And again we seem taught that the development of our Hellenising instincts, seeking ardently the intelligible law of things, and making a stream of fresh thought play freely about our stock notions and habits, is what is most wanted by us at present.

Well, then, from all sides, the more we go into the matter, the currents seem to converge, and together to bear us along towards culture. If we look at the world outside us we find a disquieting absence of sure authority. We discover that only in right reason can we get a source of sure authority; and culture brings us towards right reason. If we look at our own inner world, we find all manner of confusion arising out of the habits of unintelligent routine and one-sided growth, to which a too exclusive worship of fire, strength, earnestness, and action, has brought us. What we want is a fuller harmonious development of our humanity, a free play of thought upon our routine notions, spontaneity of consciousness, sweetness and light; and these are just what culture generates and fosters. We will not stickle for a name, and the name of culture one might easily give up, if only those who decry the frivolous and pedantic sort of culture, but wish at bottom for the same things as we do, would be careful on their part, not, in disparaging and discrediting the false culture, to unwittingly disparage and discredit, among a people with little natural reverence for it, the true also. But what we are concerned for is the thing, not the name; and the thing, call it by what name we will, is simply the enabling ourselves, by getting to know, whether through reading, observing, or thinking, the best that can at present be known in the world, to come as near as we can to the firm intelligible law of things, and thus to get a basis for a less confused action and a more complete perfection than we have at present.

And now, therefore, when we are accused of preaching up a spirit of cultivated inaction, of provoking the earnest lovers of action, of refusing to lend a hand at uprooting certain definite evils, of despairing to find any lasting truth to minister to the diseased spirit of our time, we shall not be so much confounded and embarrassed what to answer for ourselves. We shall say boldly that we do not at all despair of finding some lasting truth to minister to the diseased spirit of our time; but that we have discovered the best way of finding this to be not so much by lending a hand to our friends and countrymen in their actual operations for the removal of certain definite evils, but rather in getting our friends and countrymen to seek culture, to let their consciousness play freely round their present operations and the stock notions on which they are founded, show what these are like, and how related to the intelligible law of things, and auxiliary to true human perfection.

CHAPTER VI

# Our Liberal Practitioners

But an unpretending writer, without a philosophy based on inter-dependent, subordinate, and coherent principles, must not presume to indulge himself too much in generalities. He must keep close to the level ground of common fact, the only safe ground for understandings without a scientific equipment. Therefore, since I have spoken so slightingly of the practical operations in which my friends and countrymen are at this moment engaged for the removal of certain definite evils, I am bound to take, before concluding, some of those operations, and to make them, if I can, show the truth of what I have advanced.

Probably I could hardly give a greater proof of my confessed inex-pertness in reasoning and arguing, than by taking, for my first exam-ple of an operation of this kind, the proceedings for the disestablishment of the Irish Church,[a] which we are now witnessing.[1] It seems so clear that this is surely one of those operations for the uprooting of a certain definite evil in which one's Liberal friends engage, and have a right to complain, and to get impatient, and to reproach one with delicate Conservative scepticism and cultivated inaction, if one does not lend a hand to help them. This does, indeed, seem evident; and yet this operation comes so prominently before us at this moment,[2]—it so challenges everybody's regard,—that one

[1] Written in 1868.     [2] 1868.

[a] The Established (i.e. Anglican) Church in Ireland enjoyed many financial and legal privileges, which were deeply resented by the overwhelmingly Catholic population. In the 1860s Gladstone proposed to 'disestablish' the Irish Church, i.e. to end its uniquely privileged position, but many leading Dissenters in England objected because this meant giving public funds and official status to the Catholic Church.

153

seems cowardly in blinking it. So let us venture to try and see whether this conspicuous operation is one of those round which we need to let our consciousness play freely and reveal what manner of spirit we are of in doing it; or whether it is one which by no means admits the application of this doctrine of ours, and one to which we ought to lend a hand immediately.

# I

Now it seems plain that the present Church-establishment in Ireland is contrary to reason and justice, in so far as the Church of a very small minority of the people there takes for itself all the Church-property of the Irish people. And one would think, that property, assigned for the purpose of providing for a people's religious worship when that worship was one, the State should, when that worship is split into several forms, apportion between those several forms. But the apportionment should be made with due regard to circumstances, taking account only of great differences, which are likely to be lasting, and of considerable communions, which are likely to represent profound and widespread religious characteristics. It should overlook petty differences, which have no serious reason for lasting, and inconsiderable communions, which can hardly be taken to express any broad and necessary religious lineaments of our common nature. This is just in accordance with that maxim about the State which we have more than once used: *The State is of the religion of all its citizens, without the fanaticism of any of them.* Those who deny this, either think so poorly of the State that they do not like to see religion condescend to touch the State, or they think so poorly of religion that they do not like to see the State condescend to touch religion. But no good statesman will easily think thus unworthily either of the State or of religion.

Our statesmen of both parties were inclined, one may say, to follow the natural line of the State's duty, and to make in Ireland some fair apportionment of Church-property between large and radically divided religious communions in that country. But then it was discovered that in Great Britain the national mind, as it is called, is grown averse to endowments for religion and will make no new ones; and though this in itself looks general and solemn enough, yet there were found political philosophers to give it a look of more generality and more solemnity still, and to elevate, by their dexterous command of powerful and beautiful language, this supposed edict of the British national mind into a sort of formula for expressing a great law of religious transition and progress for all the world.

But we, who, having no coherent philosophy, must not let ourselves philosophise, only see that the English and Scotch Nonconformists have a great horror of establishments and endowments for religion, which, they assert, were forbidden by Jesus Christ when he said: "My kingdom is not of this world;" and that the Nonconformists will be delighted to aid statesmen in disestablishing any church, but will suffer none to be established or endowed if they can help it. Then we see that the Nonconformists make the strength of the Liberal Majority in the House of Commons; and that, therefore, the leading Liberal statesmen, to get the support of the Nonconformists, forsake the notion of fairly apportioning Church-property in Ireland among the chief religious communions, declare that the national mind has decided against new endowments, and propose simply to disestablish and disendow the present establishment in Ireland without establishing or endowing any other. The actual power, in short, by virtue of which the Liberal party in the House of Commons is now trying to disestablish the Irish Church, is not the power of reason and justice, it is the power of the Nonconformists' antipathy to Church establishments.

Clearly it is this; because Liberal statesmen, relying on the power of reason and justice to help them, proposed something quite different from what they now propose; and they proposed what they now propose, and talked of the decision of the national mind, because they had to rely on the English and Scotch Nonconformists. And clearly the Nonconformists are actuated by antipathy to establishments, not by antipathy to the injustice and irrationality of the present appropriation of Church-property in Ireland; because Mr. Spurgeon, in his eloquent and memorable letter, expressly avowed that he would sooner leave things as they are in Ireland, that is, he would sooner let the injustice and irrationality of the present appropriation continue, than do anything to set up the Roman image,—that is, than give the Catholics their fair and reasonable share of Church-property.[b] Most indisputably, therefore, we may affirm that the real moving power by

---

[b] Charles Haddon Spurgeon (1834–92), leading Baptist preacher (who had opened his great Tabernacle in 1861), addressed a letter to the Liberal leaders in April 1868 emphatically objecting to any scheme which would 'see Popery endowed with the national property'.

which the Liberal party are now operating the overthrow of the Irish establishment is the antipathy of the Nonconformists to Church-establishments, and not the sense of reason or justice, except so far as reason and justice may be contained in this antipathy. And thus the matter stands at present.

Now surely we must all see many inconveniences in performing the operation of uprooting this evil, the Irish Church-establishment, in this particular way. As was said about industry and freedom and gymnastics, we shall never awaken love and gratitude by this mode of operation; for it is pursued, not in view of reason and justice and human perfection and all that enkindles the enthusiasm of men, but it is pursued in view of a certain stock notion, or fetish, of the Nonconformists, which proscribes Church-establishments. And yet, evidently, one of the main benefits to be got by operating on the Irish Church is to win the affections of the Irish people. Besides this, an operation performed in virtue of a mechanical rule, or fetish, like the supposed decision of the English national mind against new endowments, does not easily inspire respect in its adversaries, and make their opposition feeble and hardly to be persisted in, as an operation evidently done in virtue of reason and justice might. For reason and justice have in them something persuasive and irresistible; but a fetish or mechanical maxim, like this of the Nonconformists, has in it nothing at all to conciliate either the affections or the understanding. Nay, it provokes the counter-employment of other fetishes or mechanical maxims on the opposite side, by which the confusion and hostility already prevalent are heightened. Only in this way can be explained the apparition of such fetishes as are beginning to be set up on the Conservative side against the fetish of the Nonconformists:— *The Constitution in danger! The bulwark of British freedom menaced! The lamp of the Reformation put out! No Popery!*—and so on. To elevate these against an operation relying on reason and justice to back it, is not so easy, or so tempting to human infirmity, as to elevate them against an operation relying on the Nonconformists' antipathy to Church-establishments to back it. For after all, *No Popery!* is a rallying cry which touches the human spirit quite as vitally as *No Church-establishments!*—that is to say, neither the one nor the other, in themselves, touch the human spirit vitally at all.

Ought the believers in action, then, to be so impatient with us, if we say, that even for the sake of this operation of theirs itself and its

satisfactory accomplishment, it is more important to make our consciousness play freely round the stock notion or habit on which their
operation relies for aid, than to lend a hand to it straight away? Clearly
they ought not; because nothing is so effectual for operating as reason
and justice, and a free play of thought will either disengage the reason
and justice lying hid in the Nonconformist fetish, and make them
effectual, or else it will help to get this fetish out of the way, and to let
statesmen go freely where reason and justice take them.

So, suppose we take this absolute rule, this mechanical maxim of
Mr. Spurgeon and the Nonconformists, that Church-establishments
are bad things because Jesus Christ said: "My kingdom is not of this
world." Suppose we try and make our consciousness bathe and float
this piece of petrifaction,—for such it now is,—and bring it within the
stream of the vital movement of our thought, and into relation with
the whole intelligible law of things. An enemy and a disputant might
probably say that much of the machinery which Nonconformists
themselves employ,—the Liberation Society which exists already, and
the Nonconformist Union which Mr. Spurgeon desires to see existing,—come within the scope of Christ's words as well as Church-
establishments.[c] This, however, is merely a negative and contentious
way of dealing with the Nonconformist maxim; whereas what we
desire is to bring this maxim within the positive and vital movement of
our thought. We say, therefore, that Jesus Christ's words mean that
his religion is a force of inward persuasion acting on the soul, and not
a force of outward constraint acting on the body; and if the Nonconformist maxim against Church-establishments and Church-endow-
ments has warrant given to it from what Christ thus meant, then their
maxim is good, even though their own practice in the matter of the
Liberation Society may be at variance with it.

And here we cannot but remember what we have formerly said
about religion, Miss Cobbe, and the British College of Health in the
New Road.[d] In religion there are two parts, the part of thought and
speculation, and the part of worship and devotion. Jesus Christ
certainly meant his religion, as a force of inward persuasion acting on
the soul, to employ both parts as perfectly as possible. Now thought

[c] The Society for the Liberation of Religion from State Patronage and Control had been
founded in 1853 by Edward Miall (see above p. 93) in succession to the equally
vehement Anti-State-Church Association.
[d] See above pp. 45–6.

and speculation is eminently an individual matter, and worship and devotion is eminently a collective matter. It does not help me to think a thing more clearly that thousands of other people are thinking the same; but it does help me to worship with more emotion that thousands of other people are worshipping with me. The consecration of common consent, antiquity, public establishment, long-used rites, national edifices, is everything for religious worship. "Just what makes worship impressive," says Joubert, "is its publicity, its external manifestation, its sound, its splendour, its observance universally and visibly holding its way through all the details both of our outward and of our inward life." Worship, therefore, should have in it as little as possible of what divides us, and should be as much as possible a common and public act; as Joubert says again: "The best prayers are those which have nothing distinct about them, and which are thus of the nature of simple adoration." For, "the same devotion," as he says in another place, "unites men far more than the same thought and knowledge."[e] Thought and knowledge, as we have said before, is eminently something individual, and of our own; the more we possess it as strictly of our own, the more power it has on us. Man worships best, therefore, with the community; he philosophises best alone.

So it seems that whoever would truly give effect to Jesus Christ's declaration that his religion is a force of inward persuasion acting on the soul, would leave our thought on the intellectual aspects of Christianity as individual as possible, but would make Christian worship as collective as possible. Worship, then, appears to be eminently a matter for public and national establishment; for even Mr. Bright, who, when he stands in Mr. Spurgeon's great Tabernacle, is so ravished with admiration, will hardly say that the great Tabernacle and its worship are in themselves, as a temple and service of religion, so impressive and affecting as the public and national Westminster Abbey, or Notre Dame, with their worship. And when, immediately after the great Tabernacle, one comes plump down to the mass of private and individual establishments of religious worship, establishments falling, like the British College of Health in the New Road, conspicuously short of what a public and national establishment might be, then one cannot but feel that Jesus Christ's command to make his religion a force of persuasion to the soul, is, so far as one main source of persuasion is concerned, altogether set at nought.

[e] See above p. 33.

But perhaps the Nonconformists worship so unimpressively because they philosophise so keenly; and one part of religion, the part of public national worship, they have subordinated to the other part, the part of individual thought and knowledge? This, however, their organisation in congregations forbids us to admit. They are members of congregations, not isolated thinkers; and a free play of individual thought is at least as much impeded by membership of a small congregation as by membership of a great Church. Thinking by batches of fifties is to the full as fatal to free thought as thinking by batches of thousands. Accordingly, we have had occasion already to notice that Nonconformity does not at all differ from the Established Church by having worthier or more philosophical ideas about God, and the ordering of the world, than the Established Church has. It has very much the same ideas about these as the Established Church has, but it differs from the Established Church in that its worship is a much less collective and national affair.

So Mr. Spurgeon and the Nonconformists seem to have misapprehended the true meaning of Christ's words, *My kingdom is not of this world*. Because, by these words, Christ meant that his religion was to work on the soul. And of the two parts of the soul on which religion works,—the thinking and speculative part, and the feeling and imaginative part,—Nonconformity satisfies the first no better than the Established Churches, which Christ by these words is supposed to have condemned, satisfy it; and the second part it satisfies even worse than the Established Churches. And thus the balance of advantage seems to rest with the Established Churches; and they seem to have apprehended and applied Christ's words, if not with perfect adequacy, at least less inadequately than the Nonconformists.

Might it not, then, be urged with great force that the way to do good, in presence of this operation for uprooting the Church-establishment in Ireland by the power of the Nonconformists' antipathy to publicly establishing or endowing religious worship, is not by lending a hand straight away to the operation, and Hebraising,—that is, in this case, taking an uncritical interpretation of certain Bible words as our absolute rule of conduct,—with the Nonconformists? It may be very well for born Hebraisers, like Mr. Spurgeon, to Hebraise; but for Liberal statesmen to Hebraise is surely unsafe, and to see poor old Liberal hacks Hebraising, whose real self belongs to a kind of negative Hellenism,—a state of moral indifference without intellectual ardour,—is even painful. And when, by our Hebraising, we neither do what the better mind of statesmen prompted them to do, nor win the affections of the people we want to conciliate, nor yet reduce the opposition of our adversaries but rather heighten it, surely it may not be unreasonable to Hellenise a little, to let our thought and consciousness play freely about our proposed operation and its motives, dissolve these motives if they are unsound,—which certainly they have some appearance, at any rate, of being,—and create in their stead, if they are, a set of sounder and more persuasive motives conducting to a more solid operation. May not the man who promotes this be giving the best help towards finding some lasting truth to minister to the diseased spirit of his time, and does he really deserve that the believers in action should grow impatient with him?

# II

But now to take another operation which does not at this moment so excite people's feelings as the disestablishment of the Irish Church, but which, I suppose, would also be called exactly one of those operations of simple, practical, common-sense reform, aiming at the removal of some particular abuse, and rigidly restricted to that object, to which a Liberal ought to lend a hand, and deserves that other Liberals should grow impatient with him if he does not. This operation I had the great advantage of with my own ears hearing discussed in the House of Commons, and recommended by a powerful speech from that famous speaker, Mr. Bright. So that the effeminate horror which, it is alleged, I have of practical reforms of this kind, was put to a searching test; and if it survived, it must have, one would think, some reason or other to support it, and can hardly quite merit the stigma of its present name.

The operation I mean was that which the Real Estate Intestacy Bill aimed at accomplishing, and the discussion on this bill I heard in the House of Commons.[f] The bill proposed, as every one knows, to prevent the land of a man who dies intestate from going, as it goes

---

[f] Several Real Estate Intestacy Bills were introduced into the Commons during Arnold's lifetime; he mocked them because they merely proposed to control the distribution of estates of men who died intestate (i.e. without leaving a valid will), but did not attempt to limit the power of bequest in any way (see also his discussion in 'Equality', pp. 215–17 below). John Bright had spoken in the debate on one such bill in June 1866.

now, to his eldest son, and was thought, by its friends and by its enemies, to be a step towards abating the now almost exclusive possession of the land of this country by the people whom we call the Barbarians. Mr. Bright, and other speakers on his side, seemed to hold that there is a kind of natural law or fitness of things which assigns to all a man's children a right to equal shares in the enjoyment of his property after his death; and that if, without depriving a man of an Englishman's prime privilege of doing what he likes by making what will he chooses, you provide that when he makes none his land shall be divided among his family, then you give the sanction of the law to the natural fitness of things, and inflict a sort of check on the present violation of this by the Barbarians.

It occurred to me, when I saw Mr. Bright and his friends proceeding in this way, to ask myself a question. If the almost exclusive possession of the land of this country by the Barbarians is a bad thing, is this practical operation of the Liberals, and the stock notion, on which it seems to rest, about the natural right of children to share equally in the enjoyment of their father's property after his death, the best and most effective means of dealing with it? Or is it best dealt with by letting one's thought and consciousness play freely and naturally upon the Barbarians, this Liberal operation, and the stock notion at the bottom of it, and trying to get as near as we can to the intelligible law of things as to each of them?

Now does any one, if he simply and naturally reads his consciousness, discover that he has any rights at all? For my part, the deeper I go in my own consciousness, and the more simply I abandon myself to it, the more it seems to tell me that I have no rights at all, only duties; and that men get this notion of rights from a process of abstract reasoning, inferring that the obligations they are conscious of towards others, others must be conscious of towards them, and not from any direct witness of consciousness at all. But it is obvious that the notion of a right, arrived at in this way, is likely to stand as a formal and petrified thing, deceiving and misleading us; and that the notions got directly from our consciousness ought to be brought to bear upon it, and to control it. So it is unsafe and misleading to say that our children have rights against us; what is true and safe to say is, that we have duties towards our children. But who will find among these natural duties, set forth to us by our consciousness, the obligation to leave to all our children an equal share in the enjoyment of our property? Or, though consciousness tells us we ought to provide for our children's welfare, whose consciousness tells him that the enjoyment of property is in itself welfare? Whether our children's welfare is best served by their all sharing equally in our property, depends on circumstances and on the state of the community in which we live. With this equal sharing, society could not, for example, have organised itself afresh out of the chaos left by the fall of the Roman Empire; and to have an organised society to live in is more for a child's welfare than to have an equal share of his father's property.

So we see how little convincing force the stock notion on which the Real Estate Intestacy Bill was based,—the notion that in the nature and fitness of things all a man's children have a right to an equal share in the enjoyment of what he leaves,— really has; and how powerless, therefore, it must of necessity be to persuade and win any one who has habits and interests which disincline him to it. On the other hand, the practical operation proposed relies entirely, if it is to be effectual in altering the present practice of the Barbarians, on the power of truth and persuasiveness in the notion which it seeks to consecrate; for it leaves to the Barbarians full liberty to continue their present practice, to which all their habits and interests incline them, unless the promulgation of a notion, which we have seen to have no vital efficacy and hold upon our consciousness, shall hinder them.

Are we really to adorn an operation of this kind, merely because it proposes to *do* something, with all the favourable epithets of simple, practical, common-sense, definite; to enlist on its side all the zeal of the believers in action, and to call indifference to it an effeminate horror of useful reforms? It seems to me quite easy to show that a free disinterested play of thought on the Barbarians and their land-holding is a thousand times more really practical, a thousand times more likely to lead to some effective result, than an operation such as that of which we have been now speaking. For if, casting aside the impediments of stock notions and mechanical action, we try to find the intelligible law of things respecting a great land-owning class such as we have in this country, does not our consciousness readily tell us that whether the perpetuation of such a class is for its own real good and for the real good of the community, depends on the actual circumstances of this class and of the community? Does it not readily tell us that wealth, power, and consideration are,—and above all when inherited and not earned,—in themselves trying and dangerous things? as Bishop Wilson excellently says: "Riches are almost always abused without a very extraordinary grace." But this extraordinary grace was in great measure supplied by the circumstances of the feudal epoch, out of which our land-holding class, with its rules of inheritance, sprang. The labour and contentions of a rude, nascent, and struggling society supplied it. These perpetually were trying, chastising, and forming the class whose predominance was then needed by society to give it points of cohesion, and was not so harmful to themselves because they were thus sharply tried and exercised. But in a luxurious, settled and easy society, where wealth offers the means of enjoyment a thousand times more, and the temptation to abuse them is thus made a thousand times greater, the exercising discipline is at the same time taken away, and the feudal class is left exposed to the full operation of the natural law well put by the French moralist: *Pouvoir sans savoir est fort dangereux.* And, for my part, when I regard the young people of this class, it is above all by the trial and shipwreck made of their own welfare by the circumstances in which they live that I am struck. How far better it would have been for nine out of every ten among them, if they had had their own way to make in the world, and not been tried by a condition for which they had not the extra-ordinary grace requisite!

This, I say, seems to be what a man's consciousness, simply consulted, would tell him about the actual welfare of our Barbarians themselves. Then, as to the effect upon the welfare of the community, how can that be salutary, if a class which, by the very possession of wealth, power and consideration, becomes a kind of ideal or standard for the rest of the community, is tried by ease and pleasure more than it can well bear, and almost irresistibly carried away from excellence and strenuous virtue? This must certainly be what Solomon meant when he said: "As he who putteth a stone in a sling, so is he that giveth honour to a fool."

For any one can perceive how this honouring of a false ideal, not of intelligence and strenuous virtue, but of wealth and station, pleasure and ease, is as a stone from a sling to kill in our great middle class, in us who are called Philistines, the desire before spoken of, which by nature for ever carries all men towards that which is lovely; and to leave instead of it only a blind deteriorating pursuit, for ourselves also, of the false ideal. And in those among us Philistines whom the desire does not wholly abandon, yet, having no excellent ideal set forth to nourish and to steady it, it meets with that natural bent for the bathos which together with this desire itself is implanted at birth in the breast of man, and is by that force twisted awry, and borne at random hither and thither, and at last flung upon those grotesque and hideous forms of popular religion which the more respectable part among us Philistines mistake for the true goal of man's desire after all that is lovely. And for the Populace this false idea is a stone which kills the desire before it can even arise; so impossible and unattainable for them do the conditions of that which is lovely appear according to this ideal to be made, so necessary to the reaching of them by the few seems the falling short of them by the many. So that, perhaps, of the actual vulgarity of our Philistines and brutality of our Populace, the Barbarians and their feudal habits of succession, enduring out of their due time and place, are involuntarily the cause in a great degree; and they hurt the welfare of the rest of the community at the same time that, as we have seen, they hurt their own.

But must not, now, the working in our minds of considerations like these, to which culture, that is, the disinterested and active use of reading, reflection, and observation, in the endeavour to know the best that can be known, carries us, be really much more effectual to the dissolution of feudal habits and rules of succession in land than an operation like the Real Estate Intestacy Bill, and a stock notion like that of the natural right of all a man's children to an equal share in the enjoyment of his property; since we have seen that this mechanical maxim is unsound, and that, if it is unsound, the operation relying upon it cannot possibly be effective? If truth and reason have, as we believe, any natural, irresistible effect on the mind of man, it must. These considerations, when culture has called them forth and given them free course in our minds, will live and work. They will work gradually, no doubt, and will not bring us ourselves to the front to sit in high place and put them into effect; but so they will be all the more beneficial. Everything teaches us how gradually nature would have all profound changes brought about; and we can even see, too, where the absolute abrupt stoppage of feudal habits has worked harm. And appealing to the sense of truth and reason, these considerations will, without doubt, touch and move all those of even the Barbarians themselves, who are (as are some of us Philistines also, and some of the Populace) beyond their fellows quick of feeling for truth and reason. For indeed this is just one of the advantages of sweetness and light over fire and strength, that sweetness and light make a feudal class quietly and gradually drop its feudal habits because it sees them at variance with truth and reason, while fire and strength are for tearing them passionately off, because this class applauded Mr. Lowe when he called, or was supposed to call, the working class drunken and venal.

# III

But when once we have begun to recount the practical operations by which our Liberal friends work for the removal of definite evils, and in which if we do not join them they are apt to grow impatient with us, how can we pass over that very interesting operation,—the attempt to enable a man to marry his deceased wife's sister? This operation, too, like that for abating the feudal customs of succession in land, I have had the advantage of myself seeing and hearing my Liberal friends labour at.

I was lucky enough to be present when Mr. Chambers brought forward in the House of Commons his bill for enabling a man to marry his deceased wife's sister, and I heard the speech which Mr. Chambers then made in support of his bill.[g] His first point was that God's law,—the name he always gave to the Book of Leviticus,—did not really forbid a man to marry his deceased wife's sister. God's law not forbidding it, the Liberal maxim, that a man's prime right and happiness is to do as he likes, ought at once to come into force, and to annul any such check upon the assertion of personal liberty as the prohibition to marry one's deceased wife's sister. A distinguished Liberal supporter of Mr. Chambers, in the debate which followed the introduction of the bill, produced a formula of much beauty and neatness for conveying in brief the Liberal notions on this head: "Liberty," said he, "is the law of human life." And, therefore, the moment it is ascertained that God's law, the Book of Leviticus, does not stop the way, man's law, the law of liberty, asserts its right, and makes us free to marry our deceased wife's sister.

And this exactly falls in with what Mr. Hepworth Dixon, who may almost be called the Colenso of love and marriage,—such a revolution

---

[g] On 2 May 1866 Thomas Chambers (1814–91), MP for Marylebone, moved the second reading of his bill to allow a man to marry his deceased wife's sister, which was at that time illegal in England.

does he make in our ideas on these matters, just as Dr. Colenso does in our ideas on religion,—tells us of the notions and proceedings of our kinsmen in America. With that affinity of genius to the Hebrew genius which we have already noticed, and with the strong belief of our race that liberty is the law of human life, so far as that fixed, perfect, and paramount rule of conscience, the Bible, does not expressly control it, our American kinsmen go again, Mr. Hepworth Dixon tells us, to their Bible, the Mormons to the patriarchs and the Old Testament, Brother Noyes to St. Paul and the New, and having never before read anything else but their Bible, they now read their Bible over again, and make all manner of great discoveries there. All these discoveries are favourable to liberty, and in this way is satisfied that double craving so characteristic of our Philistine, and so eminently exemplified in that crowned Philistine, Henry the Eighth,—the craving for forbidden fruit and the craving for legality.

Mr. Hepworth Dixon's eloquent writings give currency, over here, to these important discoveries; so that now, as regards love and marriage, we seem to be entering, with all our sails spread, upon what Mr. Hepworth Dixon, its apostle and evangelist, calls a Gothic Revival, but what one of the many newspapers that so greatly admire Mr. Hepworth Dixon's lithe and sinewy style and form their own style upon it, calls, by a yet bolder and more striking figure, "a great sexual insurrection of our Anglo-Teutonic race." For this end we have to avert our eyes from everything Hellenic and fanciful, and to keep them steadily fixed upon the two cardinal points of the Bible and liberty. And one of those practical operations in which the Liberal party engage, and in which we are summoned to join them, directs itself entirely, as we have seen, to these cardinal points, and may almost be regarded, perhaps, as a kind of first instalment, or public and parliamentary pledge, of the great sexual insurrection of our Anglo-Teutonic race.

But here, as elsewhere, what we seek is the Philistine's perfection, the development of his best self, not mere liberty for his ordinary self. And we no more allow absolute validity to his stock maxim, *Liberty is the law of human life*, than we allow it to the opposite maxim, which is just as true, *Renouncement is the law of human life*. For we know that the only perfect freedom is, as our religion says, a service; not a service to any stock maxim, but an elevation of our best self, and a harmonising in subordination to this, and to the idea of a perfected humanity, all the multitudinous, turbulent, and blind impulses of our ordinary selves. Now, the Philistine's great defect being a defect in delicacy of perception, to cultivate in him this delicacy, to render it independent of external and mechanical rule, and a law to itself, is what seems to make most for his perfection, his true humanity. And his true humanity, and therefore his happiness, appears to lie much more, so far as the relations of love and marriage are concerned, in becoming alive to the finer shades of feeling which arise within these relations, in being able to enter with tact and sympathy into the subtle instinctive propensions and repugnances of the person with whose life his own life is bound up, to make them his own, to direct and govern in harmony with them the arbitrary range of his personal action, and thus to enlarge his spiritual and intellectual life and liberty, than in remaining insensible to these finer shades of feeling and this delicate sympathy, in giving unchecked range, so far as he can, to his mere personal action, in allowing no limits or government to this except such as a mechanical external law imposes, and in thus really narrowing, for the satisfaction of his ordinary self, his spiritual and intellectual life and liberty.

Still more must this be so when his fixed eternal rule, his God's law, is supplied to him from a source which is less fit, perhaps, to supply final and absolute instructions on this particular topic of love and marriage than on any other relation of human life. Bishop Wilson, who is full of examples of that fruitful Hellenising within the limits of Hebraism itself, of that renewing of the stiff and stark notions of Hebraism by turning upon them a stream of fresh thought and consciousness, which we have already noticed in St. Paul, — Bishop Wilson gives an admirable lesson to rigid Hebraisers, like Mr. Chambers, asking themselves: Does God's law (that is, the Book of Leviticus) forbid us to marry our wife's sister? — Does God's law (that is, again, the Book of Leviticus) allow us to marry our wife's sister? — when he says: "Christian duties are founded on reason, not on the sovereign authority of God commanding what He pleases; God cannot command us what is not fit to be believed or done, all his commands being founded in the necessities of our nature." And, immense as is our debt to the Hebrew race and its genius, incomparable as is its authority on certain profoundly important sides of our human nature, worthy as it is to be described as having uttered, for those sides, the voice of the deepest necessities of our nature, the statutes of the divine and eternal order of things, the law of God,—who, that is not manacled and hoodwinked by his Hebraism, can believe that, as to love and marriage, our reason and the necessities of our humanity have their true, sufficient, and divine law expressed for them by the voice of any Oriental and polygamous nation like the Hebrews? Who, I say, will believe, when he really considers the matter, that where the feminine nature, the feminine ideal, and our relations to them, are brought into question, the delicate and apprehensive genius of the Indo-European race, the race which invented the Muses, and chivalry, and the Madonna, is to find its last word on this question in the institutions of a Semitic people, whose wisest king had seven hundred wives and three hundred concubines?

# IV

If here again, therefore, we minister better to the diseased spirit of our time by leading it to think about the operation our Liberal friends have in hand, than by lending a hand to this operation ourselves, let us see, before we dismiss from our view the practical operations of our Liberal friends, whether the same thing does not hold good as to their celebrated industrial and economical labours also. Their great work of this kind is, of course, their free-trade policy. This policy, as having enabled the poor man to eat untaxed bread, and as having wonderfully augmented trade, we are accustomed to speak of with a kind of thankful solemnity.[h] It is chiefly on their having been our leaders in this policy that Mr. Bright founds for himself and his friends the claim, so often asserted by him, to be considered guides of the blind, teachers of the ignorant, benefactors slowly and laboriously developing in the Conservative party and in the country that which Mr. Bright is fond of calling *the growth of intelligence*,—the object, as is well known, of all the friends of culture also, and the great end and aim of the culture that we preach.

Now, having first saluted free-trade and its doctors with all respect, let us see whether even here, too, our Liberal friends do not pursue their operations in a mechanical way, without reference to any firm intelligible law of things, to human life as a whole, and human happi-

[h] The repeal of the Corn Laws in 1846, which was the central element in the policy of Free Trade, had owed much to the pressure of Bright, Cobden, and their predominantly middle-class Anti-Corn-Law League.

ness; and whether it is not more for our good, at this particular moment at any rate, if, instead of worshipping free-trade with them Hebraistically, as a kind of fetish, and helping them to pursue it as an end in and for itself, we turn the free stream of our thought upon their treatment of it, and see how this is related to the intelligible law of human life, and to national well-being and happiness. In short, suppose we Hellenise a little with free-trade, as we Hellenised with the Real Estate Intestacy Bill, and with the disestablishment of the Irish Church by the power of the Nonconformists' antipathy to religious establishments, and see whether what our reprovers beautifully call ministering to the diseased spirit of our time is best done by the Hellenising method of proceeding, or by the other.

But first let us understand how the policy of free-trade really shapes itself for our Liberal friends, and how they practically employ it as an instrument of national happiness and salvation. For as we said that it seemed clearly right to prevent the Church-property of Ireland from being all taken for the benefit of the Church of a small minority, so it seems clearly right that the poor man should eat untaxed bread, and, generally, that restrictions and regulations which, for the supposed benefit of some particular person or class of persons, make the price of things artificially high here, or artificially low there, and interfere with the natural flow of trade and commerce, should be done away with. But in the policy of our Liberal friends free-trade means more than this, and is specially valued as a stimulant to the production of wealth, as they call it, and to the increase of the trade, business, and population of the country. We have already seen how these things,— trade, business, and population,—are mechanically pursued by us as ends precious in themselves, and are worshipped as what we call fetishes; and Mr. Bright, I have already said, when he wishes to give the working class a true sense of what makes glory and greatness, tells it to look at the cities it has built, the railroads it has made, the manufactures it has produced. So to this idea of glory and greatness the free-trade which our Liberal friends extol so solemnly and devoutly, has served,—to the increase of trade, business, and population; and for this it is prized. Therefore, the untaxing of the poor man's bread has, with this view of national happiness, been used not so much to make the existing poor man's bread cheaper or more abundant, but rather to create more poor men to eat it; so that we cannot precisely say that we have fewer poor men than we had before free-trade, but we can say with truth that we have many more centres of industry, as they are called, and much more business, population, and manufactures. And if we are sometimes a little troubled by our multitude of poor men, yet we know the increase of manufactures and population to be such a salutary thing in itself, and our free-trade policy begets such an admirable movement, creating fresh centres of industry and fresh poor men here, while we were thinking about our poor men there, that we are quite dazzled and borne away, and more and more industrial movement is called for, and our social progress seems to become one triumphant and enjoyable course of what is sometimes called, vulgarly, outrunning the constable.

If, however, taking some other criterion of man's well-being than the cities he has built and the manufactures he has produced, we persist in thinking that our social progress would be happier if there were not so many of us so very poor, and in busying ourselves with notions of in some way or other adjusting the poor man and business one to the other, and not multiplying the one and the other mechanically and blindly, then our Liberal friends, the appointed doctors of free-trade, take us up very sharply. "Art is long," says the *Times*, "and life is short; for the most part we settle things first and understand them afterwards. Let us have as few theories as possible; what is wanted is not the light of speculation. If nothing worked well of which the theory was not perfectly understood, we should be in sad confusion. The relations of labour and capital, we are told, are not understood, yet trade and commerce, on the whole, work satisfactorily." I quote from the *Times* of only the other day.[3] But thoughts like these, as I have often pointed out, are thoroughly British thoughts, and we have been familiar with them for years.

Or, if we want more of a philosophy of the matter than this, our free-trade friends have two axioms for us, axioms laid down by their justly esteemed doctors, which they think ought to satisfy us entirely. One is, that, other things being equal, the more population increases, the more does production increase to keep pace with it; because men by their numbers and contact call forth all manner of activities and resources in one another and in nature, which, when men are few and sparse, are never developed. The other is, that, although population always tends to equal the means of subsistence, yet people's notions of

[3] Written in 1868.

what subsistence is enlarge as civilisation advances, and take in a number of things beyond the bare necessaries of life; and thus, therefore, is supplied whatever check on population is needed. But the error of our friends is precisely, perhaps, that they apply axioms of this sort as if they were self-acting laws which will put themselves into operation without trouble or planning on our part, if we will only pursue free-trade, business, and population zealously and staunchly. Whereas the real truth is, that, however the case might be under other circumstances, yet in fact, as we now manage the matter, the enlarged conception of what is included in *subsistence* does not operate to prevent the bringing into the world of numbers of people who but just attain to the barest necessaries of life or who even fail to attain to them; while, again, though production may increase as population increases, yet it seems that the production may be of such a kind, and so related, or rather non-related, to population, that the population may be little the better for it.

For instance, with the increase of population since Queen Elizabeth's time the production of silk-stockings has wonderfully increased, and silk-stockings have become much cheaper, and procurable in greater abundance by many more people, and tend perhaps, as population and manufactures increase, to get cheaper and cheaper, and at last to become, according to Bastiat's favourite image, a common free property of the human race, like light and air.[i] But bread and bacon have not become much cheaper with the increase of population since Queen Elizabeth's time, nor procurable in much greater abundance by many more people; neither do they seem at all to promise to become, like light and air, a common free property of the human race. And if bread and bacon have not kept pace with our population, and we have many more people in want of them now than in Queen Elizabeth's time, it seems vain to tell us that silk-stockings have kept pace with our population, or even more than kept pace with it, and that we are to get our comfort out of that.

In short, it turns out that our pursuit of free-trade, as of so many other things, has been too mechanical. We fix upon some object, which in this case is the production of wealth, and the increase of manufactures, population, and commerce through free-trade, as a kind of one thing needful, or end in itself; and then we pursue it

---

[i] Frédéric Bastiat (1801–50), French political economist who was a prominent advocate of Free Trade.

staunchly and mechanically, and say that it is our duty to pursue it staunchly and mechanically, not to see how it is related to the whole intelligible law of things and to full human perfection, or to treat it as the piece of machinery, of varying value as its relations to the intelligible law of things vary, which it really is.

So it is of no use to say to the *Times*, and to our Liberal friends rejoicing in the possession of their talisman of free-trade, that about one in nineteen of our population is a pauper,[4] and that, this being so, trade and commerce can hardly be said to prove by their satisfactory working that it matters nothing whether the relations between labour and capital are understood or not; nay, that we can hardly be said not to be in sad confusion. For here our faith in the staunch mechanical pursuit of a fixed object comes in, and covers itself with that imposing and colossal necessitarianism of the *Times* which we have before noticed. And this necessitarianism, taking for granted that an increase in trade and population is a good in itself, one of the chiefest of goods, tells us that disturbances of human happiness caused by ebbs and flows in the tide of trade and business, which, on the whole, steadily mounts, are inevitable and not to be quarrelled with. This firm philosophy I seek to call to mind when I am in the East of London, whither my avocations often lead me; and, indeed, to fortify myself against the depressing sights which on these occasions assail us, I have transcribed from the *Times* one strain of this kind, full of the finest economical doctrine, and always carry it about with me. The passage is this:—

"The East End is the most commercial, the most industrial, the most fluctuating region of the metropolis. It is always the first to suffer; for it is the creature of prosperity, and falls to the ground the instant there is no wind to bear it up. The whole of that region is covered with huge docks, shipyards, manufactories, and a wilderness of small houses, all full of life and happiness in brisk times, but in dull times withered and lifeless, like the deserts we read of in the East. Now their brief spring is over. There is no one to blame for this; it is the result of Nature's simplest laws!" We must all agree that it is impossible that anything can be firmer than this, or show a surer faith in the working of free-trade, as our Liberal friends understand and employ it.

---

[4] This was in 1868.

But, if we still at all doubt whether the indefinite multiplication of manufactories and small houses can be such an absolute good in itself as to counterbalance the indefinite multiplication of poor people, we shall learn that this multiplication of poor people, too, is an absolute good in itself, and the result of divine and beautiful laws. This is indeed a favourite thesis with our Philistine friends, and I have already noticed the pride and gratitude with which they receive certain articles in the *Times*, dilating in thankful and solemn language on the majestic growth of our population. But I prefer to quote now, on this topic, the words of an ingenious young Scotch writer, Mr. Robert Buchanan, because he invests with so much imagination and poetry this current idea of the blessed and even divine character which the multiplying of population is supposed in itself to have. "We move to multiplicity," says Mr. Robert Buchanan. "If there is one quality which seems God's, and his exclusively, it seems that divine philoprogenitiveness, that passionate love of distribution and expansion into living forms. Every animal added seems a new ecstasy to the Maker; every life added, a new embodiment of his love. He would *swarm* the earth with beings. There are never enough. Life, life, life,—faces gleaming, hearts beating, must fill every cranny. Not a corner is suffered to remain empty. The whole earth breeds, and God glories."[j]

It is a little unjust, perhaps, to attribute to the Divinity exclusively this philoprogenitiveness, which the British Philistine, and the poorer class of Irish, may certainly claim to share with him; yet how inspiriting is here the whole strain of thought! and these beautiful words, too, I carry about with me in the East of London, and often read them there. They are quite in agreement with the popular language one is accustomed to hear about children and large families, which describes children as *sent*. And a line of poetry, which Mr. Robert Buchanan throws in presently after the poetical prose I have quoted, —

"Tis the old story of the fig-leaf time" —

this fine line, too, naturally connects itself, when one is in the East of London, with the idea of God's desire to *swarm* the earth with beings; because the swarming of the earth with beings does indeed, in the

<hr />

[j] Robert Buchanan (1841–1901), minor poet and essayist; his *David Gray and Other Essays* (1868), which Arnold quotes here, contained an attack on Arnold's 'Culture' articles.

East of London, so seem to revive *the old story of the fig-leaf time*, such a number of the people one meets there having hardly a rag to cover them; and the more the swarming goes on, the more it promises to revive this old story. And when the story is perfectly revived, the swarming quite completed, and every cranny choke-full, then, too, no doubt, the faces in the East of London will be gleaming faces, which Mr. Robert Buchanan says it is God's desire they should be, and which every one must perceive they are not at present, but, on the contrary, very miserable.

But to prevent all this philosophy and poetry from quite running away with us, and making us think with the *Times*, and our practical Liberal free-traders, and the British Philistines generally, that the increase of houses and manufactories, or the increase of population, are absolute goods in themselves, to be mechanically pursued, and to be worshipped like fetishes,—to prevent this, we have got that notion of ours immovably fixed, of which I have long ago spoken, the notion that culture, or the study of perfection, leads us to conceive of no perfection as being real which is not a *general* perfection, embracing all our fellow-men with whom we have to do. Such is the sympathy which binds humanity together, that we are indeed, as our religion says, members of one body, and if one member suffer, all the members suffer with it. Individual perfection is impossible so long as the rest of mankind are not perfected along with us. "The *multitude* of the wise is the welfare of the world," says the wise man. And to this effect that excellent and often-quoted guide of ours, Bishop Wilson, has some striking words:—"It is not," says he, "so much our neighbour's interest as our own that we love him." And again he says: "Our salvation does in some measure depend upon that of others." And the author of the *Imitation* puts the same thing admirably when he says:— "*Obscurior etiam via ad cœlum videbatur quando tam pauci regnum cœlorum quærere curabant*; the fewer there are who follow the way to perfection, the harder that way is to find." So all our fellow-men, in the East of London and elsewhere, we must take along with us in the progress towards perfection, if we ourselves really, as we profess, want to be perfect; and we must not let the worship of any fetish, any machinery, such as manufacturers or population,—which are not, like perfection, absolute goods in themselves, though we think them so,— create for us such a multitude of miserable, sunken, and ignorant human beings, that to carry them all along with us is impossible, and perforce they must for the most part be left by us in their degradation and wretchedness. But evidently the conception of free-trade, on which our Liberal friends vaunt themselves, and in which they think they have found the secret of national prosperity,— evidently, I say, the mere unfettered pursuit of the production of wealth, and the mere mechanical multiplying, for this end, of manufactures and population, threatens to create for us, if it has not created already, those vast, miserable, unmanageable masses of sunken people, to the existence of which we are, as we have seen, absolutely forbidden to reconcile ourselves, in spite of all that the philosophy of the *Times* and the poetry of Mr. Robert Buchanan may say to persuade us.

Hebraism in general seems powerless, almost as powerless as our free-trading Liberal friends, to deal efficaciously with our ever-accumulating masses of pauperism, and to prevent their accumulating still more. Hebraism builds churches, indeed, for these masses, and sends missionaries among them; above all, it sets itself against the social necessitarianism of the *Times*, and refuses to accept their degradation as inevitable. But with regard to their ever-increasing accumulation, it seems to be led to the very same conclusions, though from a point of view of its own, as our free-trading Liberal friends. Hebraism, with that mechanical and misleading use of the letter of Scripture on which we have already commented, is governed by such texts as: *Be fruitful and multiply*, the edict of God's law, as Mr. Chambers would say; or by the declaration of what he would call God's word in the Psalms, that the man who has a great number of children is thereby made happy. And in conjunction with such texts as these, Hebraism is apt to place another text: *The poor shall never cease out of the land.* Thus Hebraism is conducted to nearly the same notion as the popular mind and as Mr. Robert Buchanan, that children are *sent*, and that the divine nature takes a delight in swarming the East End of London with paupers. Only, when they are perishing in their helplessness and wretchedness, it asserts the Christian duty of succouring them, instead of saying, like the *Times*: "Now their brief spring is over; there is nobody to blame for this; it is the result of Nature's simplest laws!" But, like the *Times*, Hebraism despairs of any help from knowledge and says that "what is wanted is not the light of speculation."

I remember, only the other day, a good man looking with me upon a multitude of children who were gathered before us in one of the most miserable regions of London,—children eaten up with disease, half-sized, half-fed, half-clothed, neglected by their parents, without health, without home, without hope,—said to me: "The one thing really needful is to teach these little ones to succour one another, if only with a cup of cold water; but now, from one end of the country to the other, one hears nothing but the cry for knowledge, knowledge, knowledge!" And yet surely, so long as these children are there in these festering masses, without health, without home, without hope, and so long as their multitude is perpetually swelling, charged with misery they must still be for themselves, charged with misery they must still be for us, whether they help one another with a cup of cold water or no; and the knowledge how to prevent their accumulating is necessary, even to give their moral life and growth a fair chance!

May we not, therefore, say, that neither the true Hebraism of this good man, willing to spend and be spent for these sunken multitudes, nor what I may call the spurious Hebraism of our free-trading Liberal friends,—mechanically worshipping their fetish of the production of wealth and of the increase of manufactures and population, and looking neither to the right nor left so long as this increase goes on,—avail us much here; and that here, again, what we want is Hellenism, the letting our consciousness play freely and simply upon the facts before us, and listening to what it tells us of the intelligible law of things as concerns them? And surely what it tells us is, that a man's children are not really *sent*, any more than the pictures upon his wall, or the horses in his stable are *sent*; and that to bring people into the world, when one cannot afford to keep them and oneself decently and not too precariously, or to bring more of them into the world than one can afford to keep thus, is, whatever the *Times* and Mr. Robert Buchanan may say, by no means an accomplishment of the divine will or a fulfilment of Nature's simplest laws, but is just as wrong, just as contrary to reason and the will of God, as for a man to have horses, or carriages, or pictures, when he cannot afford them, or to have more of them than he can afford; and that, in the one case as in the other, the larger the scale on which the violation of reason's law is practised, and the longer it is persisted in, the greater must be the confusion and final trouble. Surely no laudations of free-trade, no meetings of bishops and clergy in the East End of London, no reading of papers and reports, can tell us anything about our social condition which it more concerns us to know than that! and not only to know, but habitually to have the knowledge present, and to act upon it as one acts upon the knowledge that water wets and fire burns! And not only the sunken populace of our great cities are concerned to know it, and the pauper twentieth of our population; we Philistines of the middle class, too, are concerned to know it, and all who have to set themselves to make progress in perfection.

But we all know it already! some one will say; it is the simplest law of prudence. But how little reality must there be in our knowledge of it; how little can we be putting it in practice; how little is it likely to penetrate among the poor and struggling masses of our population, and to better our condition, so long as an unintelligent Hebraism of one sort keeps repeating as an absolute eternal word of God the psalm-verse which says that the man who has a great many children is happy; or an unintelligent Hebraism of another sort,—that is to say, a blind following of certain stock notions as infallible,—keeps assigning as an absolute proof of national prosperity the multiplying of manufactures and population! Surely, the one set of Hebraisers have to learn that their psalm-verse was composed at the resettlement of Jerusalem after the Captivity, when the Jews of Jerusalem were a handful, an undermanned garrison, and every child was a blessing; and that the word of God, or the voice of the divine order of things, declares the possession of a great many children to be a blessing only when it really is so! And the other set of Hebraisers, have they not to learn that if they call their private acquaintances imprudent or unlucky, when, with no means of support for them or with precarious means, they have a large family of children, then they ought not to call the State well managed and prosperous merely because its manufactures and its citizens multiply, if the manufactures, which bring new citizens into existence just as much as if they had actually begotten them, bring more of them into existence than they can maintain, or are too precarious to go on maintaining those whom for a while they maintained?

Hellenism, surely, or the habit of fixing our mind upon the intelligible law of things, is most salutary if it makes us see that the only absolute good, the only absolute and eternal object prescribed to us by God's law, or the divine order of things, is the progress towards perfection,—our own progress towards it and the progress of humanity. And therefore, for every individual man, and for every society of men, the possession and multiplication of children, like the possession and multiplication of horses and pictures, is to be accounted good or bad, not in itself, but with reference to this object and the progress towards it. And as no man is to be excused in having horses or pictures, if his having them hinders his own or others' progress towards perfection and makes them lead a servile and ignoble life, so is no man to be excused for having children if his having them makes him or others lead this. Plain thoughts of this kind are surely the spontaneous product of our consciousness, when it is allowed to play freely and disinterestedly upon the actual facts of our social condition, and upon our stock notions and stock habits in respect to it. Firmly grasped and simply uttered, they are more likely, one cannot but think, to better that condition, than is the mechanical pursuit of free-trade by our Liberal friends.

# V

So that, here as elsewhere, the practical operations of our Liberal friends, by which they set so much store, and in which they invite us to join them and to show what Mr. Bright calls a commendable interest, do not seem to us so practical for real good as they think; and our Liberal friends seem to us themselves to need to Hellenise, as we say, a little,—that is, to examine into the nature of real good, and to listen to what their consciousness tells them about it,—rather than to pursue with such heat and confidence their present practical operations. And it is clear that they have no just cause, so far as regards several operations of theirs which we have canvassed, to reproach us with delicate Conservative scepticism. For often by Hellenising we seem to subvert stock Conservative notions and usages more effectually than they subvert them by Hebraising. But, in truth, the free spontaneous play of consciousness with which culture tries to float our stock habits of thinking and acting, is by its very nature, as has been said, disinterested. Sometimes the result of floating them may be agreeable to this party, sometimes to that; now it may be unwelcome to our so-called Liberals, now to our so-called Conservatives; but what culture seeks is, above all, to *float* them, to prevent their being stiff and stark pieces of petrifaction any longer. It is mere Hebraising, if we stop short, and refuse to let our consciousness play freely, whenever we or our friends do not happen to like what it discovers to us. This is to make the Liberal party, or the Conservative party, our one thing needful, instead of human perfection; and we have seen what mischief arises from making an even greater thing than the Liberal or the Conservative party, — the predominance of the moral side in man, — our one thing needful. But wherever the free play of our consciousness leads us, we shall follow; believing that in this way we shall tend to make good at all points what is wanting to us, and so shall be brought nearer to our complete human perfection.

Everything, in short, confirms us in the doctrine, so unpalatable to the believers in action, that our main business at the present moment is not so much to work away at certain crude reforms of which we have already the scheme in our own mind, as to create, through the help of that culture which at the very outset we began by praising and recommending, a frame of mind out of which the schemes of really fruitful reforms may with time grow. At any rate, we ourselves must put up with our friends' impatience, and with their reproaches against cultivated inaction, and must still decline to lend a hand to their practical operations, until we, for our own part at least, have grown a little clearer about the nature of real good, and have arrived nearer to a condition of mind out of which really fruitful and solid operations may spring.

In the meanwhile, since our Liberal friends keep loudly and resolutely assuring us that their actual operations at present are fruitful and solid, let us in each case keep testing these operations in the simple way we have indicated, by letting the natural stream of our consciousness flow over them freely; and if they stand this test successfully, then let us give them our interest, but not else.

# Conclusion

And so we bring to an end what we had to say in praise of culture, and in evidence of its special utility for the circumstances in which we find ourselves, and the confusion which environs us. Through culture seems to lie our way, not only to perfection, but even to safety. Resolutely refusing to lend a hand to the imperfect operations of our Liberal friends, disregarding their impatience, taunts, and reproaches, firmly bent on trying to find in the intelligible laws of things a firmer and sounder basis for future practice than any which we have at present, and believing this search and discovery to be, for our generation and circumstances, of yet more vital and pressing importance than practice itself, we nevertheless may do more, perhaps, we poor disparaged followers of culture, to make the actual present, and the frame of society in which we live, solid and sea-worthy, than all which our bustling politicians can do.

For we have seen how much of our disorders and perplexities is due to the disbelief, among the classes and combinations of men, Barbarian or Philistine, which have hitherto governed our society, in right reason, in a paramount best self; to the inevitable decay and break-up of the organisations by which, asserting and expressing in these organisations their ordinary self only, they have so long ruled us; and to their irresolution, when the society, which their conscience tells them they have made and still manage not with right reason but with their ordinary self, is rudely shaken, in offering resistance to its subverters. But for us,—who believe in right reason, in the duty and possibility of extricating and elevating our best self, in the progress of humanity towards perfection,—for us the framework of society, that theatre on which this august drama has to unroll itself, is sacred; and whoever administers it, and however we may seek to remove them from their tenure of administration, yet, while they administer, we steadily and with undivided heart support them in repressing anarchy and disorder; because without order there can be no society, and without society there can be no human perfection.

And this opinion of the intolerableness of anarchy we can never forsake, however our Liberal friends may think a little rioting, and what they call popular demonstrations, useful sometimes to their own interests and to the interests of the valuable practical operations they have in hand, and however they may preach the right of an Englishman to be left to do as far as possible what he likes, and the duty of his government to indulge him and connive as much as possible and abstain from all harshness of repression. And even when they artfully show us operations which are undoubtedly precious, such as the abolition of the slave-trade, and ask us if, for their sake, foolish and obstinate governments may not wholesomely be frightened by a little disturbance, the good design in view and the difficulty of overcoming opposition to it being considered, — still we say no, and that monster-processions in the streets and forcible irruptions into the parks, even in professed support of this good design, ought to be unflinchingly forbidden and repressed; and that far more is lost than is gained by permitting them. Because a State in which law is authoritative and sovereign, a firm and settled course of public order, is requisite if man is to bring to maturity anything precious and lasting now, or to found anything precious and lasting for the future.

Thus, in our eyes, the very framework and exterior order of the State, whoever may administer the State, is sacred; and culture is the most resolute enemy of anarchy, because of the great hopes and designs for the State which culture teaches us to nourish. But as, believing in right reason, and having faith in the progress of humanity towards perfection, and ever labouring for this end, we grow to have clearer sight of the ideas of right reason, and of the elements and helps of perfection, and come gradually to fill the framework of the State with them, to fashion its internal composition and all its laws and institutions conformably to them, and to make the State more and more the expression, as we say, of our best self, which is not manifold, and vulgar, and unstable, and contentious, and ever-varying, but one, and noble, and secure, and peaceful, and the same for all mankind, —

with what aversion shall we not *then* regard anarchy, with what firmness shall we not check it, when there is so much that is so precious which it will endanger!

So that, for the sake of the present, but far more for the sake of the future, the lovers of culture are unswervingly and with a good conscience the opposers of anarchy. And not as the Barbarians and Philistines, whose honesty and whose sense of humour make them shrink, as we have seen, from treating the State as too serious a thing, and from giving it too much power;—for indeed the only State they know of, and think they administer, is the expression of their ordinary self. And though the headstrong and violent extreme among them might gladly arm this with full authority, yet their virtuous mean is, as we have said, pricked in conscience at doing this; and so our Barbarian Secretaries of State let the Park railings be broken down, and of our Philistine Alderman-Colonels; and to tell them, that it is not really in behalf of their own ordinary self that they are called to our ordinary self, but even already, as it were, the appointed frame and prepared vessel of our best self, and, for the future, our best self's powerful, beneficent, and sacred expression and organ,—we are willing and resolved, even now, to strengthen against anarchy the trembling hands of our Barbarian Home Secretaries, and the feeble knees of our Philistine Alderman- Colonels; and to tell them, that it is not really in behalf of their own ordinary self that they are called to protect the Park railings, and to suppress the London roughs, but in behalf of the best self both of themselves and of all of us in the future.

Nevertheless, though for resisting anarchy the lovers of culture may prize and employ fire and strength, yet they must, at the same time, bear constantly in mind that it is not at this moment true, what the majority of people tell us, that the world wants fire and strength more than sweetness and light, and that things are for the most part to be settled first and understood afterwards. We have seen how much of our present perplexities and confusion this untrue notion of the majority of people amongst us has caused, and tends to perpetuate. Therefore the true business of the friends of culture now is, to dissipate this false notion, to spread the belief in right reason and in a firm intelligible law of things, and to get men to try, in preference to staunchly acting with imperfect knowledge, to obtain some sounder basis of knowledge on which to act. This is what the friends and lovers of culture have to do, however the believers in action may grow impatient with us for saying so, and may insist on our lending a hand to their practical operations and showing a commendable interest in them.

To this insistence we must indeed turn a deaf ear. But neither, on the other hand, must the friends of culture expect to take the believers in action by storm, or to be visibly and speedily important, and to rule and cut a figure in the world. Aristotle says that those for whom alone ideas and the pursuit of the intelligible law of things can, in general, have much attraction, are principally the young, filled with generous spirit and with a passion for perfection; but the mass of mankind, he says, follow seeming goods for real, bestowing hardly a thought upon true sweetness and light;—"and to *their* lives," he adds mournfully, "who can give another and a better rhythm?" But, although those chiefly attracted by sweetness and light will probably always be the young and enthusiastic, and culture must not hope to take the mass of mankind by storm, yet we will not therefore, for our own day and for our own people, admit and rest in the desponding sentence of Aristotle. For is not this the right crown of the long discipline of Hebraism, and the due fruit of mankind's centuries of painful school- ing in self-conquest, and the just reward, above all, of the strenuous energy of our own nation and kindred in dealing honestly with itself and walking steadfastly according to the best light it knows,—that when in the fulness of time it has reason and beauty offered to it, and the law of things as they really are, it should at last walk by this true light with the same staunchness and zeal with which it formerly walked by its imperfect light? And thus man's two great natural forces, Hebraism and Hellenism, will no longer be dissociated and rival, but will be a joint force of right thinking and strong doing to carry him on towards perfection. This is what the lovers of culture may perhaps dare to augur for such a nation as ours.

Therefore, however great the changes to be accomplished, and however dense the array of Barbarians, Philistines, and Populace, we will neither despair on the one hand, nor, on the other, threaten violent revolution and change. But we will look forward cheerfully and hopefully to "a revolution," as the Duke of Wellington said, "by due course of law;" though not exactly such laws as our Liberal friends are now, with their actual lights, fond of offering to us.

But if despondency and violence are both of them forbidden to the believer in culture, yet neither, on the other hand, is public life and direct political action much permitted to him. For it is his business, as we have seen, to get the present believers in action, and lovers of political talking and doing, to make a return upon their own minds, scrutinise their stock notions and habits much more, value their present talking and doing much less; in order that, by learning to think more clearly, they may come at last to act less confusedly. But how shall we persuade our Barbarian to hold lightly to his feudal usages; how shall we persuade our Nonconformist that his time spent in agitating for the abolition of church-establishments would have been better spent in getting worthier ideas of God and the ordering of the world, or his time spent in battling for voluntaryism in education better spent in learning to value and found a public and national culture; how shall we persuade, finally, our Alderman-Colonel not to be content with sitting in the hall of judgment or marching at the head of his men of war, without some knowledge how to perform judgment and how to direct men of war,—how, I say, shall we persuade all these of this, if our Alderman-Colonel sees that we want to get his leading-staff and his scales of justice for our own hands; or the Nonconform-ist, that we want for ourselves his platform; or the Barbarian, that we want for ourselves his pre-eminence and function? Certainly they will be less slow to believe, as we want them to believe, that the intelligible law of things has in itself something desirable and precious, and that all place, function, and bustle are hollow goods without it, if they see that we ourselves can content ourselves with this law, and find in it our satisfaction, without making it an instrument to give us for our-selves place, function, and bustle.

And although Mr. Sidgwick says that social usefulness really means "losing oneself in a mass of disagreeable, hard, mechanical details," and though all the believers in action are fond of asserting the same thing, yet, as to lose ourselves is not what we want, but to find ourselves through finding the intelligible law of things, this assertion too we shall not blindly accept, but shall sift and try it a little first.[a] And if we see that because the believers in action, forgetting Goethe's maxim, "to act is easy, to think is hard," imagine there is some wonderful virtue in losing oneself in a mass of mechanical details, therefore they excuse themselves from much thought about the clear ideas which ought to govern these details, then we shall give our chief

<hr/>

[a] See above p. 140.

care and pains to seeking out those ideas and to setting them forth; being persuaded that if we have the ideas firm and clear, the mechanical details for their execution will come a great deal more simply and easily than we now suppose.

At this exciting juncture, then, while so many of the lovers of new ideas, somewhat weary, as we too are, of the stock performances of our Liberal friends upon the political stage, are disposed to rush valiantly upon this public stage themselves, we cannot at all think that for a wise lover of new ideas this stage is the right one. Plenty of people there will be without us, — country gentlemen in search of a club, demagogues in search of a tub, lawyers in search of a place, industrialists in search of gentility, — who will come from the east and from the west, and will sit down at that Thyesteän banquet of claptrap which English public life for these many years past has been. And, so long as those old organisations, of which we have seen the insufficiency, — those expressions of our ordinary self, Barbarian or Philistine, — have force anywhere, they will have force in Parliament. There, the man whom the Barbarians send, cannot but be impelled to please the Barbarians' ordinary self, and their natural taste for the bathos; and the man whom the Philistines send, cannot but be impelled to please those of the Philistines. Parliamentary Conservatism will and must long mean there, that the Barbarians should keep their heritage; and Parliamentary Liberalism, that the Barbarians should pass away, as they will pass away, and that into their heritage the Philistines should enter. This seems, indeed, to be the true and authentic promise of which our Liberal friends and Mr. Bright believe themselves the heirs, and the goal of that great man's labours. Presently, perhaps, Mr. Odger and Mr. Bradlaugh will be there with their mission to oust both Barbarians and Philistines, and to get the heritage for the Populace.[b]

We, on the other hand, are for giving the heritage neither to the Barbarians nor to the Philistines, nor yet to the Populace; but we are for the transformation of each and all of these according to the law of perfection. Through the length and breadth of our nation a sense, — vague and obscure as yet, — of weariness with the old organisations, of desire for this transformation, works and grows. In the House of Commons the old organisations must inevitably be most enduring and

---

[b] See above pp. 72, 98; Bradlaugh was elected to Parliament, Odger was not.

strongest, the transformation must inevitably be longest in showing itself; and it may truly be averred, therefore, that at the present juncture the centre of movement is not in the House of Commons. It is in the fermenting mind of the nation; and his is for the next twenty years the real influence who can address himself to this.

Pericles was perhaps the most perfect public speaker who ever lived, for he was the man who most perfectly combined thought and wisdom with feeling and eloquence. Yet Plato brings in Alcibiades declaring, that men went away from the oratory of Pericles, saying it was very fine, it was very good, and afterwards thinking no more about it; but they went away from hearing Socrates talk, he says, with the point of what he had said sticking fast in their minds, and they could not get rid of it. Socrates has drunk his hemlock and is dead; but in his own breast does not every man carry about with him a possible Socrates, in that power of a disinterested play of consciousness upon his stock notions and habits, of which this wise and admirable man gave all through his lifetime the great example, and which was the secret of his incomparable influence? And he who leads men to call forth and exercise in themselves this power, and who busily calls it forth and exercises it in himself, is at the present moment, perhaps, as Socrates was in his time, more in concert with the vital working of men's minds, and more effectually significant, than any House of Commons' orator, or practical operator in politics.

Every one is now boasting of what he has done to educate men's minds and to give things the course they are taking. Mr. Disraeli educates, Mr. Bright educates, Mr. Beales educates. We, indeed, pretend to educate no one, for we are still engaged in trying to clear and educate ourselves. But we are sure that the endeavour to reach, through culture, the firm intelligible law of things, we are sure that the detaching ourselves from our stock notions and habits, that a more free play of consciousness, an increased desire for sweetness and light, and all the bent which we call Hellenising, is the master-impulse even now of the life of our nation and of humanity,— somewhat obscurely perhaps for this actual moment, but decisively and certainly for the immediate future; and that those who work for this are the sovereign educators.

Docile echoes of the eternal voice, pliant organs of the infinite will, such workers are going along with the essential movement of the world; and this is their strength, and their happy and divine fortune.

For if the believers in action, who are so impatient with us and call us effeminate, had had the same good fortune, they would, no doubt, have surpassed us in this sphere of vital influence by all the superiority of their genius and energy over ours. But now we go the way the human race is going, while they abolish the Irish Church by the power of the Nonconformists' antipathy to establishments, or they enable a man to marry his deceased wife's sister.

# Preface to *Culture and Anarchy* (1869)

My foremost design in writing this Preface is to address a word of exhortation to the Society for Promoting Christian Knowledge. In the essay which follows, the reader will often find Bishop Wilson quoted.[a] To me and to the members of the Society for Promoting Christian Knowledge his name and writings are still, no doubt, familiar. But the world is fast going away from old-fashioned people of his sort, and I learnt with consternation lately from a brilliant and distinguished votary of the natural sciences, that he had never so much as heard of Bishop Wilson, and that he imagined me to have invented him. At a moment when the Courts of Law have just taken off the embargo from the recreative religion furnished on Sundays by my gifted acquaintance and others, and when St. Martin's Hall and the Alhambra will soon be beginning again to resound with their pulpit-eloquence, it distresses one to think that the new lights should not only have, in general, a very low opinion of the preachers of the old religion, but that they should have it without knowing the best that these preachers can do.[b] And that they are in this case is owing in part, certainly, to the negligence of the Christian Knowledge Society. In the old times they used to print and spread abroad Bishop Wilson's *Maxims of Piety and Christianity*. The copy of this work which I use is one of their publications, bearing their imprint, and bound in the

---

[a] On Bishop Wilson, see above p. 60.

[b] The scientist in question was T.H. Huxley (see above p. 70); in November 1868 the courts ruled that lectures on science and other subjects given under the aegis of the 'Recreative Religionists' did not contravene the law prohibiting 'entertainments' on Sundays.

well-known brown calf which they made familiar to our childhood; but the date of my copy is 1812. I know of no copy besides, and I believe the work is no longer one of those printed and circulated by the Society.[1] Hence the error, flattering, I own, to me personally, yet in itself to be regretted, of the distinguished physicist already mentioned.

But Bishop Wilson's *Maxims* deserve to be circulated as a religious book, not only by comparison with the cartloads of rubbish circulated at present under this designation, but for their own sake, and even by comparison with the other works of the same author. Over the far better known *Sacra Privata* they have this advantage, that they were prepared by him for his own private use, while the *Sacra Privata* were prepared by him for the use of the public. The *Maxims* were never meant to be printed, and have on that account, like a work of, doubtless, far deeper emotion and power, the *Meditations* of Marcus Aurelius, something peculiarly sincere and first-hand about them. Some of the best things from the *Maxims* have passed into the *Sacra Privata*. Still, in the *Maxims*, we have them as they first arose; and whereas, too, in the *Sacra Privata* the writer speaks very often as one of the clergy, and as addressing the clergy, in the *Maxims* he almost always speaks solely as a man. I am not saying a word against the *Sacra Privata*, for which I have the highest respect; only the *Maxims* seem to me a better and more edifying book still. They should be read, as Joubert says Nicole should be read, with a direct aim at practice. The reader will leave on one side things which, from the change of time and from the changed point of view which the change of time inevitably brings with it, no longer suit him; enough will remain to serve as a sample of the very best, perhaps, which our nation and race can do in the way of religious writing. M. Michelet makes it a reproach to us that, in all the doubt as to the real author of the *Imitation*, no one has ever dreamed of ascribing that work to an Englishman. It is true, the *Imitation* could not well have been written by an Englishman; the religious delicacy and the profound asceticism of that admirable book are hardly in our nature. This would be more of a reproach to us if in poetry, which requires, no less than religion, a true delicacy of spiritual perception, our race had not done great things; and if the *Imitation*, exquisite as it is, did not, as I have elsewhere remarked,

[1] The Christian Knowledge Society has, since 1869, republished the *Maxims* of Bishop Wilson

belong to a class of works in which the perfect balance of human nature is lost, and which have therefore, as spiritual productions, in their contents something excessive and morbid, in their form something not thoroughly sound. On a lower range than the *Imitation*, and awakening in our nature chords less poetical and delicate, the *Maxims* of Bishop Wilson are, as a religious work, far more solid. To the most sincere ardour and unction, Bishop Wilson unites, in these *Maxims*, that downright honesty and plain good sense which our English race has so powerfully applied to the divine impossibilities of religion; by which it has brought religion so much into practical life, and has done its allotted part in promoting upon earth the kingdom of God.

With ardour and unction religion, as we all know, may still be fanatical; with honesty and good sense, it may still be prosaic; and the fruit of honesty and good sense united with ardour and unction is often only a prosaic religion held fanatically. Bishop Wilson's excellence lies in a balance of the four qualities, and in a fulness and perfection of them, which makes this untoward result impossible. His unction is so perfect, and in such happy alliance with his good sense, that it becomes tenderness and fervent charity. His good sense is so perfect, and in such happy alliance with his unction, that it becomes moderation and insight. While, therefore, the type of religion exhibited in his *Maxims* is English, it is yet a type of a far higher kind than is in general reached by Bishop Wilson's countrymen; and yet, being English, it is possible and attainable for them. And so I conclude as I began, by saying that a work of this sort is one which the Society for Promoting Christian Knowledge should not suffer to remain out of print and out of currency.

And now to pass to the matters canvassed in the following essay. The whole scope of the essay is to recommend culture as the great help out of our present difficulties; culture being a pursuit of our total perfection by means of getting to know, on all the matters which most concern us, the best which has been thought and said in the world; and through this knowledge, turning a stream of fresh and free thought upon our stock notions and habits, which we now follow staunchly but mechanically, vainly imagining that there is a virtue in following them staunchly which makes up for the mischief of following them mechanically. This, and this alone, is the scope of the following essay. And the culture we recommend is, above all, an inward operation.

But we are often supposed, when we criticise by the help of culture some imperfect doing or other, to have in our eye some well-known rival plan of doing, which we want to serve and recommend. Thus, for instance, because we have freely pointed out the dangers and inconveniences to which our literature is exposed in the absence of any centre of taste and authority like the French Academy, it is constantly said that we want to introduce here in England an institution like the French Academy.ᶜ We have, indeed, expressly declared that we wanted no such thing; but let us notice how it is just our worship of machinery, and of external doing, which leads to this charge being brought; and how the inwardness of culture makes us seize, for watching and cure, the faults to which our want of an Academy inclines us, and yet prevents us from trusting to an arm of flesh, as the Puritans say,—from blindly flying to this outward machinery of an Academy, in order to help ourselves. For the very same culture and free inward play of thought which shows how the Corinthian style, or the whimsies about the One Primeval Language, are generated and strengthened in the absence of an Academy, shows us, too, how little any Academy, such as we should be likely to get, would cure them. Every one who knows the characteristics of our national life, and the tendencies so fully discussed in the following pages, knows exactly what an English Academy would be like. One can see the happy family in one's mind's eye as distinctly as if it were already constituted. Lord Stanhope, the Dean of St. Paul's,² the Bishop of Oxford,³ Mr. Gladstone, the Dean of Westminster, Mr. Froude, Mr. Henry Reeve,—everything which is influential, accomplished, and distinguished; and then, some fine morning, a dissatisfaction of the public mind with this brilliant and select coterie, a flight of Corinthian leading articles, and an irruption of Mr. G. A. Sala.ᵈ Clearly, this is not what will do us good. The very same

---

² The late Dean Milman.
³ The late Bishop Wilberforce

ᶜ In 'The Literary Influence of Academies' (1864 and included in *Essays in Criticism*), Arnold had emphasized the beneficial influence of the *Académie Française*, but had not urged the establishment of an Academy in England.
ᵈ George Augustus Sala (1828–96), prominent journalist on the *Daily Telegraph* and a favourite target of Arnold's; the implication here is that Sala would have no difficulty in arousing public resentment at the hypothetical proceedings of the distinguished persons mentioned earlier in the sentence.

faults,—the want of sensitiveness of intellectual conscience, the disbelief in right reason, the dislike of authority,—which have hindered
our having an Academy and have worked injuriously in our literature,
would also hinder us from making our Academy, if we established it,
one which would really correct them. And culture, which shows us
truly the faults to be corrected, shows us this also just as truly.

Natural, as we have said, the sort of misunderstanding just noticed
is; yet our usefulness depends upon our being able to clear it away,
and to convince those who mechanically serve some stock notion or
operation, and thereby go astray, that it is not culture's work or aim to
give the victory to some rival fetish, but simply to turn a free and fresh
stream of thought upon the whole matter in question. In a thing of
more immediate interest, just now, than any question of an Academy,
the like misunderstanding prevails; and until it is dissipated, culture
can do no good work in the matter. When we criticise the present
operation of disestablishing the Irish Church, not by the power of
reason and justice, but by the power of the antipathy of the Protestant
Nonconformists, English and Scotch, to establishments, we are called
enemies of the Nonconformists, blind partisans of the Anglican
Establishment, possessed with the one desire to help the clergy and to
harm the Dissenters. More than a few words we must give to showing
how erroneous are these charges; because if they were true, we
should be actually subverting our own design, and playing false to that
culture which it is our very purpose to recommend.

Certainly we are no enemies of the Nonconformists; for, on the
contrary, what we aim at is their perfection. But culture, which is the
study of perfection, leads us, as we in the following pages have shown,
to conceive of true human perfection as a *harmonious* perfection,
developing all sides of our humanity; and as a *general* perfection,
developing all parts of our society. For if one member suffer, the
other members must suffer with it; and the fewer there are that follow
the true way of salvation, the harder that way is to find. And while the
Nonconformists, the successors and representatives of the Puritans,
and like them staunchly walking by the best light they have, make a
large part of what is strongest and most serious in this nation, and
therefore attract our respect and interest, yet all which, in what follows, is said about Hebraism and Hellenism, has for its main result to
show how our Puritans, ancient and modern, have not enough added
to their care for walking staunchly by the best light they have, a care

that that light be not darkness; how they have developed one side of their humanity at the expense of all others, and have become incomplete and mutilated men in consequence. Thus falling short of harmonious perfection, they fail to follow the true way of salvation. Therefore that way is made the harder for others to find, general perfection is put further off out of our reach, and the confusion and perplexity in which our society now labours is increased by the Nonconformists rather than diminished by them. So, while we praise and esteem the zeal of the Nonconformists in walking staunchly by the best light they have, and desire to take no whit from it, we seek to add to this what we call sweetness and light, and to develop their full humanity more perfectly. To seek this is certainly not to be the enemy of the Nonconformists.

But now, with these ideas in our head, we come upon the operation for disestablishing the Irish Church by the power of the Nonconformists' antipathy to religious establishments and endowments. And we see Liberal statesmen, for whose purpose this antipathy happens to be convenient, flattering it all they can; saying that though they have no intention of laying hands on an Establishment which is efficient and popular, like the Anglican Establishment here in England, yet it is in the abstract a fine and good thing that religion should be left to the voluntary support of its promoters, and should thus gain in energy and independence; and Mr. Gladstone has no words strong enough to express his admiration of the refusal of State-aid by the Irish Roman Catholics, who have never yet been seriously asked to accept it, but who would a good deal embarrass him if they demanded it. And we see philosophical politicians with a turn for swimming with the stream, and philosophical divines with the same turn, seeking to give a sort of grand stamp of generality and solemnity to this antipathy of the Nonconformists, and to dress it out as a law of human progress in the future. Now, nothing can be pleasanter than swimming with the stream; and we might gladly, if we could, try in our unsystematic way to take part in labours at once so philosophical and so popular. But we have got fixed in our minds that a more full and harmonious development of their humanity is what the Nonconformists most want, that narrowness, one-sidedness, and incompleteness is what they most suffer from; in a word, that in what we call *provinciality* they abound, but in what we may call *totality* they fall short.

And they fall short more than the members of Establishments. The great works by which, not only in literature, art, and science generally, but in religion itself, the human spirit has manifested its approaches to totality and to a full, harmonious perfection, and by which it stimulates and helps forward the world's general perfection, come, not from Nonconformists, but from men who either belong to Establishments or have been trained in them. A Nonconformist minister, the Rev. Edward White, who has written a temperate and well-reasoned pamphlet against Church Establishments, says that "the unendowed and unestablished communities of England exert full as much moral and ennobling influence upon the conduct of statesmen as that Church which is both established and endowed." That depends upon what one means by moral and ennobling influence. The believer in machinery may think that to get a Government to abolish Church-rates or to legalise marriage with a deceased wife's sister is to exert a moral and ennobling influence upon Government. But a lover of perfection, who looks to inward ripeness for the true springs of conduct, will surely think that as Shakspeare has done more for the inward ripeness of our statesmen than Dr. Watts,[e] and has, therefore, done more to moralise and ennoble them, so an Establishment which has produced Hooker, Barrow, Butler, has done more to moralise and ennoble English statesmen and their conduct than communities which have produced the Nonconformist divines.[f] The fruitful men of English Puritanism and Nonconformity are men who were trained within the pale of the Establishment,—Milton, Baxter, Wesley. A generation or two outside the Establishment, and Puritanism produces men of national mark no more. With the same doctrine and discipline, men of national mark are produced in Scotland; but in an Establishment. With the same doctrine and discipline, men of national and even European mark are produced in Germany, Switzerland, France; but in Establishments. Only two religious disciplines seem exempted, or comparatively exempted, from the operation of the law which appears to forbid the rearing, outside of national Churches, of men of the highest spiritual significance. These two are the Roman Catholic and the Jewish. And these, both of them, rest on Establishments, which, though not indeed national, are cosmopolitan; and perhaps here, what the individual man does not lose by these

[e] Issac Watts (1674–1748), prolific hymn- writer.
[f] Richard Hooker (1554–1600), Isaac Barrow (1630–77), and Joseph Butler, Bishop of Durham (1692–1752) were all leading Anglican churchmen.

conditions of his rearing, the citizen, and the State of which he is a citizen, loses.

What, now, can be the reason of this undeniable provincialism of the English Puritans and Protestant Nonconformists? Men of genius and character are born and reared in this medium as in any other. From the faults of the mass such men will always be comparatively free, and they will always excite our interest; yet in this medium they seem to have a special difficulty breaking through what bounds them, and in developing their totality. Surely the reason is, that the Nonconformist is not in contact with the main current of national life, like the member of an Establishment. In a matter of such deep and vital concern as religion, this separation from the main current of the national life has peculiar importance. In the following essay we have discussed at length the tendency in us to *Hebraise*, as we call it; that is, to sacrifice all other sides of our being to the religious side. This tendency has its cause in the divine beauty and grandeur of religion, and bears affecting testimony to them. But we have seen that it has dangers for us, we have seen that it leads to a narrow and twisted growth of our religious side itself, and to a failure in perfection. But if we tend to Hebraise even in an Establishment, with the main current of national life flowing round us, and reminding us in all ways of the variety and fulness of human existence,—by a Church which is historical as the State itself is historical, and whose order, ceremonies, and monuments reach, like those of the State, far beyond any fancies and devisings of ours; and by institutions such as the Universities, formed to defend and advance that very culture and many-sided development which it is the danger of Hebraising to make us neglect,—how much more must we tend to Hebraise when we lack these preventives. One may say that to be reared a member of a national Church is in itself a lesson of religious moderation, and a help towards culture and harmonious perfection. Instead of battling for his own private forms for expressing the inexpressible and defining the undefinable, a man takes those which have commended themselves most to the religious life of his nation; and while he may be sure that within those forms the religious side of his own nature may find its satisfaction, he has leisure and composure to satisfy other sides of his nature as well.

But with the member of a Nonconforming or self-made religious community, how different! The sectary's *eigene grosse Erfindungen*, as

Goethe calls them,—the precious discoveries of himself and his friends for expressing the inexpressible and defining the undefinable in peculiar forms of their own, cannot but, as he has voluntarily chosen them, and is personally responsible for them, fill his whole mind. He is zealous to do battle for them and affirm them; for in affirming them he affirms himself, and that is what we all like. Other sides of his being are thus neglected, because the religious side, always tending in every serious man to predominance over our other spiritual sides, is in him made quite absorbing and tyrannous by the condition of self-assertion and challenge which he has chosen for himself. And just what is not essential in religion he comes to mistake for essential, and a thousand times the more readily because he has chosen it for himself; and religious activity he fancies to consist in battling for it. All this leaves him little leisure or inclination for culture; to which, besides, he has no great institutions not of his own making, like the Universities connected with the national Church to invite him; but only such institutions as, like the order and discipline of his religion, he may have invented for himself, and invented under the sway of the narrow and tyrannous notions of religion fostered in him as we have seen. Thus, while a national establishment of religion favours totality, *hole-and-corner* forms of religion (to use an expressive popular word) inevitably favour provincialism.

But the Nonconformists, and many of our Liberal friends along with them, have a plausible plan for getting rid of this provincialism, if, as they can hardly quite deny, it exists. "Let us all be in the same boat," they cry; "open the Universities to everybody, and let there be no establishment of religion at all!" Open the Universities by all means; but, as to the second point about establishment, let us sift the proposal a little. It does seem at first a little like that proposal of the fox, who had lost his own tail, to put all the other foxes in the same case by a general cutting off of tails; and we know that moralists have decided that the right course here was, not to adopt this plausible suggestion, and cut off tails all round, but rather that the other foxes should keep their tails, and that the fox without a tail should get one. And so we might be inclined to urge, that, to cure the evil of the Nonconformists' provincialism, the right way can hardly be to provincialise us all round.

However, perhaps we shall not be provincialised. For Mr. White says that probably, "when all good men alike are placed in a condition of religious equality, and the whole complicated iniquity of Government Church patronage is swept away, more of moral and ennobling influence than ever will be brought to bear upon the action of statesmen."

We already have an example of religious equality in our colonies. "In the colonies," says *The Times*, "we see religious communities unfettered by State-control, and the State relieved from one of the most troublesome and irritating responsibilities." But America is the great example alleged by those who are against establishments for religion. Our topic at this moment is the influence of religious establishments on culture; and it is remarkable that Mr. Bright, who has taken lately to representing himself as, above all, a promoter of reason and of the simple natural truth of things, and his policy as a fostering of the growth of intelligence,—just the aims, as is well known, of culture also,—Mr. Bright, in a speech at Birmingham about education, seized on the very point which seems to concern our topic, when he said: "I believe the people of the United States have offered to the world more valuable information during the last forty years, than all Europe put together." So America, without religious establishments, seems to get ahead of us all, even in light and the things of the mind.

On the other hand, another friend of reason and the simple natural truth of things, M. Renan, says of America, in a book he has recently published, what seems to conflict violently with what Mr. Bright says. Mr. Bright avers that not only have the United States thus informed Europe, but they have done it without a great apparatus of higher and scientific instruction, and by dint of all classes in America being "sufficiently educated to be able to read, and to comprehend, and to think; and that, I maintain, is the foundation of all subsequent progress." And then comes M. Renan, and says: "The sound instruction of the people is an effect of the high culture of certain classes. *The countries which, like the United States, have created a considerable popular instruction without any serious higher instruction, will long have to expiate this fault by their intellectual mediocrity, their vulgarity of manners, their superficial spirit, their lack of general intelligence.*"[4]

---

[4] "Les pays qui, comme les Etats-Unis, ont créé un enseignement populaire considérable sans instruction supérieure sérieuse, expieront longtemps encore cette faute par leur médiocrité intellectuelle, leur grossièreté de moeurs, leur esprit superficiel, leur manque d'intelligence générale."

Now, which of these two friends of light are we to believe? M. Renan seems more to have in view what we ourselves mean by culture; because Mr. Bright always has in his eye what he calls "a commendable interest" in politics and in political agitations. As he said only the other day at Birmingham: "At this moment,—in fact, I may say at every moment in the history of a free country,—there is nothing that is so much worth discussing as politics." And he keeps repeating, with all the powers of his noble oratory, the old story, how to the thoughtfulness and intelligence of the people of great towns we owe all our improvements in the last thirty years, and how these improvements have hitherto consisted in Parliamentary reform, and free trade, and abolition of Church rates, and so on; and how they are now about to consist in getting rid of minority-members, and in introducing a free breakfast-table, and in abolishing the Irish Church by the power of the Nonconformists' antipathy to establishments, and much more of the same kind. And though our pauperism and ignorance, and all the questions which are called social, seem now to be forcing themselves upon his mind, yet he still goes on with his glorifying of the great towns, and the Liberals, and their operations for the last thirty years. It never seems to occur to him that the present troubled state of our social life has anything to do with the thirty years' blind worship of their nostrums by himself and our Liberal friends, or that it throws any doubts upon the sufficiency of this worship. But he thinks that what is still amiss is due to the stupidity of the Tories, and will be cured by the thoughtfulness and intelligence of the great towns, and by the Liberals going on gloriously with their political operations as before; or that it will cure itself. So we see what Mr. Bright means by thoughtfulness and intelligence, and in what manner, according to him, we are to grow in them. And, no doubt, in America all classes read their newspaper, and take a commendable interest in politics, more than here or anywhere else in Europe.

But in the following essay we have been led to doubt the sufficiency of all this political operating, pursued mechanically as our race pursues it; and we found that *general intelligence*, as M. Renan calls it, or, as we say, attention to the reason of things, was just what we were without, and that we were without it because we worshipped our machinery so devoutly. Therefore, we conclude that M. Renan, more than Mr. Bright, means by reason and intelligence the same thing as we do. And when M. Renan says that America, that chosen home of newspapers and politics, is without general intelligence, we think it likely, from the circumstances of the case, that this is so; and that in the things of the mind, and in culture and totality, America, instead of surpassing us all, falls short.

And,—to keep to our point of the influence of religious establishments upon culture and a high development of our humanity,—we can surely see reasons why, with all her energy and fine gifts, America does not show more of this development, or more promise of this. In the following essay it will be seen how our society distributes itself into Barbarians, Philistines, and Populace; and America is just ourselves, with the Barbarians quite left out, and the Populace nearly. This leaves the Philistines for the great bulk of the nation;—a livelier sort of Philistine than ours, and with the pressure and false ideal of our Barbarians taken away, but left all the more to himself and to have his full swing. And as we have found that the strongest and most vital part of English Philistinism was the Puritan and Hebraising middle class, and that its Hebraising keeps it from culture and totality, so it is notorious that the people of the United States issues from this class, and reproduces its tendencies,—its narrow conception of man's spiritual range and of his one thing needful. From Maine to Florida, and back again, all America Hebraises. Difficult as it is to speak of a people merely from what one reads, yet that, I think, one may without much fear of contradiction say. I mean, when in the United States any spiritual side in man is wakened to activity, it is generally the religious side, and the religious side in a narrow way. Social reformers go to Moses or St. Paul for their doctrines, and have no notion there is anywhere else to go to; earnest young men at schools and universities, instead of conceiving salvation as a harmonious perfection only to be won by unreservedly cultivating many sides in us, conceive of it in the old Puritan fashion, and fling themselves ardently upon it in the old, false ways of this fashion, which we know so well, and such as Mr. Hammond, the American revivalist, has lately at Mr. Spurgeon's Tabernacle been refreshing our memory with.[g]

Now, if America thus Hebraises more than either England or Germany, will any one deny that the absence of religious establishments has much to do with it? We have seen how establishments tend

---

[g] Edward Payson Hammond (1831–1910), American Evangelist preacher who conducted a series of emotional revival meetings at Spurgeon's Tabernacle in November 1868.

to give us a sense of a historical life of the human spirit, outside and beyond our own fancies and feelings; how they thus tend to suggest new sides and sympathies in us to cultivate; how, further, by saving us from having to invent and fight for our own forms of religion, they give us leisure and calm to steady our view of religion itself,—the most overpowering of objects, as it is the grandest,—and to enlarge our first crude notions of the one thing needful. But, in a serious people, where every one has to choose and strive for his own order and discipline of religion, the contention about these non-essentials occupies his mind. His first crude notions about the one thing needful do not get purged, and they invade the whole spiritual man in him, and then, making a solitude, they call it heavenly peace.

I remember a Nonconformist manufacturer, in a town of the Midland counties, telling me that when he first came there, some years ago, the place had no Dissenters; but he had opened an Independent chapel in it, and now Church and Dissent were pretty equally divided, with sharp contests between them. I said that this seemed a pity. "A pity?" cried he; "not at all! Only think of all the zeal and activity which the collision calls forth!" "Ah, but, my dear friend," I answered, "only think of all the nonsense which you now hold quite firmly, which you would never have held if you had not been contradicting your adversary in it all these years!" The more serious the people, and the more prominent the religious side in it, the greater is the danger of this side, if set to choose out forms for itself and fight for existence, swelling and spreading till it swallows all other spiritual sides up, intercepts and absorbs all nutriment which should have gone to them, and leaves Hebraism rampant in us and Hellenism stamped out.

Culture, and the harmonious perfection of our whole being, and what we call totality, then become quite secondary matters. And even the institutions, which should develop these, take the same narrow and partial view of humanity and its wants as the free religious communities take. Just as the free churches of Mr. Beecher or Brother Noyes, with their provincialism and want of centrality, make mere Hebraisers in religion, and not perfect men, so the university of Mr. Ezra Cornell, a really noble monument of his munificence, yet seems to rest on a misconception of what culture truly is, and to be calculated to produce miners, or engineers, or architects, not sweetness and light.[h]

---

[h] Henry Ward Beecher (1813–87) was a leading American Congregationalist preacher;

And, therefore, when Mr. White asks the same kind of question about America that he has asked about England, and wants to know whether, without religious establishments, as much is not done in America for the higher national life as is done for that life here, we answer in the same way as we did before, that as much is not done. Because to enable and stir up people to read their Bible and the newspapers, and to get a practical knowledge of their business, does not serve to the higher spiritual life of a nation so much as culture, truly conceived, serves; and a true conception of culture is, as M. Renan's words show, just what America fails in.

To the many who think that spirituality, and sweetness, and light, are all moonshine, this will not appear to matter much; but with us, who value them, and who think that we have traced much of our present discomfort to the want of them, it weighs a great deal. So not only do we say that the Nonconformists have got provincialism and lost totality by the want of a religious establishment, but we say that the very example which they bring forward to help their case makes against them; and that when they triumphantly show us America without religious establishments, they only show us a whole nation touched, amidst all its greatness and promise, with that provincialism which it is our aim to extirpate in the English Nonconformists.

But now to evince the disinterestedness which culture teaches us. We have seen the narrowness generated in Puritanism by its hole-and-corner organisation, and we propose to cure it by bringing Puritanism more into contact with the main current of national life. Here we are fully at one with the Dean of Westminster; and, indeed, he and we were trained in the same school to mark the narrowness of Puritanism, and to wish to cure it.[i] But he and others seem disposed simply to give to the present Anglican Establishment a character the most latitudinarian, as it is called, possible; availing themselves for this purpose of the diversity of tendencies and doctrines which does undoubtedly exist already in the Anglican formularies; and then they would say to the Puritans: "Come all of you into this liberally conceived Anglican Establishment." But to say this is hardly, perhaps, to take sufficient account of the course of history, or of the strength of

John Humphrey Noyes (1811–86) was the founder of the Oneida Community, an idealistic group supposedly committed to 'free love'; Cornell University in New York State was founded by Ezra Cornell (1807–74) to promote, in particular, the study of agriculture and technology.

[i] A.P. Stanley (see above p. 43) had, like Arnold himself, been a pupil at Dr Arnold's Rugby.

men's feelings in what concerns religion, or of the gravity which may have come to attach to points of religious order and discipline merely. When Mr. White talks of "sweeping away the whole complicated iniquity of Government Church patronage," he uses language which has been forced upon him by his position, but which is devoid of all real solidity. But when he talks of the religious communities "which have for three hundred years contended for the power of the congregation in the management of their own affairs," then he talks history; and his language has behind it, in my opinion, facts which make the latitudinarianism of our Broad Churchmen quite illusory.

Certainly, culture will never make us think it an essential of religion whether we have in our Church discipline "a popular authority of elders," as Hooker calls it, or whether we have Episcopal jurisdiction. Certainly, Hooker himself did not think it an essential; for in the dedication of his *Ecclesiastical Polity*, speaking of these questions of church-discipline which gave occasion to his great work, he says they are "in truth, for the greatest part, such silly things, that very easiness doth make them hard to be disputed of in serious manner." Hooker's great work against the impugners of the order and discipline of the Church of England was written (and this is too indistinctly seized by many who read it), not because Episcopalianism is essential, but because its impugners maintained that Presbyterianism is essential, and that Episcopalianism is sinful. Neither the one nor the other is either essential or sinful, and much may be said on behalf of both. But what is important to be remarked is, *that both were in the Church of England at the Reformation*, and that Presbyterianism was only extruded gradually. We have mentioned Hooker, and nothing better illustrates what has just been asserted than the following incident in Hooker's own career, which every one has read, for it is related in Isaac Walton's *Life of Hooker*, but of which, probably, the significance has been fully grasped by very few of those who have read it.

Hooker was through the influence of Archbishop Whitgift appointed, in 1585, Master of the Temple; but a great effort had first been made to obtain the place for a Mr. Walter Travers, well known in that day, though now it is Hooker's name which alone preserves his. This Travers was then afternoon-lecturer at the Temple. The Master whose death made the vacancy, Alvey, recommended on his deathbed Travers for his successor. The Society was favourable to Travers, and he had the support of the Lord Treasurer Burghley. Although

Hooker was appointed to the Mastership, Travers remained after-
noon-lecturer, and combated in the afternoons the doctrine which
Hooker preached in the mornings. Now, this Travers, originally a
Fellow of Trinity College, Cambridge, afterwards afternoon-lecturer
at the Temple, recommended for the Mastership by the foregoing
Master whose opinions, it is said, agreed with his, favoured by the
Society of the Temple and supported by the Prime Minister,—this
Travers was not an Episcopally ordained clergyman at all. He was a
Presbyterian, a partisan of the Geneva church-discipline, as it was
then called, and "had taken orders," says Walton, "by the Presbyters
in Antwerp." In another place Walton speaks of his orders yet more
fully:—"He had disowned," he says, "the English Established
Church and Episcopacy, and went to Geneva, and afterwards to
Antwerp, to be ordained minister, as he was by Villers and Cartwright
and others the heads of a congregation there; and so came back again
more confirmed for the discipline." Villers and Cartwright are in like
manner examples of Presbyterianism within the Church of England,
which was common enough at that time. But perhaps nothing can
better give us a lively sense of its presence there than this history of
Travers, which is as if Mr. Binney were now[5] afternoon-reader at
Lincoln's Inn or the Temple; were to be a candidate, favoured by the
Benchers and by the Prime Minister, for the Mastership; and were
only kept out of the post by the accident of the Archbishop of Canterbury's influence with the Queen carrying a rival candidate.[j]

Presbyterianism, with its popular principle of the power of the
congregation in the management of their own affairs, was extruded
from the Church of England, and men like Travers can no longer
appear in her pulpits. Perhaps if a government like that of Elizabeth,
with secular statesmen like the Cecils, and ecclesiastical statesmen
like Whitgift, could have been prolonged, Presbyterianism might, by a
wise mixture of concession and firmness, have been absorbed in the
Establishment. Lord Bolingbroke, on a matter of this kind a very
clear-judging and impartial witness, says, in a work far too little read,
his *Remarks on English History:*—"The measures pursued and the
temper observed in Queen Elizabeth's time tended to diminish the
religious opposition by a slow, a gentle, and for that very reason an

[5] 1869.
[j] Thomas Binney (1798–1874) was at the time the best known Congregationalist minister
in England.

effectual progression. There was even room to hope that when the first fire of the Dissenters' zeal was passed, reasonable terms of union with the Established Church might be accepted by such of them as were not intoxicated with fanaticism. These were friends to order, though they disputed about it. If these friends of Calvin's discipline had been once incorporated with the Established Church, the remaining sectaries would have been of little moment, either for numbers or reputation; and the very means which were proper to gain these friends were likewise the most effectual to hinder the increase of them, and of the other sectaries in the meantime." The temper and ill judgment of the Stuarts made shipwreck of all policy of this kind. Yet speaking even of the time of the Stuarts, but their early time, Clarendon says that if Bishop Andrewes had succeeded Bancroft at Canterbury, the disaffection of separatists might have been stayed and healed. This, however, was not to be; and Presbyterianism, after exercising for some years the law of the strongest, itself in Charles the Second's reign suffered under this law, and was finally cast out from the Church of England.

Now the points of church-discipline at issue between Presbyterianism and Episcopalianism are, as has been said, not essential. They might probably once have been settled in a sense altogether favourable to Episcopalianism. Hooker may have been right in thinking that there were in his time circumstances which made it essential that they should be settled in this sense, though the points in themselves were not essential. But by the very fact of the settlement not having then been effected, of the breach having gone on and widened, of the Nonconformists not having been amicably incorporated with the Establishment but violently cast out from it, the circumstances are now altogether altered. Isaac Walton, a fervent Churchman, complains that "the principles of the Nonconformists grew at last to such a height and were vented so daringly, that, beside the loss of life and limbs, the Church and State were both forced to use such other severities as will not admit of an excuse, if it had not been to prevent confusion and the perilous consequences of it." But those very severities have of themselves made union on an Episcopalian footing impossible. Besides, Presbyterianism, the popular authority of elders, the power of the congregation in the management of their own affairs, has that warrant given to it by Scripture and by the proceedings of the early Christian Churches, it is so consonant with the spirit of Protestantism which made the Reformation and which has great strength in this country, it is so predominant in the practice of other Reformed Churches, it was so strong in the original Reformed Church of England, that one cannot help doubting whether any settlement which suppressed it could have been really permanent, and whether it would not have kept appearing again and again, and causing dissension.

Well, then, if culture is the disinterested endeavour after man's perfection, will it not make us wish to cure the provincialism of the Nonconformists, not by rendering Churchmen provincial along with them, but by letting their popular church-discipline, formerly present in the national Church and still present in the affections and practice of a good part of the nation, appear in the national Church once more; and thus to bring Nonconformists into contact again, as their greater fathers were, with the main stream of national life? Why should not a Presbyterian Church, based on this considerable and important, though not essential principle, of the congregation's share in the church-management, be established, — with equal rank for its chiefs with the chiefs of Episcopacy, and with admissibility of its ministers, under a revised system of patronage and preferment, to benefices, — side by side with the Episcopal Church, as the Calvinist and Lutheran Churches are established side by side in France and Germany? Such a Presbyterian Church would unite the main bodies of Protestants who are now separatists; and separation would cease to be the law of their religious order. And thus, — through this concession on a really considerable point of difference, — that endless splitting into hole-and-corner churches on quite inconsiderable points of difference, which must prevail so long as separatism is the first law of a Nonconformist's religious existence, would be checked. Culture would then find a place among English followers of the popular authority of Elders, as it has long found it among the followers of Episcopal jurisdiction. And this we should gain by merely recognising, regularising, and restoring an element which appeared once in the reformed national Church, and which is considerable and national enough to have a sound claim to appear there still.

So far, then, is culture from making us unjust to the Nonconformists because it forbids us to worship their fetishes, that it even leads us to propose to do more for them than they themselves venture to claim. It leads us, also, to respect what is solid and respectable in their convictions. Not that the forms in which the human spirit tries to to express the inexpressible, or the forms by which man tries to worship, have or can have, as has been said, for the follower of perfection, anything necessary or eternal. If the New Testament and the practice of the primitive Christians sanctioned the popular form of church-government a thousand times more expressly than they do, if the Church since Constantine were a thousand times more of a departure from the scheme of primitive Christianity than it can be shown to be, that does not at all make, as is supposed by men in bondage to the letter, the popular form of church-government alone and always sacred and binding, or the work of Constantine a thing to be regretted.

What is alone and always sacred and binding for man is the making progress towards his total perfection; and the machinery by which he does this varies in value according as it helps him to do it. The planters of Christianity had their roots in deep and rich grounds of human life and achievement, both Jewish and also Greek; and had thus a comparatively firm and wide basis amidst all the vehement inspiration of their mighty movement and change. By their strong inspiration they carried men off the old basis of life and culture, whether Jewish or Greek, and generations arose who had their roots in neither world, and were in contact therefore with no full and great stream of human life. If it had not been for some such change as that of the fourth century, Christianity might have lost itself in a multitude of hole-and-corner churches like the churches of English Nonconformity after its founders departed; churches without great men, and without furtherance for the higher life of humanity. At a critical moment came Constantine, and placed Christianity,—or let us rather say, placed the human spirit, whose totality was endangered,— in contact with the main current of human life. And his work was justified by its fruits, in men like Augustine and Dante, and indeed in all the great men of Christianity, Catholics or Protestants, ever since.

And one may go beyond this. M. Albert Réville, whose religious writings are always interesting, says that the conception which cultivated and philosophical Jews now entertain of Christianity and its Founder, is probably destined to become the conception which Christians themselves will entertain.[k] Socinians are fond of saying the

---

[k] Albert Réville (1826–1906), a French Protestant theologian and historian of 'advanced' views.

same thing about the Socinian conception of Christianity. Now, even if this were true, it would still have been better for a man, during the last eighteen hundred years, to have been a Christian and a member of one of the great Christian communions, than to have been a Jew or a Socinian; because the being in contact with the main stream of human life is of more moment for a man's total spiritual growth, and for his bringing to perfection the gifts committed to him, which is his business on earth, than any speculative opinion which he may hold or think he holds. Luther,—whom we have called a Philistine of genius, and who, because he was a Philistine, had a coarseness and lack of spiritual delicacy which have harmed his disciples, but who, because he was a genius, had splendid flashes of spiritual insight,—Luther says admirably in his Commentary on the Book of Daniel: "A God is simply *that* whereon the human heart rests with trust, faith, hope, and love. If the resting is right, then the God too is right; if the resting is wrong, then the God too is illusory." In other words, the worth of what a man thinks about God and the objects of religion depends on what the man *is*; and what the man *is*, depends upon his having more or less reached the measure of a perfect and total man.

Culture, disinterestedly seeking in its aim at perfection to see things as they really are, shows us how worthy and divine a thing is the religious side in man, though it is not the whole of man. But while recognising the grandeur of the religious side in man, culture yet makes us also eschew an inadequate conception of man's totality. Therefore to the worth and grandeur of the religious side in man, culture is rejoiced and willing to pay any tribute, except the tribute of man's totality. Unless it is proved that contact with the main current of national life is of no value (and we have shown that it is of the greatest value), we cannot safely, even to please the Nonconformists in a matter where we would please them as much as possible, admit their doctrines of disestablishment and separation.

Culture, again, can be disinterested enough to perceive and avow, that for Ireland the ends of human perfection might be best served by establishing,—that is, by bringing into contact with the main current of the national life,—the Roman Catholic and the Presbyterian Churches along with the Anglican Church. It can perceive and avow that we should really, in this way, be working to make reason and the will of God prevail; because we should be making Roman Catholics better citizens, and both Protestants and Roman Catholics larger-minded and more complete men. Undoubtedly there are great difficulties in such a plan as this; and the plan is not one which looks very likely to be adopted. The Churchman must rise above his ordinary self in order to favour it. And the Nonconformist has worshipped his fetish of separatism so long that he is likely to wish to remain, like Ephraim, "a wild ass alone by himself." It is a plan more for a time of creative statesmen, like the time of Elizabeth, than for a time of instrumental statesman like the present. The centre of power being where it is, our statesmen have every temptation, when they must act, to go along as they do with the ordinary self of those on whose favour they depend, to adopt as their own its desires, and to serve them with fidelity, and even, if possible, with ardour. This is the more easy for them, because there are not wanting,—and there never will be wanting,—thinkers to call the desires of the ordinary self of any great section of the community edicts of the national mind and laws of human progress, and to give them a general, a philosophic, and imposing expression. Therefore a plan such as that which we have indicated does not seem a plan so likely to find favour as a plan for abolishing the Irish Church by the power of the Nonconformists' antipathy to establishments.

But although culture makes us fond stickers to no machinery, not even our own, and therefore we are willing to grant that perfection can be reached without it,—with free churches as with established churches, and with instrumental statesmen as with creative statesmen,—yet perfection can never be reached without seeing things as they really are; and it is to this, therefore, and to no machinery in the world, that we stick. We insist that men should not mistake, as they are prone to mistake, their natural taste for the bathos for a relish for the sublime. And if statesmen, either with their tongue in their cheek or with a fine impulsiveness, tell people that their natural taste for the bathos is a relish for the sublime, there is the more need to tell them the contrary.

It is delusion on this point which is fatal, and against delusion on this point culture works. It is not fatal to our Liberal friends to labour for free trade, extension of the suffrage, and abolition of church-rates, instead of graver social ends; but it is fatal to them to be told by their flatterers, and to believe, with our social condition what it is, that they have performed a great, a heroic work, by occupying themselves exclusively, for the last thirty years, with these Liberal nostrums, and that the right and good course for them now is to go on occupying themselves with the like for the future. It is not fatal to Americans to have no religious establishments and no effective centres of high culture; but it is fatal to them to be told by their flatterers, and to believe, that they are the most intelligent people in the whole world, when of intelligence, in the true and fruitful sense of the word, they even singularly, as we have seen, come short. It is not fatal to the Nonconformists to remain with their separated churches; but it is fatal to them to be told by their flatterers, and to believe, that theirs is the one true way of worshipping God, that provincialism and loss of totality have not come to them from following it, or that provincialism and loss of totality are not evils. It is not fatal to the English nation to abolish the Irish Church by the power of the Nonconformists' antipathy to establishments; but it is fatal to it to be told by its flatterers, and to believe, that it is abolishing it through reason and justice, when it is really abolishing it through this power: or to expect the fruits of reason and justice from anything but the spirit of reason and justice themselves.

Now culture, because of its keen sense of what is really fatal, is all the more disposed to be rather indifferent about what is not fatal. And because machinery is the one concern of our actual politics, and an inward working, and not machinery, is what we most want, we keep advising our ardent young Liberal friends to think less of machinery, to stand more aloof from the arena of politics at present, and rather to try and promote, with us, an inward working. They do not listen to us, and they rush into the arena of politics, where their merits, indeed, seem to be little appreciated as yet; and then they complain of the reformed constituencies, and call the new Parliament a Philistine Parliament.[1] As if a nation, nourished and reared as ours has been, could give us, just yet, anything but a Philistine Parliament! —and would a Barbarian Parliament be even so good, or a Populace Parliament? For our part, we rejoice to see our dear old friends, the Hebraising Philistines, gathered in force in the Valley of Jehoshaphat

---

[1] The Parliament of 1868, in which Gladstone and the Liberals held a majority in favour of disestablishing the Irish Church, was the first to be elected following the broadening of the franchise by the 1867 Reform Act.

previous to their final conversion, which will certainly come. But, to attain this conversion, we must not try to oust them from their places and to contend for machinery with them, but we must work on them inwardly and cure their spirit. Ousted they will not be, but transformed. Ousted they do not deserve to be, and will not be.

For *the days of Israel are innumerable*; and in its blame of Hebraising too, and in its praise of Hellenising, culture must not fail to keep its flexibility, and to give to its judgments that passing and provisional character which we have seen it impose on its preferences and rejections of machinery. Now, and for us, it is a time to Hellenise, and to praise knowing; for we have Hebraised too much, and have overvalued doing. But the habits and discipline received from Hebraism remain for our race an eternal possession; and, as humanity is constituted, one must never assign to them the second rank to-day, without being prepared to restore to them the first rank to-morrow. Let us conclude by marking this distinctly.

To walk staunchly by the best light one has, to be strict and sincere with oneself, not to be of the number of those who say and do not, to be in earnest,—this is the discipline by which alone man is enabled to rescue his life from thraldom to the passing moment and to his bodily senses, to ennoble it, and to make it eternal. And this discipline has been nowhere so effectively taught as in the school of Hebraism. The intense and convinced energy with which the Hebrew, both of the Old and of the New Testament, threw himself upon his ideal of righteousness, and which inspired the incomparable definition of the great Christian virtue, faith,—*the substance of things hoped for, the evidence of things not seen,*—this energy of devotion to its ideal has belonged to Hebraism alone. As our idea of perfection widens beyond the narrow limits to which the over-rigour of Hebraising has tended to confine it, we shall yet come again to Hebraism for that devout energy in embracing our ideal, which alone can give to man the happiness of doing what he knows. "If ye know these things, happy are ye if ye do them!"—the last word for infirm humanity will always be that. For this word, reiterated with a power now sublime, now affecting, but always admirable, our race will, as long as the world lasts, return to Hebraism; and the Bible, which preaches this word, will for ever remain, as Goethe called it, not only a national book, but the Book of the Nations. Again and again, after what seemed breaches and separations, the prophetic promise to Jerusalem will still be true: — *Lo, thy sons come, whom thou sentest away; they come gathered from the west unto the east by the word of the Holy One, rejoicing in the remembrance of God.*

# Equality[1]

There is a maxim which we all know, which occurs in our copy-books, which occurs in that solemn and beautiful formulary against which the Nonconformist genius is just now so angrily chafing,—the Burial Service.[a] The maxim is this: "Evil communications corrupt good manners." It is taken from a chapter of the First Epistle to the Corinthians; but originally it is a line of poetry, of Greek poetry. *Quid Athenis et Hierosolymis?* asks a Father; what have Athens and Jerusalem to do with one another? Well, at any rate, the Jerusalemite Paul, exhorting his converts, enforces what he is saying by a verse of Athenian comedy,—a verse, probably, from the great master of that comedy, a man unsurpassed for fine and just observation of human life, Menander: Φθείρουσιν ἤθη χρήσθ᾽ ὁμιλίαι κακαί—"Evil communications corrupt good manners."

In that collection of single, sententious lines, printed at the end of Menander's fragments, where we now find the maxim quoted by St. Paul, there is another striking maxim, not alien certainly to the language of the Christian religion, but which has not passed into our copy-books: "Choose equality and flee greed." The same profound observer, who laid down the maxim so universally accepted by us that it has become commonplace, the maxim that evil communications corrupt good manners, laid down also, as a no less sure result of the accurate study of human life, this other maxim as well: "Choose

---

[1] Address delivered at the Royal Institution.

[a] The lesson read in the Church of England Burial Service was 1 Corinthians 15:20–58. The Dissenters protested against being required to use the Anglican Book of Common Prayer for burials in the parish churchyard.

equality and flee greed"—'Ισότητα δ' αἱροῦ καὶ πλεονεξίαν φύγε.

*Pleonexia*, or greed, the wishing and trying for the bigger share, we know under the name of covetousness. We understand by covetousness something different from what *pleonexia* really means: we understand by it the longing for other people's goods: and covetousness, so understood, it is a commonplace of morals and of religion with us that we should shun. As to the duty of pursuing equality, there is no such consent amongst us. Indeed, the consent is the other way, the consent is against equality. Equality before the law we all take as a matter of course; that is not the equality which we mean when we talk of equality. When we talk of equality, we understand social equality; and for equality in this Frenchified sense of the term almost everybody in England has a hard word. About four years ago Lord Beaconsfield held it up to reprobation in a speech to the students at Glasgow;[b]—a speech so interesting, that being asked soon afterwards to hold a discourse at Glasgow, I said that if one spoke there at all at that time it would be impossible to speak on any other subject but equality. However, it is a great way to Glasgow, and I never yet have been able to go and speak there.

But the testimonies against equality have been steadily accumulating from the date of Lord Beaconsfield's Glasgow speech down to the present hour. Sir Erskine May winds up his new and important *History of Democracy* by saying: "France has aimed at social equality. The fearful troubles through which she has passed have checked her prosperity, demoralised her society, and arrested the intellectual growth of her people."[c] Mr. Froude, again, who is more his own master than I am, has been able to go to Edinburgh and to speak there upon equality. Mr. Froude told his hearers that equality splits a nation into a "multitude of disconnected units," that "the masses require leaders whom they can trust," and that "the natural leaders in a healthy country are the gentry."[d] And only just before the *History of Democracy* came out, we had that exciting passage of arms between Mr. Lowe and Mr. Gladstone, where equality, poor thing, received

---

[b] Benjamin Disraeli (Lord Beaconsfield) (1804–81), leader of the Tory Party, *Inaugural Address . . . as Lord Rector of the University of Glasgow* (1873).

[c] Thomas Erskine May (1815–86), *Democracy in Europe: a History* (1878).

[d] J.A. Froude (1818–94), 'On the Uses of a Landed Gentry', *Short Studies on Great Subjects* (1877).

blows from them both. Mr. Lowe declared that "no concession should be made to the cry for equality, unless it appears that the State is menaced with more danger by its refusal than by its admission. No such case exists now or ever has existed in this country." And Mr. Gladstone replied that equality was so utterly unattractive to the people of this country, inequality was so dear to their hearts, that to talk of concessions being made to the cry for equality was absurd. "There is no broad political idea," says Mr. Gladstone quite truly, "which has entered less into the formation of the political system of this country than the love of equality." And he adds: "It is not the love of equality which has carried into every corner of the country the distinct undeniable popular preference, wherever other things are equal, for a man who is a lord over a man who is not. The love of freedom itself is hardly stronger in England than the love of aristocracy." Mr. Gladstone goes on to quote a saying of Sir William Molesworth, that with our people the love of aristocracy "is religion." And he concludes in his copious and eloquent way: "Call this love of inequality by what name you please,—the complement of the love of freedom, or its negative pole, or the shadow which the love of freedom casts, or the reverberation of its voice in the halls of the constitution,—it is an active, living, and life-giving power, which forms an inseparable essential element in our political habits of mind, and asserts itself at every step in the processes of our system."[e]

And yet, on the other side, we have a consummate critic of life like Menander, delivering, as if there were no doubt at all about the matter, the maxim: "Choose equality!" An Englishman with any curiosity must surely be inclined to ask himself how such a maxim can ever have got established, and taken rank along with "Evil communications corrupt good manners." Moreover, we see that among the French, who have suffered so grievously, as we hear, from choosing equality, the most gifted spirits continue to believe passionately in it nevertheless. "The human ideal, as well as the social ideal, is," says George Sand, "to achieve equality." She calls equality "the goal of man and the law of the future." She asserts that France is the most

---

[e] Robert Lowe (see above p. 74) and the Liberal leader William Ewart Galdstone (1809–98) debated the question of extending the franchise in a series of articles in the *Fortnightly Review* and the *Nineteenth Century* in the course of 1877.

civilised of nations, and that its pre-eminence in civilisation it owes to equality.[f]

But Menander lived a long while ago, and George Sand was an enthusiast. Perhaps their differing from us about equality need not trouble us much. France, too, counts for but one nation, as England counts for one also. Equality may be a religion with the people of France, as inequality, we are told, is a religion with the people of England. But what do other nations seem to think about the matter?

Now, my discourse to-night is most certainly not meant to be a disquisition on law, and on the rules of bequest. But it is evident that in the societies of Europe, with a constitution of property such as that which the feudal Middle Age left them with,—a constitution of property full of inequality,—the state of the law of bequest shows us how far each society wishes the inequality to continue. The families in possession of great estates will not break them up if they can help it. Such owners will do all they can, by entail and settlement, to prevent their successors from breaking them up. They will preserve inequality. Freedom of bequest, then, the power of making entails and settlements, is sure, in an old European country like ours, to maintain inequality. And with us, who have the religion of inequality, the power of entailing and settling, and of willing property as one likes, exists, as is well known, in singular fulness,—greater fulness than in any country of the Continent. The proposal of a measure such as the Real Estates Intestacy Bill is, in a country like ours, perfectly puerile.[g] A European country like ours, wishing not to preserve inequality but to abate it, can only do so by interfering with the freedom of bequest. This is what Turgot, the wisest of French statesmen, pronounced before the Revolution to be necessary, and what was done in France at the great Revolution. The *Code Napoléon*, the actual law of France, forbids entails altogether, and leaves a man free to dispose of but one-fourth of his property, of whatever kind, if he have three children or more, of one-third if he have two children, of one-half if he have but one child. Only in the rare case, therefore, of a man's having but one child, can that child take the whole of his

[f] George Sand (*nom de plume* of Armandine Lucile Aurore Dupin, 1804–76) was a prolific French novelist whom Arnold admired and about whom he wrote a very favourable essay which also appeared in *Mixed Essays*.

[g] The Real Estate Intestacy Bill of 1878 was defeated in Parliament; for Arnold's view of the inadequacy of such proposals, see above p. 160.

father's property. If there are two children, two-thirds of the property must be equally divided between them; if there are more than two, three-fourths. In this way has France, desiring equality, sought to bring equality about.

Now the interesting point for us is, I say, to know how far other European communities, left in the same situation with us and with France, having immense inequalities of class and property created for them by the Middle Age, have dealt with these inequalities by means of the law of bequest. Do they leave bequest free, as we do? then, like us, they are for inequality. Do they interfere with the freedom of bequest, as France does? then, like France, they are for equality. And we shall be most interested, surely, by what the most civilised European communities do in this matter,—communities such as those of Germany, Italy, Belgium, Holland, Switzerland. And among those communities we are most concerned, I think, with such as, in the conditions of freedom and of self-government which they demand for their life, are most like ourselves. Germany, for instance, we shall less regard, because the conditions which the Germans seem to accept for their life are so unlike what we demand for ours; there is so much personal government there, so much *junkerism*, militarism, officialism; the community is so much more trained to submission than we could bear, so much more used to be, as the popular phrase is, sat upon. Countries where the community has more a will of its own, or can more show it, are the most important for our present purpose,— such countries as Belgium, Holland, Italy, Switzerland. Well, Belgium adopts purely and simply, as to bequest and inheritance, the provisions of the *Code Napoléon*. Holland adopts them purely and simply. Italy has adopted them substantially. Switzerland is a republic, where the general feeling against inequality is strong, and where it might seem less necessary, therefore, to guard against inequality by interfering with the power of bequest. Each Swiss canton has its own law of bequest. In Geneva, Vaud, and Zurich,—perhaps the three most distinguished cantons,—the law is identical with that of France. In Berne, one-third is the fixed proportion which a man is free to dispose of by will; the rest of his property must go among his children equally. In all the other cantons there are regulations of a like kind. Germany, I was saying, will interest us less than these freer countries. In Germany,—though there is not the English freedom of bequest, but the rule of the Roman law prevails, the rule obliging the parent to assign a certain portion to each child,—in Germany entails and settlements in favour of an eldest son are generally permitted. But there is a remarkable exception. The Rhine countries, which in the early part of this century were under French rule, and which then received the *Code Napoléon*, these countries refused to part with it when they were restored to Germany; and to this day Rhenish Prussia, Rhenish Hesse, and Baden, have the French law of bequest, forbidding entails, and dividing property in the way we have seen.

The United States of America have the English liberty of bequest. But the United States are, like Switzerland, a republic, with the republican sentiment for equality. Theirs is, besides, a new society; it did not inherit the system of classes and of property which feudalism established in Europe. The class by which the United States were settled was not a class with feudal habits and ideas. It is notorious that to acquire great landed estates and to entail them upon an eldest son, is neither the practice nor the desire of any class in America. I remember hearing it said to an American in England: "But, after all, you have the same freedom of bequest and inheritance as we have, and if a man to-morrow chose in your country to entail a great landed estate rigorously, what could you do?" The American answered: "Set aside the will on the ground of insanity."

You see we are in a manner taking the votes for and against equality. We ought not to leave out our own colonies. In general they are, of course, like the United States of America, new societies. They have the English liberty of bequest. But they have no feudal past, and were not settled by a class with feudal habits and ideas. Nevertheless it happens that there have arisen, in Australia, exceedingly large estates, and that the proprietors seek to keep them together. And what have we seen happen lately? An Act has been passed which in effect inflicts a fine upon every proprietor who holds a landed estate of more than a certain value. The measure has been severely blamed in England; to Mr. Lowe such a "concession to the cry for equality" appears, as we might expect, pregnant with warnings. At present I neither praise it nor blame it; I simply count it as one of the votes for equality. And is it not a singular thing, I ask you, that while we have the religion of inequality, and can hardly bear to hear equality spoken of, there should be, among the nations of Europe which have politically most in common with us, and in the United States of America, and in our own colonies, this diseased appetite, as we must think it, for equality? Perhaps Lord Beaconsfield may not have turned your minds to this subject as he turned mine, and what Menander or George Sand happens to have said may not interest you much; yet surely, when you think of it, when you see what a practical revolt against inequality there is amongst so many people not so very unlike to ourselves, you must feel some curiosity to sift the matter a little further, and may be not ill-disposed to follow me while I try to do so.

I have received a letter from Clerkenwell, in which the writer reproaches me for lecturing about equality at this which he calls "the most aristocratic and exclusive place out."[h] I am here because your secretary invited me. But I am glad to treat the subject of equality before such an audience as this. Some of you may remember that I have roughly divided our English society into Barbarians, Philistines, Populace, each of them with their prepossessions, and loving to hear what gratifies them. But I remarked at the same time, that scattered throughout all these classes were a certain number of generous and humane souls, lovers of man's perfection, detached from the prepossessions of the class to which they might naturally belong, and desirous that he who speaks to them should, as Plato says, not try to please his fellow-servants, but his true and legitimate masters—the heavenly Gods. I feel sure that among the members and frequenters of an institution like this, such humane souls are apt to congregate in numbers. Even from the reproach which my Clerkenwell friend brings against you of being too aristocratic, I derive some comfort. Only I give to the term *aristocratic* a rather wide extension. An accomplished American, much known and much esteemed in this country, the late Mr. Charles Sumner, says that what particularly struck him in England was the large class of gentlemen as distinct from the nobility, and the abundance amongst them of serious knowledge, high accomplishment, and refined taste,—taste fastidious perhaps, says Mr. Sumner, to excess, but erring on virtue's side. And he goes on: "I do not know that there is much difference between the manners and social observances of the highest classes of England and those of the corresponding classes of France and Germany; but in the rank immediately below the highest, — as among the professions, or military men, or literary men, — there you will find that the Englishmen have the advantage. They are better educated and better bred, more

---

[h] The subject of Arnold's lecture had been advertised in advance; Clerkenwell was an unfashionable district of London.

careful in their personal habits and in social conventions, more refined."[i] Mr. Sumner's remark is just and important; this large class of gentlemen in the professions, the services, literature, politics,—and a good contingent is now added from business also,—this large class, not of the nobility, but with the accomplishments and taste of an upper class, is something peculiar to England. Of this class I may probably assume that my present audience is in large measure composed. It is aristocratic in this sense, that it has the tastes of a cultivated class, a certain high standard of civilisation. Well, it is in its effects upon *civilisation* that equality interests me. And I speak to an audience with a high standard of civilisation. If I say that certain things in certain classes do not come up to a high standard of civilisation, I need not prove how and why they do not; you will feel instinctively whether they do or no. If they do not, I need not prove that this is a bad thing, that a high standard of civilisation is desirable; you will instinctively feel that it is. Instead of calling this "the most aristocratic and exclusive place out," I conceive of it as a *civilised* place; and in speaking about civilisation half one's labour is saved when one speaks about it among those who are civilised.

Politics are forbidden here; but equality is not a question of English politics. The abstract right to equality may, indeed, be a question of speculative politics. French equality appeals to this abstract natural right as its support. It goes back to a state of nature where all were equal, and supposes that "the poor consented," as Rousseau says, "to the existence of rich people," reserving always a natural right to return to the state of nature. It supposes that a child has a natural right to his equal share in his father's goods. The principle of abstract right, says Mr. Lowe, has never been admitted in England, and is false. I so entirely agree with him, that I run no risk of offending by discussing equality upon the basis of this principle. So far as I can sound human consciousness, I cannot, as I have often said, perceive that man is really conscious of any abstract natural rights at all. The natural right to have work found for one to do, the natural right to have food found for one to eat—rights sometimes so confidently and so indignantly asserted—seem to me quite baseless. It cannot be too often repeated: peasants and workmen have no natural rights, not one. Only we ought instantly to add, that kings and nobles have none

[i] Edward L. Pierce, *Memoir and Letters of Charles Sumner, 1811–1845* (1877).

either. If it is the sound English doctrine that all rights are created by law and are based on expediency, and are alterable as the public advantage may require, certainly that orthodox doctrine is mine. Property is created and maintained by law. It would disappear in that state of private war and scramble which legal society supersedes. Legal society creates, for the common good, the right of property; and for the common good that right is by legal society limitable. That property should exist, and that it should be held with a sense of security and with a power of disposal, may be taken, by us here at any rate, as a settled matter of expediency. With these conditions a good deal of inequality is inevitable. But that the power of disposal should be practically *unlimited*, that the inequality should be *enormous*, or that the degree of inequality admitted at one time should be admitted *always*,—this is by no means so certain. The right of bequest was in early times, as Sir Henry Maine and Mr. Mill have pointed out, seldom recognised.[j] In later times it has been limited in many countries in the way that we have seen; even in England itself it is not formally quite unlimited. The question is one of expediency. It is assumed, I grant, with great unanimity amongst us, that our signal inequality of classes and property is expedient for our civilisation and welfare. But this assumption, of which the distinguished personages who adopt it seem so sure that they think it needless to produce grounds for it, is just what we have to examine.

Now, there is a sentence of Sir Erskine May, whom I have already quoted, which will bring us straight to the very point that I wish to raise. Sir Erskine May, after saying, as you have heard, that France has pursued social equality, and has come to fearful troubles, demoralisation, and intellectual stoppage by doing so, continues thus: "Yet is she high, if not the first, in the scale of civilised nations." Why, here is a curious thing, surely! A nation pursues social equality, supposed to be an utterly false and baneful ideal; it arrives, as might have been expected, at fearful misery and deterioration by doing so; and yet, at the same time, it is high, if not the first, in the scale of civilised nations. What do we mean by *civilised*? Sir Erskine May does not seem to have asked himself the question, so we will try to answer it

[j] H.S. Maine, *Ancient Law* (1861); J.S. Mill, *Principles of Political Economy* (1848). In the 1862 and subsequent edition of his *Principles* Mill inserted a very favourable discussion of Maine's account of the absence of the right of bequest in earlier societies.

for ourselves. Civilisation is the humanisation of man in society. To be humanised is to comply with the true law of our human nature: *servare modum, finemque tenere, Naturamque sequi,* says Lucan; "to keep our measure, and to hold fast our end, and to follow Nature." To be humanised is to make progress towards this, our true and full humanity. And to be civilised is to make progress towards this in civil society; in that civil society "without which," says Burke, "man could not by any possibility arrive at the perfection of which his nature is capable, nor even make a remote and faint approach to it." To be the most civilised of nations, therefore, is to be the nation which comes nearest to human perfection, in the state which that perfection essentially demands. And a nation which has been brought by the pursuit of social equality to moral deterioration, intellectual stoppage, and fearful troubles, is perhaps the nation which has come nearest to human perfection in that state which such perfection essentially demands! Michelet himself, who would deny the demoralisation and the stoppage, and call the fearful troubles a sublime expiation for the sins of the whole world, could hardly say more for France than this. Certainly Sir Erskine May never intended to say so much. But into what a difficulty has he somehow run himself, and what a good action would it be to extricate him from it! Let us see whether the performance of that good action may not also be a way of clearing our minds as to the uses of equality.

When we talk of man's advance towards his full humanity, we think of an advance, not along one line only, but several. Certain races and nations, as we know, are on certain lines pre-eminent and representative. The Hebrew nation was pre-eminent on one great line. "What nation," it was justly asked by their lawgiver, "hath statutes and judgments so righteous as the law which I set before you this day? Keep therefore and do them; for this is your wisdom and your understanding in the sight of the nations which shall hear all these statutes and say: Surely this great nation is a wise and understanding people!" The Hellenic race was pre-eminent on other lines. Isocrates could say of Athens: "Our city has left the rest of the world so far behind in philosophy and eloquence, that those educated by Athens have become the teachers of the rest of mankind; and so well has she done her part, that the name of Greeks seems no longer to stand for a race but to stand for intelligence itself, and they who share in our culture are called Greeks even before those who are merely of our own blood." The power of intellect and science, the power of beauty, the power of social life and manners, — these are what Greece so felt, and fixed, and may stand for. They are great elements in our humanisation. The power of conduct is another great element; and this was so felt and fixed by Israel that we can never with justice refuse to permit Israel, in spite of all his shortcomings, to stand for it.

So you see that in being humanised we have to move along several lines, and that on certain lines certain nations find their strength and take a lead. We may elucidate the thing yet further. Nations now existing may be said to feel or to have felt the power of this or that element in our humanisation so signally that they are characterised by it. No one who knows this country would deny that it is characterised, in a remarkable degree, by a sense of the power of conduct. Our feeling for religion is one part of this; our industry is another. What foreigners so much remark in us, — our public spirit, our love, amidst all our liberty, for public order and for stability, — are parts of it too. Then the power of beauty was so felt by the Italians that their art revived, as we know, the almost lost idea of beauty, and the serious and successful pursuit of it. Cardinal Antonelli,[k] speaking to me about the education of the common people in Rome, said that they were illiterate indeed, but whoever mingled with them at any public show, and heard them pass judgment on the beauty or ugliness of what came before them, — "*è brutto*," "*è bello*," — would find that their judgment agreed admirably, in general, with just what the most cultivated people would say. Even at the present time, then, the Italians are pre-eminent in feeling the power of beauty. The power of knowledge, in the same way, is eminently an influence with the Germans. This by no means implies, as is sometimes supposed, a high and fine general culture. What it implies is a strong sense of the necessity of knowing *scientifically*, as the expression is, the things which have to be known by us; of knowing them systematically, by the regular and right process, and in the only real way. And this sense the Germans especially have. Finally, there is the power of social life and manners. And even the Athenians themselves, perhaps, have hardly felt this power so much as the French.

Voltaire, in a famous passage where he extols the age of Louis the

---

[k] Arnold had been presented to Cardinal Antonelli, the Papal Secretary of State, during his tour of the Continent in 1865 to gather information for the Taunton Commission on middle-class schools.

Fourteenth and ranks it with the chief epochs in the civilisation of our race, has to specify the gift bestowed on us by the age of Louis the Fourteenth, as the age of Pericles, for instance, bestowed on us its art and literature, and the Italian Renascence its revival of art and literature. And Voltaire shows all his acuteness in fixing on the gift to name. It is not the sort of gift which we expect to see named. The great gift of the age of Louis the Fourteenth to the world, says Voltaire, was this: *l'esprit de société*, the spirit of society, the social spirit. And another French writer, looking for the good points in the old French nobility, remarks that this at any rate is to be said in their favour: they established a high and charming ideal of social inter- course and manners, for a nation formed to profit by such an ideal, and which has profited by it ever since. And in America, perhaps, we see the disadvantages of having social equality before there has been any such high standard of social life and manners formed.

We are not disposed in England, most of us, to attach all this importance to social intercourse and manners. Yet Burke says: "There ought to be a system of manners in every nation which a well- formed mind would be disposed to relish." And the power of social life and manners is truly, as we have seen, one of the great elements in our humanisation. Unless we have cultivated it, we are incomplete. The impulse for cultivating it is not, indeed, a moral impulse. It is by no means identical with the moral impulse to help our neighbour and to do him good. Yet in many ways it works to a like end. It brings men together, makes them feel the need of one another, be considerate of one another, understand one another. But, above all things, it is a promoter of equality. It is by the humanity of their manners that men are made equal. "A man thinks to show himself my equal," says Goethe, "by being *grob*, — that is to say, coarse and rude; he does not show himself my equal, he shows himself *grob*." But a community having humane manners is a community of equals, and in such a community great social inequalities have really no meaning, while they are at the same time a menace and an embarrassment to perfect ease of social intercourse. A community with the spirit of society is eminently, therefore, a community with the spirit of equality. A nation with a genius for society, like the French or the Athenians, is irresist- ibly drawn towards equality. From the first moment when the French people, with its congenital sense for the power of social intercourse and manners, came into existence, it was on the road to equality.

When it had once got a high standard of social manners abundantly established, and at the same time the natural, material necessity for the feudal inequality of classes and property pressed upon it no longer, the French people introduced equality and made the French Revolution. It was not the spirit of philanthropy which mainly impelled the French to that Revolution, neither was it the spirit of envy, neither was it the love of abstract ideas, though all these did something towards it; but what did most was the spirit of society.

The well-being of the many comes out more and more distinctly, in proportion as time goes on, as the object we must pursue. An individual or a class, concentrating their efforts upon their own well-being exclusively, do but beget troubles both for others and for themselves also. No individual life can be truly prosperous, passed, as Obermann says, in the midst of men who suffer; *passée au milieu des générations qui souffrent.* To the noble soul, it cannot be happy; to the ignoble, it cannot be secure. Socialistic and communistic schemes have generally, however, a fatal defect; they are content with too low and material a standard of well-being. That instinct of perfection, which is the master-power in humanity, always rebels at this, and frustrates the work. Many are to be made partakers of well-being, true; but the ideal of well-being is not to be, on that account, lowered and coarsened. M. de Laveleye, the political economist, who is a Belgian and a Protestant, and whose testimony therefore we may the more readily take about France, says that France, being the country of Europe where the soil is more divided than anywhere except in Switzerland and Norway, is at the same time the country where material well-being is most widely spread, where wealth has of late years increased most, and where population is least outrunning the limits which, for the comfort and progress of the working classes themselves, seem necessary.[1] This may go for a good deal. It supplies an answer to what Sir Erskine May says about the bad effects of equality upon French prosperity. But I will quote to you from Mr. Hamerton what goes, I think, for yet more. Mr. Hamerton is an excellent observer and reporter, and has lived for many years in France. He says of the French peasantry that they are exceedingly ignorant. So they are. But he adds: "They are at the same time full of intelligence; their manners are excellent, they have delicate percep-

[1] Emile de Laveleye, 'Le socialisme contemporain en Allemagne', *Revue des Deux Mondes* (1876).

tions, they have tact, they have a certain refinement which a brutalised peasantry could not possibly have. If you talk to one of them at his own home, or in his field, he will enter into conversation with you quite easily, and sustain his part in a perfectly becoming way, with a pleasant combination of dignity and quiet humour. The interval between him and a Kentish labourer is enormous."[m]

This is indeed worth your attention. Of course all mankind are, as Mr. Gladstone says, of our own flesh and blood.[n] But you know how often it happens in England that a cultivated person, a person of the sort that Mr. Charles Sumner describes, talking to one of the lower class, or even of the middle class, feels, and cannot but feel, that there is somehow a wall of partition between himself and the other, that they seem to belong to two different worlds. Thoughts, feelings, perceptions, susceptibilities, language, manners, — everything is different. Whereas, with a French peasant, the most cultivated man may find himself in sympathy, may feel that he is talking to an equal. This is an experience which has been made a thousand times, and which may be made again any day. And it may be carried beyond the range of mere conversation, it may be extended to things like pleasures, recreations, eating and drinking, and so on. In general the pleasures, recreations, eating and drinking of English people, when once you get below that class which Mr. Charles Sumner calls the class of gentlemen, are to one of that class unpalatable and impossible. In France there is not this incompatibility. Whether he mix with high or low, the gentleman feels himself in a world not alien or repulsive, but a world where people make the same sort of demands upon life, in things of this sort, which he himself does. In all these respects France is the country where the people, as distinguished from a wealthy refined class, most lives what we call a humane life, the life of civilised man.

Of course, fastidious persons can and do pick holes in it. There is just now, in France, a *noblesse* newly revived, full of pretension, full of airs and graces and disdains; but its sphere is narrow, and out of its own sphere no one cares very much for it. There is a general equality

[m] Philip Gilbert Hamerton, *Round My House: Notes of Rural Life in France in Peace and War* (1876); Hamerton was an English artist and art critic who had married a French wife and settled in France.
[n] During the Reform Bill debates of March 1866, Mr Gladstone had responded to Robert Lowe's assertion of the ignorance and violence of the working class (see above p. 115) by insisting that they were 'our fellow-Christians, our own flesh and blood'.

in a humane kind of life. This is the secret of the passionate attachment with which France inspires all Frenchmen, in spite of her fearful troubles, her checked prosperity, her disconnected units, and the rest of it. There is so much of the goodness and agreeableness of life there, and for so many. It is the secret of her having been able to attach so ardently to her the German and Protestant people of Alsace, while we have been so little able to attach the Celtic and Catholic people of Ireland. France brings the Alsatians into a social system so full of the goodness and agreeableness of life; we offer to the Irish no such attraction. It is the secret, finally, of the prevalence which we have remarked in other continental countries of a legislation tending, like that of France, to social equality. The social system which equality creates in France is, in the eyes of others, such a giver of the goodness and agreeableness of life, that they seek to get the goodness by getting the equality.

Yet France has had her fearful troubles, as Sir Erskine May justly says. She suffers too, he adds, from demoralisation and intellectual stoppage. Let us admit, if he likes, this to be true also. His error is that he attributes all this to equality. Equality, as we have seen, has brought France to a really admirable and enviable pitch of humanisation in one important line. And this, the work of equality, is so much a good in Sir Erskine May's eyes, that he has mistaken it for the whole of which it is a part, frankly identifies it with civilisation, and is inclined to pronounce France the most civilised of nations.

But we have seen how much goes to full humanisation, to true civilisation, besides the power of social life and manners. There is the power of conduct, the power of intellect and knowledge, the power of beauty. The power of conduct is the greatest of all. And without in the least wishing to preach, I must observe, as a mere matter of natural fact and experience, that for the power of conduct France has never had anything like the same sense which she has had for the power of social life and manners. Michelet, himself a Frenchman, gives us the reason why the Reformation did not succeed in France. It did not succeed, he says, because *la France ne voulait pas de réforme morale* — moral reform France would not have; and the Reformation was above all a moral movement.° The sense in France for the power of conduct

---

° Arnold quoted this remark in several of his essays (see R.H. Super's note in *Complete Prose Works*, VIII, p. 456); the remark may have been made in conversation when Arnold had visited Michelet in Paris in 1859 (see above p. 84).

has not greatly deepened, I think, since. The sense for the power of intellect and knowledge has not been adequate either. The sense for beauty has not been adequate. Intelligence and beauty have been, in general, but so far reached as they can be and are reached by men who, of the elements of perfect humanisation, lay thorough hold upon one only,—the power of social intercourse and manners. I speak of France in general; she has had, and she has, individuals who stand out and who form exceptions. Well then, if a nation laying no sufficient hold upon the powers of beauty and knowledge, and a most failing and feeble hold upon the power of conduct, comes to demoralisation and intellectual stoppage and fearful troubles, we need not be inordinately surprised. What we should rather marvel at is the healing and bountiful operation of Nature, whereby the laying firm hold on one real element in our humanisation has had for France results so beneficent.

And thus, when Sir Erskine May gets bewildered between France's equality and fearful troubles on the one hand, and the civilisation of France on the other, let us suggest to him that perhaps he is bewildered by his data because he combines them ill. France has not exemplary disaster and ruin as the fruits of equality, and at the same time, and independently of this, an exemplary civilisation. She has a large measure of happiness and success as the fruits of equality, and she has a very large measure of dangers and troubles as the fruits of something else.

We have more to do, however, than to help Sir Erskine May out of his scrape about France. We have to see whether the considerations which we have been employing may not be of use to us about England.

We shall not have much difficulty in admitting whatever good is to be said of ourselves, and we will try not to be unfair by excluding all that is not so favourable. Indeed, our less favourable side is the one which we should be the most anxious to note, in order that we may mend it. But we will begin with the good. Our people has energy and honesty as its good characteristics. We have a strong sense for the chief power in the life and progress of man,—the power of conduct. So far we speak of the English people as a whole. Then we have a rich, refined, and splendid aristocracy. And we have, according to Mr. Charles Sumner's acute and true remark, a class of gentlemen, not of the nobility, but well-bred, cultivated, and refined, larger than is to be found in any other country. For these last we have Mr. Sumner's testimony. As to the splendour of our aristocracy, all the world is agreed. Then we have a middle class and a lower class; and they, after all, are the immense bulk of the nation.

Let us see how the civilisation of these classes appears to a Frenchman, who has witnessed, in his own country, the considerable humanisation of these classes by equality. To such an observer our middle class divides itself into a serious portion and a gay or rowdy portion; both are a marvel to him. With the gay or rowdy portion we need not much concern ourselves; we shall figure it to our minds sufficiently if we conceive it as the source of that war-song produced in these recent days of excitement:

> "We don't want to fight, but by jingo, if we do,
>    We've got the ships, we've got the men, and we've got the
>    money too."[p]

We may also partly judge its standard of life, and the needs of its nature, by the modern English theatre, perhaps the most contemptible in Europe. But the real strength of the English middle class is in its serious portion. And of this a Frenchman, who was here some little time ago as the correspondent, I think, of the *Siècle* newspaper, and whose letters were afterwards published in a volume, writes as follows. He had been attending some of the Moody and Sankey meetings,[q] and he says: "To understand the success of Messrs. Moody and Sankey, one must be familiar with English manners, one must know the mind-deadening influence of a narrow Biblism, one must have experienced the sense of acute ennui, which the aspect and the frequentation of this great division of English society produce in others, the want of elasticity and the chronic ennui which characterise this class itself, petrified in a narrow Protestantism and in a perpetual reading of the Bible."

You know the French;—a little more Biblism, one may take leave to say, would do them no harm. But an audience like this,—and here, as I said, is the advantage of an audience like this,—will have no diffi-

---

[p] A popular music-hall song in 1878 when Britain was threatening to intervene on behalf of Turkey in the Russo-Turkish war; it is the origin of the term 'jingoism'.

[q] D.L. Moody and I.D. Sankey were American revivalist preachers who toured Britain in 1873–5, attracting huge crowds.

culty in admitting the amount of truth which there is in the French-man's picture. It is the picture of a class which, driven by its sense for the power of conduct, in the beginning of the seventeenth century entered, — as I have more than once said, and as I may more than once have occasion in future to say, — *entered the prison of Puritanism, and had the key turned upon its spirit there for two hundred years.*[r] They did not know, good and earnest people as they were, that to the building up of human life there belong all those other powers also, — the power of intellect and knowledge, the power of beauty, the power of social life and manners. And something, by what they became, they gained, and the whole nation with them; they deepened and fixed for this nation the sense of conduct. But they created a type of life and manners, of which they themselves indeed are slow to recognise the faults, but which is fatally condemned by its hideousness, its immense ennui, and against which the instinct of self-preservation in humanity rebels.

Partisans fight against facts in vain. Mr. Goldwin Smith, a writer of eloquence and power, although too prone to acerbity, is a partisan of the Puritans, and of the Nonconformists who are the special inheritors of the Puritan tradition.[s] He angrily resents the imputation upon that Puritan type of life, by which the life of our serious middle class has been formed, that it was doomed to hideousness, to immense ennui. He protests that it had beauty, amenity, accomplish-ment. Let us go to facts. Charles the First, who, with all his faults, had the just idea that art and letters are great civilisers, made, as you know, a famous collection of pictures, — our first National Gallery. It was, I suppose, the best collection at that time north of the Alps. It contained nine Raphaels, eleven Correggios, twenty-eight Titians. What became of that collection? The journals of the House of Com-mons will tell you. There you may see the Puritan Parliament dispos-ing of this Whitehall or York House collection as follows: "Ordered, that all such pictures and statues there as are without any superstition, shall be forthwith sold. ... Ordered, that all such pictures there as have the representation of the Second Person in Trinity upon them,

[r] Arnold had used this phrase in several of his writings, beginning with his 1863 essay on Heine reprinted in *Essays in Criticism*; see also above p. 136.
[s] Goldwin Smith (1823–1910), historian and Liberal polemicist, fiercely attacked the account Arnold had given of the Puritans in his essay on the seventeeth-century states-man Falkland; Goldwin Smith, 'Falkland and the Puritans: a Reply to Mr Matthew Arnold', *Contemporary Review* (1877).

shall be forthwith burnt." There we have the weak side of our parliamentary government and our serious middle class. We are incapable of sending Mr. Gladstone to be tried at the Old Bailey because he proclaims his antipathy to Lord Beaconsfield. A majority in our House of Commons is incapable of hailing, with frantic laughter and applause, a string of indecent jests against Christianity and its Founder.[f] But we are not, or were not, incapable of producing a Parliament which burns or sells the masterpieces of Italian art. And one may surely say of such a Puritan Parliament, and of those who determine its line for it, that they had not the spirit of beauty.

What shall we say of amenity? Milton was born a humanist, but the Puritan temper, as we know, mastered him. There is nothing more unlovely and unamiable than Milton the Puritan disputant. Some one answers his *Doctrine and Discipline of Divorce.* "I mean not," rejoins Milton, "to dispute philosophy with this pork, who never read any." However, he does reply to him, and throughout the reply Milton's great joke is, that his adversary, who was anonymous, is a servingman. "Finally, he winds up his text with much doubt and trepidation; for it may be his trenchers were not scraped, and that which never yet afforded corn of savour to his noddle,—the salt-cellar,—was not rubbed; and therefore, in this haste, easily granting that his answers fall foul upon each other, and praying you would not think he writes as a prophet, but as a man, he runs to the black jack, fills his flagon, spreads the table, and serves up dinner." There you have the same spirit of urbanity and amenity, as much of it, and as little, as generally informs the religious controversies of our Puritan middle class to this day.

But Mr. Goldwin Smith insists, and picks out his own exemplar of the Puritan type of life and manners; and even here let us follow him. He picks out the most favourable specimen he can find,—Colonel Hutchinson, whose well-known memoirs, written by his widow, we have all read with interest.[u] "Lucy Hutchinson," says Mr. Goldwin Smith, "is painting what she thought a perfect Puritan would be; and her picture presents to us not a coarse, crop-eared, and snuffling

---

[f] An allusion to an episode in the predominantly anti-clerical French Chamber of Deputies in 1877, referred to disapprovingly in Britain.

[u] *Memoirs of the Life of Colonel Hutchinson,* by his widow, Lucy; John Hutchinson (1615–64) was one of the Members of the Long Parliament who signed the death warrant for Charles I.

fanatic, but a highly accomplished, refined, gallant, and most amiable, though religious and seriously minded, gentleman." Let us, I say, in this example of Mr. Goldwin Smith's own choosing, lay our finger upon the points where this type deflects from the truly humane ideal.

Mrs. Hutchinson relates a story which gives us a good notion of what the amiable and accomplished social intercourse, even of a picked Puritan family, was. Her husband was governor of Nottingham. He had occasion, she says, "to go and break up a private meeting in the cannoneer's chamber"; and in the cannoneer's chamber "were found some notes concerning paedobaptism, which, being brought into the governor's lodgings, his wife having perused them and compared them with the Scriptures, found not what to say against the truths they asserted concerning the misapplication of that ordinance to infants." Soon afterwards she expects her confinement, and communicates the cannoneer's doubts about paedobaptism to her husband. The fatal cannoneer makes a breach in him too. "Then he bought and read all the eminent treatises on both sides, which at that time came thick from the presses, and still was cleared in the error of the paedobaptists." Finally, Mrs. Hutchinson is confined. Then the governor "invited all the ministers to dinner, and propounded his doubt and the ground thereof to them. None of them could defend their practice with any satisfactory reason, but the tradition of the Church from the primitive times, and their main buckler of federal holiness, which Tombs and Denne had excellently overthrown. He and his wife then, professing themselves unsatisfied, desired their opinions." With the opinions I will not trouble you, but hasten to the result: "Whereupon that infant was not baptized."

No doubt to a large division of English society at this very day, that sort of dinner and discussion, and, indeed, the whole manner of life and conversation here suggested by Mrs. Hutchinson's narrative, will seem both natural and amiable, and such as to meet the needs of man as a religious and social creature. You know the conversation which reigns in thousands of middle-class families at this hour, about nunneries, teetotalism, the confessional, eternal punishment, ritualism, disestablishment. It goes wherever the class goes which is moulded on the Puritan type of life. In the long winter evenings of Toronto Mr. Goldwin Smith has had, probably, abundant experience of it.[v] What is

---

[v] Goldwin Smith left England in 1868, and lived in Toronto from 1871 till his death.

its enemy? The instinct of self-preservation in humanity. Men make crude types and try to impose them, but to no purpose. "*L'homme s'agite, Dieu le mène,*" says Bossuet. "There are many devices in a man's heart; nevertheless the counsel of the Eternal, that shall stand." Those who offer us the Puritan type of life offer us a religion not true, the claims of intellect and knowledge not satisfied, the claim of beauty not satisfied, the claim of manners not satisfied. In its strong sense for conduct that life touches truth; but its other imperfections hinder it from employing even this sense aright. The type mastered our nation for a time. Then came the reaction. The nation said: "This type, at any rate, is amiss; we are not going to be all like *that!*" The type retired into our middle class, and fortified itself there. It seeks to endure, to emerge, to deny its own imperfections, to impose itself again;—impossible! If we continue to live, we must outgrow it. The very class in which it is rooted, our middle class, will have to acknowledge the type's inadequacy, will have to acknowledge the hideousness, the immense ennui of the life which this type has created, will have to transform itself thoroughly. It will have to admit the large part of truth which there is in the criticisms of our Frenchman, whom we have too long forgotten.

After our middle class he turns his attention to our lower class. And of the lower and larger portion of this, the portion not bordering on the middle class and sharing its faults, he says: "I consider this multitude to be absolutely devoid, not only of political principles, but even of the most simple notions of good and evil. Certainly it does not appeal, this mob, to the principles of '89, which you English make game of; it does not insist on the rights of man; what it wants is beer, gin, and *fun*."[2]

That is a description of what Mr. Bright would call the residuum, only our author seems to think the residuum a very large body.[w] And its condition strikes him with amazement and horror. And surely well it may. Let us recall Mr. Hamerton's account of the most illiterate class in France; what an amount of civilisation they have notwithstanding! And this is always to be understood, in hearing or reading a Frenchman's praise of England. He envies our liberty, our public

---

[2] So in the original.

[w] In the Reform Bill Debate of March 1867, Bright had described that small class which, because of their 'almost hopeless poverty and dependence', should be excluded from any extension of the franchise, as 'the residuum'.

spirit, our trade, our stability. But there is always a reserve in his mind. He never means for a moment that he would like to change with us. Life seems to him so much better a thing in France for so many more people, that, in spite of the fearful troubles of France, it is best to be a Frenchman. A Frenchman might agree with Mr. Cobden, that life is good in England for those people who have at least £5000 a year. But the civilisation of that immense majority who have not £5000 a year, or £500, or even £100,—of our middle and lower class,—seems to him too deplorable.

And now what has this condition of our middle and lower classes to tell us about equality? How is it, must we not ask, how is it that, being without fearful troubles, having so many achievements to show and so much success, having as a nation a deep sense for conduct, having signal energy and honesty, having a splendid aristocracy, having an exceptionally large class of gentlemen, we are yet so little civilised? How is it that our middle and lower classes, in spite of the individuals among them who are raised by happy gifts of nature to a more humane life, in spite of the seriousness of the middle class, in spite of the honesty and power of true work, the *virtus verusque labor*, which are to be found in abundance throughout the lower, do yet present, as a whole, the characters which we have seen?

And really it seems as if the current of our discourse carried us of itself to but one conclusion. It seems as if we could not avoid concluding, that just as France owes her fearful troubles to other things and her civilisedness to equality, so we owe our immunity from fearful troubles to other things, and our uncivilisedness to inequality. "Knowledge is easy," says the wise man, "to him that understandeth;" easy, he means, to him who will use his mind simply and rationally, and not to make him think he can know what he cannot, or to maintain, *per fas et nefas*, a false thesis with which he fancies his interests to be bound up. And to him who will use his mind as the wise man recommends, surely it is easy to see that our shortcomings in civilisation are due to our inequality; or in other words, that the great inequality of classes and property, which came to us from the Middle Age and which we maintain because we have the religion of inequality, that this constitution of things, I say, has the natural and necessary effect, under present circumstances, of materialising our upper class, vulgarising our middle class, and brutalising our lower class. And this is to fail in civilisation.

For only just look how the facts combine themselves. I have said little as yet about our aristocratic class, except that it is splendid. Yet these, "our often very unhappy brethren," as Burke calls them, are by no means matter for nothing but ecstasy. Our charity ought certainly, Burke says, to "extend a due and anxious sensation of pity to the distresses of the miserable great." Burke's extremely strong language about their miseries and defects I will not quote. For my part, I am always disposed to marvel that human beings, in a position so false, should be so good as these are. Their reason for existing was to serve as a number of centres in a world disintegrated after the ruin of the Roman Empire, and slowly re-constituting itself. Numerous centres of material force were needed, and these a feudal aristocracy supplied. Their large and hereditary estates served this public end. The owners had a positive function, for which their estates were essential. In our modern world the function is gone; and the great estates, with an infinitely multiplied power of ministering to mere pleasure and indulgence, remain. The energy and honesty of our race does not leave itself without witness in this class, and nowhere are there more conspicuous examples of individuals raised by happy gifts of nature far above their fellows and their circumstances. For distinction of all kinds this class has an esteem. Everything which succeeds they tend to welcome, to win over, to put on their side; genius may generally make, if it will, not bad terms for itself with them. But the total result of the class, its effect on society at large and on national progress, are what we must regard. And on the whole, with no necessary function to fulfil, never conversant with life as it really is, tempted, flattered, and spoiled from childhood to old age, our aristocratic class is inevitably materialised, and the more so the more the development of industry and ingenuity augments the means of luxury. Every one can see how bad is the action of such an aristocracy upon the class of newly enriched people, whose great danger is a materialistic ideal, just because it is the ideal they can easiest comprehend. Nor is the mischief of this action now compensated by signal services of a public kind. Turn even to that sphere which aristocracies think specially their own, and where they have under other circumstances been really effective, — the sphere of politics. When there is need, as now, for any large forecast of the course of human affairs, for an acquaintance with the ideas which in the end sway mankind, and for an estimate of their power, aristocracies are out of their element, and materialised aristocracies most of all. In the immense spiritual movement of our day, the English aristocracy, as I have elsewhere said,[x] always reminds me of Pilate confronting the phenomenon of Christianity. Nor can a materialised class have any serious and fruitful sense for the power of beauty. They may imagine themselves to be in pursuit of beauty; but how often, alas, does the pursuit come to little more than dabbling a little in what they are pleased to call art, and making a great deal of what they are pleased to call love!

Let us return to their merits. For the power of manners an aristocratic class, whether materialised or not, will always, from its circumstances, have a strong sense. And although for this power of social life and manners, so important to civilisation, our English race has no special natural turn, in our aristocracy this power emerges and marks them. When the day of general humanisation comes, they will have fixed the standard of manners. The English simplicity, too, makes the best of the English aristocracy more frank and natural than the best of the like class anywhere else, and even the worst of them it makes free from the incredible fatuities and absurdities of the worst. Then the sense of conduct they share with their countrymen at large. In no class has it such trials to undergo; in none is it more often and more grievously overborne. But really the right comment on this is the comment of Pepys upon the evil courses of Charles the Second and the Duke of York and the court of that day: "At all which I am sorry; but it is the effect of idleness, and having nothing else to employ their great spirits upon."

Heaven forbid that I should speak in dispraise of that unique and most English class which Mr. Charles Sumner extols—the large class of gentlemen, not of the landed class or of the nobility, but cultivated and refined. They are a seemly product of the energy and of the power to rise in our race. Without, in general, rank and splendour and wealth and luxury to polish them, they have made their own the high standard of life and manners of an aristocratic and refined class. Not having all the dissipations and distractions of this class, they are much more seriously alive to the power of intellect and knowledge, to the power of beauty. The sense of conduct, too, meets with fewer trials in this class. To some extent, however, their contiguousness to the aristocratic class has now the effect of materialising them, as it does

[x] In *Literature and Dogma* (1873).

the class of newly enriched people. The most palpable action is on the young amongst them, and on their standard of life and enjoyment. But in general, for this whole class, established facts, the materialism which they see regnant, too much block their mental horizon, and limit the possibilities of things to them. They are deficient in openness and flexibility of mind, in free play of ideas, in faith and ardour. Civilised they are, but they are not much of a civilising force; they are somehow bounded and ineffective.

So on the middle class they produce singularly little effect. What the middle class sees is that splendid piece of materialism, the aristocratic class, with a wealth and luxury utterly out of their reach, with a standard of social life and manners, the offspring of that wealth and luxury, seeming utterly out of their reach also. And thus they are thrown back upon themselves— upon a defective type of religion, a narrow range of intellect and knowledge, a stunted sense of beauty, a low standard of manners. And the lower class see before them the aristocratic class, and its civilisation, such as it is, even infinitely more out of *their* reach than out of that of the middle class; while the life of the middle class, with its unlovely types of religion, thought, beauty, and manners, has naturally, in general, no great attractions for them either. And so they too are thrown back upon themselves; upon their beer, their gin, and their *fun*. Now, then, you will understand what I meant by saying that our inequality materialises our upper class, vulgarises our middle class, brutalises our lower.

And the greater the inequality the more marked is its bad action upon the middle and lower classes. In Scotland the landed aristocracy fills the scene, as is well known, still more than in England; the other classes are more squeezed back and effaced. And the social civilisation of the lower middle class and of the poorest class, in Scotland, is an example of the consequences. Compared with the same class even in England, the Scottish lower middle class is most visibly, to vary Mr. Charles Sumner's phrase, *less* well-bred, *less* careful in personal habits and in social conventions, *less* refined. Let any one who doubts it go, after issuing from the aristocratic solitudes which possess Loch Lomond, let him go and observe the shopkeepers and the middle class in Dumbarton, and Greenock, and Gourock, and the places along the mouth of the Clyde. And for the poorest class, who that has seen it can ever forget the hardly human horror, the abjection and uncivilisedness of Glasgow?

What a strange religion, then, is our religion of inequality! Romance often helps a religion to hold its ground, and romance is good in its way; but ours is not even a romantic religion. No doubt our aristocracy is an object of very strong public interest. The *Times* itself bestows a leading article by way of epithalamium on the Duke of Norfolk's marriage[y] And those journals of a new type, full of talent, and which interest me particularly because they seem as if they were written by the young lion of our youth, — the young lion grown mellow and, as the French say, *viveur*, arrived at his full and ripe knowledge of the world, and minded to enjoy the smooth evening of his days, — those journals, in the main a sort of social gazette of the aristocracy, are apparently not read by that class only which they most concern, but are read with great avidity by other classes also. And the common people too have undoubtedly, as Mr. Gladstone says, a wonderful preference for a lord. Yet our aristocracy, from the action upon it of the Wars of the Roses, the Tudors, and the political necessities of George the Third, is for the imagination a singularly modern and uninteresting one. Its splendour of station, its wealth, show, and luxury, is then what the other classes really admire in it; and this is not an elevating admiration. Such an admiration will never lift us out of our vulgarity and brutality, if we chance to be vulgar and brutal to start with; it will rather feed them and be fed by them. So that when Mr. Gladstone invites us to call our love of inequality "the complement of the love of freedom or its negative pole, or the shadow which the love of freedom casts, or the reverberation of its voice in the halls of the constitution," we must surely answer that all this mystical eloquence is not in the least necessary to explain so simple a matter; that our love of inequality is really the vulgarity in us, and the brutality, admiring and worshipping the splendid materiality.

Our present social organisation, however, will and must endure until our middle class is provided with some better ideal of life than it has now. Our present organisation has been an appointed stage in our growth; it has been of good use, and has enabled us to do great things. But the use is at an end, and the stage is over. Ask yourselves if you do not sometimes feel in yourselves a sense, that in spite of the strenuous efforts for good of so many excellent persons amongst us, we begin somehow to flounder and to beat the air; that we seem to be finding

---

[y] A leading article in the *Times* for 22 November 1877, on the occasion of the marriage of the Duke of Norfolk, extravagantly praised the English aristocracy.

ourselves stopped on this line of advance and on that, and to be threatened with a sort of standstill. It is that we are trying to live on with a social organisation of which the day is over. Certainly equality will never of itself alone give us a perfect civilisation. But, with such inequality as ours, a perfect civilisation is impossible.

To that conclusion, facts, and the stream itself of this discourse, do seem, I think, to carry us irresistibly. We arrive at it because they so choose, not because we so choose. Our tendencies are all the other way. We are all of us politicians, and in one of two camps, the Liberal or the Conservative. Liberals tend to accept the middle class as it is, and to praise the nonconformists; while Conservatives tend to accept the upper class as it is, and to praise the aristocracy. And yet here we are at the conclusion, that whereas one of the great obstacles to our civilisation is, as I have often said, British nonconformity, another main obstacle to our civilisation in British aristocracy! And this while we are yet forced to recognise excellent special qualities as well as the general English energy and honesty, and a number of emergent humane individuals, in both nonconformists and aristocracy. Clearly such a conclusion can be none of our own seeking.

Then again, to remedy our inequality, there must be a change in the law of bequest, as there has been in France; and the faults and inconveniences of the present French law of bequest are obvious. It tends to over-divide property; it is unequal in operation, and can be eluded by people limiting their families; it makes the children, however ill they may behave, independent of the parent. To be sure, Mr. Mill and others have shown that a law of bequest fixing the maximum, whether of land or money, which any one individual may take by bequest or inheritance, but in other respects leaving the testator quite free, has none of the inconveniences of the French law, and is every way preferable.[z] But evidently these are not questions of practical politics. Just imagine Lord Hartington[aa] going down to Glasgow, and meeting his Scotch Liberals there, and saying to them: "You are ill at ease, and you are calling for change, and very justly. But the cause of your being ill at ease is not what you suppose. The cause of your being ill at ease is the profound imperfectness of your social civilisation. Your social civilisation is indeed such as I forebear

---

[z] Mill had argued this in Book II of his *Principles of Political Economy*, cited above p. 220.

[aa] Spencer Cavendish, Lord Hartington (1833–1908) was leader of the Liberal Party when he was given the Freedom of the City of Glasgow in 1877.

to characterise. But the remedy is not disestablishment. The remedy is social equality. Let me direct your attention to a reform in the law of bequest and entail." One can hardly speak of such a thing without laughing. No, the matter is at present one for the thoughts of those who think. It is a thing to be turned over in the minds of those who, on the one hand, have the spirit of scientific inquirers, bent on seeing things as they really are; and, on the other hand, the spirit of friends of the humane life, lovers of perfection. To your thoughts I commit it. And perhaps, the more you think of it, the more you will be persuaded that Menander showed his wisdom quite as much when he said *Choose equality*, as when he assured us that *Evil communications corrupt good manners*.

## Cambridge Texts in the History of Political Thought

*Titles published in the series thus far*

# Index